DEEP TALK

Reading African-American Literary Names

Debra Walker King

UNIVERSITY PRESS OF VIRGINIA

Charlottesville and London

Acknowledgments for previously published material appear on page x.

THE UNIVERSITY PRESS OF VIRGINIA

Printed in the United States of America

First published 1998

∞ The paper used in this publication meets the minimum requirements of the American National Standard for Information Sciences—Permanence of Paper for Printed Library Materials, ANSI Z39.48–1984.

Library of Congress Cataloging-in-Publication Data
King, Debra Walker, 1959–
    Deep talk : reading African-American literary names / Debra Walker King.
        p.   cm.
    Includes bibliographical references and index.
    ISBN 0-8139-1793-X (cloth : alk. paper) ; ISBN 0-8139-1852-9 (paper : alk. paper)
    1. American literature—Afro-American authors—History and criticism.   2. Literature and society—United States.   3. Names, Personal, in literature.   4. Names, Personal—Afro-American.
5. Afro-Americans in literature.   6. Afro-Americans—Names.
I. Title.
PS153.N5K44   1998
810.9'896073—dc21   98-12159

For My Parents

and

My Husband

Contents

Preface

THE QUESTIONS *Deep Talk* addresses were conceived in a moment of personal frustration and loss. As a new bride, I purchased an insurance policy for my car. When the policy arrived addressed to "Michael Anthony King and wif," I was incensed! By giving prominence and respect to my husband's name, the processor unnamed me. I was a role, wife—worse than that, I had no "e." I was "*wif.*" My identity on the address label as an abbreviated *no-name* said more about the challenges I faced in my new social role than the salesman (who, by the way, never spoke with my husband) could say using a million words. In protest against my unnaming, I canceled the policy. Still, I owe a great debt of thanks to the processor, whoever it was, and the computer program that did not have space for my name nor my "e." The incident inaugurated my quest to understand how names communicate their deep-level messages.

I chose African-American literature as my focus in this quest because it is the literature of my spirit, my flesh, and my culture. Through it I learned why I read a stranger's disrespect for the calling process as an assault upon my sense of self. The reason? Names speak. They offer a wide range of deep-level communications that reveal not only identity but shared languages, histories, behavioral expectations, resistance, creativity, and personal accountabilities. *Deep Talk* tells the story of names that speak; but, more importantly, it tells the story of women and men whose ancestors were unnamed through Middle Passage, whose public identities were erased through uncaring or careless record keeping, who used names as weapons against spiritual wounding, who understood the magic of naming and used its incantatory force to survive racist assaults. These are the ancestors to whom I owe my deepest gratitude. In this study, I attempt to honor them all by reading and writing the legacy of names and naming they left behind.

I gratefully acknowledge the National Research Council and the Ford Foundation for fellowship support and conference sponsorship. Also, for leave time and grant assistance during the research and writing of this book, I thank the Florida Board of Regents and the University of Florida's Research Development Award Program. For permission to reprint portions of my article "Reading the 'Deep Talk' of Literary Names and Naming," *Names: The Journal of the American Name Association* 42, no. 3 (Sept. 1994): 181–99, I thank the journal.

Cathie Brettschneider, at the University Press of Virginia, earns my admiration and gratitude for her enthusiasm, friendship, and commitment to this project. I also extend my thanks to Jane Curran of Winnipeg, Manitoba, and Deborah A. Oliver at the University Press of Virginia for their assistance.

I am in awe of the time several colleagues and mentors dedicated to this book, reading various versions or portions of it (many during its infant stages)—David Leverenz, Elizabeth Langland, Hortense Spillers, Richard Long, Robert Detweiler, Allen Tullos, Amy Lang, and Kathryn W. Shanley. Nora Alter, Gay Wilentz, and Jacquelyn Y. McLendon read the manuscript of the book with great care and concern. Their insights helped me tremendously.

Sometimes we receive assistance and support that does not fit easily into any category. There are people, special people, who rebuild the broken—people whose insights and guidance stop the flood of tears and renew our faith in ourselves. People who are God sent. My parents, Mollie and Peter Taylor, are two of these people; Karla Holloway, who read only a proposal of this book but endured my frantic calls for encouragement and direction, is another. I offer my humble appreciation to them for being my hope and sustenance. Because of them this book exists. For encouragement and continuing support I also acknowledge my mentors who never read this work in manuscript form but believed in it as much as I did—Sandra Govan, Trudier Harris, Harry Shaw, Mildred Hill-Lubin, Stan Patten and Ann Carver.

Accolades of praise I extend to my husband, Mike, who understood the deep talk of "seven times" and guided me patiently beyond its rewriting mandates, who filled my study with the sweet aroma of flowers as I worked, and who read *aloud* every version of this book. Through his voice I heard my words speak. A mere "thanks" is not enough for the strength and love he gives.

Finally, I thank Emmanuel, whose spirit has been my constant help.

DEEP
TALK

Introduction: Listening for the Deep Talk

DURING A 1993 interview, Maya Angelou advised her interviewer to "do as West Africans do . . . listen for the deep talk." [1] Angelou's advice and its acknowledgment of utterances existing beneath the obvious is central to this book's focus on names that speak. *Deep Talk* seeks the discourses existing beneath or alongside the primary narratives of literary texts. The readings and discussions it offers examine the metatext of names and naming, a place where names create streams of metaphoric, metonymic, allegorical, and other meanings that avail themselves of multiple interpretive possibilities. From this alternate site, poetic names give voice to the unspoken and transparency to the concealed. With the assistance of a reader who hears and interprets these utterances, stories and events develop that comment upon and transform the surface.

In the second section of *Brothers and Keepers* (1984), John Edgar Wideman describes something akin to name-motivated (or onomastic) deep talk: "You heard things . . . in Homewood names. Rules of etiquette, thumbnail character sketches, a history of the community. A dire warning to get back could be coded into the saying of a person's name, and a further inflection of the speaker's voice could tell you to ignore the facts, forget what he's just reminded you to remember and go on. Try your luck" (74). Wideman's statements move beyond discussions of names as instruments of personal designation to acknowledge the living energy of name-driven deep talk as a strategy of discourse production. Names in Homewood achieve a conspicuous actualization of what Mikhail Bakhtin calls *living words*—"language in its concrete and living totality . . . the concrete life of the word . . . the polyphonic utilization of the word." [2]

Wideman explores the unique power his grandfather's surname, *French*, has upon the actions, reactions, and perceptions of people living in his hometown. "If one of the Homewood people said, 'That's the French girl' or, 'There goes John French's daughter,' a portrait with subtle shading and complex resonance was painted by the words" (72). The discourses provoked by the deep-level communications of *French* include everything from descriptive commentaries of physical attributes to religious beliefs, personal histories, and reputation. Just mentioning the name causes men to "clean up" their thoughts concerning the young girl it designates. The name, spoken in just the right context with just the right tone and interpreted by an informed listener, can issue a threat or warning—a deep talk—that provokes fear and action.

To demonstrate this point, Wideman describes how the name influences the actions of a careless drunk, Elias Brown, who accidentally discharges a double-barreled shotgun near the play area of several children. Although the buckshot "nicks" one of John French's daughters on the knee, Elias remains intoxicated, unconcerned, and apathetic until he hears the name *French*. "Then Elias woke up real quick. His knees, his dusty butt, everything he got starts to trembling and his eyes got big as dinner plates. Then he's gone like a turkey through the corn. Nobody seen Elias for a week" (73). For Elias, *French* speaks of violent retribution and danger. It is a notice to run.

In literature the deep-level communication of poetic names such as *French*, and others not so clearly drawn, finds a place for free and rigorous play. In what follows, I examine this play, its rhapsody and creative impulses, its biblical and mythological intertextuality, and its function as a form of resistance against racist, sexist, and careless unnaming. As I understand the discursive role of poetic names, they are not static elements of language but speaking agents of narrative incantation that function effectively in both the social real and in fiction. All names contain an incantatory presence—usually in the form of historical content and meanings that define (if not also guide the destiny of) the named. Bakhtin calls this ability to mean and speak the *stylistic aura* of utterances.[3] In this study it is more than that; it is incantation.

wield the power of narrative incantation or, more specifically, the creative, procreative, and destructive spirit of the calling process. I focus on the patterns of naming, the battles for dominance, and the deep-level stories that liberate subject positions and meanings obscured by the weight of hostile forces. I chart narratives of onomastic resistance as engaged and played out beneath primary discourses; and I trace the ways poetic names speak into being the liberated "flesh" of not only various subject positions but a plethora of narrative actions and extratextual discourses.

Critics often note the importance of names and naming in black-authored literature, but before *Deep Talk* there existed no methodological discussion of African-American literary naming. By this I mean *how* a name communicates its discursive impulses, its emancipatory counter-narratives, its resistance and recovery, its revisions and redemptions. Kimberly Benston's "I Yam What I Am: The Topos of (Un)naming in Afro-American Literature," one of the most well known essays written on this subject, comes closer than any other published study to examining the methodology of African-American literary naming. As interpreted by Benston, the tradition emphasizing names (and particularly unnaming) in black texts is one of "genealogical revisionism." "All of Afro-American literature," according to Benston, "may be seen as one vast genealogical poem that attempts to restore continuity to the ruptures or discontinuities imposed by the history of black presence in America." [6] My work moves beyond Benston's essay not only by discussing the genealogical revisions that unnaming (and renaming) affirms but also by exploring the nature of literary names—their interlocutory potential and function as utterances of subversive narrative strategy. *Deep Talk* explores how names and naming function as agents of resistance—as subversive forces—that operate and speak on several levels of meaning and complexity at once.

My intent is three-fold. First, I want to describe a method for reading literary names and naming through the presentation and application of seven guiding principles (outlined below). These principles offer a methodological vehicle through which an interpreter may discover how a name identifies, defines, describes, or acts within a narrative text. Second, I am concerned with the use of naming as a strategy of covert writing. I examine this potential by exploring the contextual aims of

5

names—what I call their *onomastic desires*. This term refers to the utterances produced through the meaning potential of poetic names and name phrases, their intent as discursive strategy, and the multiple speech centers they contain and exploit. A simple way of conceptualizing onomastic desires is to think of them as what a name wants to say or what it *desires* to communicate. My third objective is to define the reader's role in the creation of name-motivated discourse. I explain how the already present, Signifyin(g) rhetoric of poetic names coaxes readers to contribute to the meaning experience.

I borrow the term *Signifyin(g)* from Henry Louis Gates Jr.'s *The Signifying Monkey*, a book to which my work is greatly indebted. Gates describes naming as a key player in the rhetorical universe of a master trope called *Signifyin(g)*. He defines *Signifyin(g)* as a rhetorical strategy that repeats, critiques, and revises the narrative form and style of literary antecedents. Gates borrows the word *Signifying(g)* from the black vernacular tradition but admits a sensation of "vertigo" when contemplating the relationship between this word and the standard English usage of its homonym, *signifying*. *Signifyin(g)* contains within its deep talk a "black difference" that relies, in part, upon impulses that rename its standard English homonym. To distinguish between these two signifiers, Gates capitalizes the vernacular word and writes the standard English word in lower case. He also brackets the final *g* of the vernacular term and explains: "The bracketed *g* enables me to connote the fact that this word is, more often than not, spoken by black people without the final *g* as 'signifyin'.' . . . The bracketed or aurally erased *g*, . . . is a figure for the Signifyin(g) black difference." Although I acknowledge the origins of black vernacular speech in my intended use of *signifying*, I emphasize that the method of reading names and naming I present is not restricted to black literature by not maintaining Gates's graphic representation of those origins and vernacular inflections. I maintain Gates's definition of *Signifyin(g)*, however, and characterize it as a rhetorical figuration dependent upon an onomastic play of difference.[7]

For Gates, naming is "a metaphor for black intertextuality" that operates as pastiche (repetition that gives homage to the original) and parody (which allows repetition to evaluate the original stringently). The innate structure of naming as outlined by Gates offers opportunities for interpretive textual layering through "calling out (of one's name)" and "loud talking," speech addressed to a second person that contains a difference (usually a metaphor) intended for a third person to overhear and understand. With this in mind, *Deep Talk* gives homage to its indomitable predecessor. It signifies upon *The Signifying Monkey* by picking up where Gates's discussion of naming stopped, but with a difference: it focuses on proper names, nicknames, and epithets.[8]

For the reader of names, the interpretive process I call *Reading through Names and Naming* means experiencing the sense of a name, discovering its deep-level meanings, acknowledging and tracing the implications of its creative force, and interpreting the acts of resistance implicit in it. I seek to dissolve the name as "body" and rebuild it as "flesh" by highlighting the metaphoric chaos and covert stories of resistance it creates. Instead of insisting that names denote singular objects or ideas exclusively, all readings presented in this study trace the proliferation of discursive value. I argue that names in African-American texts describe, "call out," "loud talk," and enact a kind of deep talk of their own within the metatext. For instance, I capitalize and italicize the gerund phrase that names this process to highlight the dualistic nature of names as storehouses of meaning and action. *Reading through Names and Naming* functions simultaneously as a gerund phrase, the description of an interpretive process, and as a name whose discursive makeup and deep talk "call out" to West African traditions of phrase naming.

Guiding Principles

By limiting my observations and the testing of my theoretical propositions to the literature of black writers, I am not designating it as the only literary culture to which my proposed strategy for reading applies. Neither am I implying that black literature is a self-contained entity, unaffected by white cultural forms of representation. Just the opposite is true, as I demonstrate in my reading of Zora Neale Hurston's *Their Eyes Were Watching God* (1937), a novel that creates deep-level discourses through the intertextual development of names from Greco-Roman mythology.

Reading through Names and Naming is a method of interpretation, and as such, all propositions can apply to other literary cultures. The discussions in this book, however, reveal the discourse production of names within African-American literature specifically. An application of this method of reading to other literatures would have to consider the culture (or rather, interlocutory community) out of which those texts originate.

A paper presented by Kathryn Shanley, Cornell University, at the 1995 Ford Fellows Conference brought this point clearly into focus for me. During her presentation, Shanley mentioned that readers unfamiliar with Blackfeet naming traditions often misinterpret the phrase name *White Man's Dog* in James Welch's *Fools Crow*. In that novel, the nickname *White Man's Dog* contains deep talk originating from legends that associate Napi, Old Man and Old Woman, with white as the north and age as wisdom. In this mythology, Napi, a trickster figure who is the creator of human life (and death), has a kit fox (a member of the dog family of carnivores) as his constant companion. Welch, a Blackfoot and Gros Ventre Indian, names a humble but bumbling character in this novel *Sinopa*, a name that means "kit fox" in Blackfoot. Like Napi's companion, Sinopa constantly follows the novel's medicine man, who is called *White Man*, a name that associates him with the legendary Napi. Because Sinopa follows White Man as a companion, he bears the nickname *White Man's Dog*.

A lack of knowledge and understanding concerning Blackfoot legend, language, and cultural naming practices may lead readers to incorrect and even offensive interpretations of this character's name and its deep talk. Shanley comments that "Because in tribal life names reflect what a person has accomplished (that can be something foolish or valorous), or are meant as blessings to ensure what a person will become (women particularly receive names reflecting hope they will be lovely and devoted to their family) or follow ancestral patterns of naming (such as a child being named after a deceased relative), *White Man's Dog* is fitting as a nickname on many scores. It is a name that should encourage [the character] to become 'his own man' in the future, since male naming frequently served as a humbling device, a bit of a tease." [9]

White Man's Dog is not a name of insult and denigration but one whose deep talk speaks of hope, encouragement, and diachronic time—

having an existence in and a knowledge of history. It honors Native Americans' awareness of "possessing something [an ancient wisdom and heritage] that is more essential than one's oppression." [10] The same name used in an African-American text would have quite a different message. For this reason, an understanding of cultural context is essential when reading names.

My use of the term *cultural* in the paragraph above refers to language cultures and literary traditions as mutable, living forces. Much like Karla Holloway's "moorings places," it "marks the starting place of my critical interpretations," not the end of them.[11] Readers who are aware of a work's cultural origins recognize the imprints of that culture and its traditions upon names and their deep talk. They understand the cultural boundaries of onomastic expression and can identify the violation of those boundaries. They can also recognize the development and struggles of competing language cultures present within literary naming patterns. To deny the mutability of diverse language cultures in conflict is to deny their existence as living forces. To deny tradition and cultural history (either literary or social) when reading names is to deny the name, to silence both its voice and its potential for radical and re-creative discursive influence (what I call its *discursive value* or *creative force*). Therefore, the readings I offer acknowledge black cultural name coding and, moving constantly through and beyond it, explore the influencing energies of its mutability.

This does not mean that every African American will read names in the same way nor that readers from diverse class, ethnic, or gender orientations are excluded from understanding onomastic deep talk because of innate differences. Black discourse is not an essentialist property shared meagerly or guarded jealously among particular groups of African Americans. It can be learned. No system of cultural language coding is homogenous, and neither are the meanings of names somehow permeated by way of skin color, class, or gender. Each is transmitted through what George Lipsitz calls *collective memory* and *social learning.*" [12] Cultural languages transmit themselves through experiences and communal interactions; they are crafted through artifice, "handed down" orally, transmitted through cultural artifacts, and learned or shared in rituals of communal and familial bonding.

My intent is to emphasize the inflections and *learned* communal utterances that speak through shared languages—their special accents and struggles for control against alien forces. I consider this position grounded in a theoretical perspective similar to that of Hazel Carby (who comments that she draws her arguments from V. N. Voloshinov, an associate of Bakhtin). Like Carby, I do not advocate the idea that one tradition informs all of black literature. Language is constructed and reconstructed on a field of struggle for social domination and linguistic control. The accents of speech and writing and the circumstances of human experiences that transform broadly shared languages develop discursive traditions or "ways of saying" that are at once culturally, geographically, and historically specific. I agree with Ann duCille, among others, who argues "against the notion of *a* black tradition, *a* common black . . . experience, or *a* shared black . . . language" (duCille's italics).[13] Even within racial categories different experiences and language constructions abound. There are *many* traditions, *many* common experiences, and *many* shared languages that inform onomastic deep talk. Each of these vehicles for historical content and interpretation brings a different type of awareness, depth, and meaning experience to the reading of names.

To varying degrees, both the namer and the reader contribute to the discourses that names produce regardless of whether either is a member of the ethnic group from which the name originates. This interplay among name, namer, and reader functions similarly in literature and the social real. The deep talk of the name *Ralph Waldo Ellison* is informed by both the namer and the creative force of this name's historical content (*Ralph Waldo Emerson*). For Ellison, an African-American writer existing within the social real and reading a name within the context of that reality, the historical content of *Ralph Waldo* speaks of an obligation to the name's original bearer—a white American, transcendentalist writer from a Unitarian family background. Similarly, in literature the historical content of poetic names includes the social, cultural, and intertextual accents associated with its previous use. The influencing power of the name is also shaped by the intent of its utterer. Thus, Ellison hears the voice of the man who named him, his father, speaking through his own name. Determining the intent of poetic names, on the other hand, includes a consideration of characters (and narrators) as speaking subjects, the reader as an interpreting subject, and the author as a writing subject.

The term *writing subject* suggests that the author of a text does not determine textual meaning—not as its ultimate authority. Since poststructuralism declared the "death of the author," the name *author* has been replaced by the *writing subject* in many critical discourses. This phrase name situates conscious authorial intent as only one of several impulses determining meaning. Cultural implications, conscious and unconscious ideological constructions, and readers also inform meaning. Since *Deep Talk* discusses interpretation as well as the author and the poetic name as manipulators of discourse, its hero is (at least) tripartite: writing subject, interpreting subject, and speaking subject.

When referring to this list of heroes, I use the phrases *hypothesized author* or *hypothesized authorial intent*. These phrase names emphasize the various influences and meanings gathered around and in a literary offering, including those inscribed by poetic names, characters, and narrators. Moreover, it speaks clearly of what we do when we attempt to pin down the meaning of name utterances through an assessment of authorial intent. We hypothesize. Jerrold Levinson explains:

> Utterance meaning is logically distinct from utterer's meaning and at the same time is necessarily related to it conceptually: we arrive at utterance meaning by aiming at utterer's meaning in the most comprehensive and informed manner we can muster as the utterance's intended recipients. Actual utterer's intention, then, is not what is determinative of the meaning of a literary offering (or other linguistic discourse) but such intention as optimally *hypothesized*, given all the resources available to us in the work's internal structure and the relevant surrounding context of creation, in all its legitimately invoked specificity [Levinson's italics].[14]

Because of their many influences, the utterances that result from an understanding of hypothetical authorial intent are not necessarily those of the text's "real" author. According to Levinson, hypothetical authorial intent is the reader's best epistemical guess considering the traditions from which the literary work originates, the author's oeuvre and cultural orientation, the historical milieu of the text's creation, and even interviews, diaries, or letters of the author (when available). As we discover new information concerning a historical event, an author, name, or an idea, new interpretations of those events, authors, names, and ideas emerge. Hypothetical authorial intent, then, is our best construction of authorial intent given our understanding of background information and the interplay of ideas and ideological constructs.

When we accept hypothetical authorial intent as a guide for interpretation, we also accept the possibility that "real" authors *do not always say what they thought they were saying*. Onomastic deep talk speaks directly to a reader, informing him or her of metaphoric (and, sometimes, masked) discursive action. The incantatory utterances of names depend upon the reader's recognition of semantic differences and sociocultural accents that often work magic beyond authorial intent. For instance, an utterance interpreted by way of its culturally familiar associations or its sound or graphic makeup (what I call *cultural, homophonic,* and *graphic imprints*) may be supported fully by its narrative situation and still not reflect what the true author intended it to mean. In fact, it may even have different interpretive meanings among its various readers.

The name *Nunkie*, appearing in chapter 15 of Zora Neale Hurston's *Their Eyes Were Watching God*, offers an example. The name and its textual proclivity remind the reader of "nookie," a term many readers find culturally familiar. While researching and writing this text, I discovered two readers who interpreted this term differently, one reading it as "sexual foreplay" and the other reading it as "the woman's sex, like the P—— word." Both readings are supported by the surface story, with one being more specific about the suggested level of achieved intimacy between the woman who bears the name *Nunkie* and the character Tea Cake, who chases her on a regular basis. I also discovered that the effects of this name's imprinted discourses conjure other meanings. The name's relationship with events and descriptions in the surface text proliferates its discourse-producing potential until it undermines surface events and offers the "inside scoop" on the playful pair's games of chase.

Besides its cultural imprint, the term *Nunkie* speaks from two homophonic imprints: *chunky*, which is Janie's description of the woman, and *none-key*, the binary opposite of Janie's subject position as possessor of what her husband, Tea Cake, suggestively calls "de keys tuh de kingdom" (181). It also speaks from a graphic imprint (nun). Although the name's cultural and homophonic imprints have physical and sexual implications, the graphic imprint does not replicate these discourses. It silences the discourses suggesting sexual flirtation by producing a name-entity that usurps surface action and transforms it within a metatext. Beneath the surface this name-entity, *nun*, inverts the games of chase played out between Tea Cake and Nunkie, transforming them into a commentary on purity. In the metatext, any suggestion of infidelity disappears through this name play. Instead of *being* chased, this name-entity *is* chaste—as in "chaste as a nun." We may now conclude that the name's deep talk offers a *nun key* that informs against the surface text and reports that Tea Cake and Nunkie's relationship is as chaste as a nun.

This reading revises the reader's interpretative focus so that questions concerning Tea Cake and his fidelity become subordinate to those about Janie and the agitators who encourage her jealousy, possessiveness, and emotional insecurity. We also discover that we have fallen victim to a supreme trickster's ruse. In Tea Cake's attempt to explain himself, he tells Janie, "Don't keer how big uh lie get told, somebody kin b'lieve it!" (205). By reading the story's nun "key," we understand that we, the readers who doubted Tea Cake's fidelity and praised Janie for exposing his lustful play, have bought a lie that encompasses the entire chapter, a "big lie" told by a master of verbal manipulation.

As re-creative forces within literary texts, names like *Nunkie* negotiate their potential for creating discursive magic through a multitude of referential, denotative, and connotative modes of expression that may or may not have been intended. My use of the term *reference* implies the concrete objects designated (the flirtatious woman, or subject persona, as a character in Hurston's novel); *connotation* is the historical content of a name—its "memory" of sociocultural, intertextual, and other meaningful accents (*nookie*, *chunky*, and *none-key* as subject positions)—and *denotation* refers to the theme, entities, or objects created by names as creative acts of onomastic deep talk (*nun* as a subject position with differentiating position effects). Through these three modes of expression, names signify upon and revise a text's surface level of interpretation by commenting on it, subverting its precepts, and undermining its construction. They provide poetic names with deep-level communications that reveal to readers alternative ways of interpreting their meanings.

Not all names take advantage of this potential for meaning. Not all names are poetic; some are muted. Their potential as creative or subversive forces does not promote clearly defined or (and this is important) textually significant meanings. Therefore, their role as utterances, as interpretable units of speech communication, is frustrated and underdetermined. In most cases these muted names appear only once and are assigned to peripheral characters. They play a minor role in the development of meaning and action within metatexts—if any role at all.

Another way a name may be muted is if it is read inactively. The effects of referential, connotative, and denotative modes of deep-level communication depend upon the presence of an active reader, one who hears, understands, and interprets a name's deep talk. This view of reading poetic names does not affect the nature of the name but describes the nature of the reader's involvement in the creation of meaning. An inactive reader views names as nothing more than marks on a page identifying characters. This reader does not seek the work of names as creative forces. She or he may intuit the deep talk of poetic names and dismiss it as interesting but outside the structures of meaning necessary for interpretation. In such readings, the discursive function of poetic names is muted by the singularity of purpose thrust upon them. The active reader, on the other hand, pursues the conditions and functions of onomastic multiplicity. For the active reader, poetic names speak from not one referential, denotative, or connotative space, but many.

Because names mask their discourses by abbreviating and embodying these discourses, their expressive functions proliferate; they gain the ability to work on the surface and beneath it. In this way they identify: subject personae, by which I mean an actor's or character's physical presence; subject positions, meaning states or modes of being; and discursive effects, which are the events and perceptual changes created or revealed through naming. These last two contextual aims represent the "flesh" of which I spoke earlier and demonstrated through my reading of *Nunkie* as a name-entity. Subject positions and discursive effects perform the work of onomastic discursive strategy.

Poetic names that designate subject positions speak from five interrelated and aggregating categories of deep talk: cultural, ancestral, social, attitudinal, and allegorical. Through constant manipulation and conflation of these categories, names communicate with readers, informing them of discourses that develop characterization as well as the stories and events of the metatext. The allegorical deep talk of the name *Pilate* in Toni Morrison's *Song of Solomon* (1977), for instance, signals the presence of a deep-level intertextual impulse that repeats and revises the biblical story of salvation and redemption from which the name originates. (I present a reading of this name and its allegorical impulses in chapter 3.)

Discursive effects, on the other hand, function as informants and liberators of intratextual and extratextual discourses. Although there are four types, each may be realized through the deep talk of a single name, as with *Nunkie*, or through the interaction (and intervention) of several poetic names. The first of these, narrative effects, are poetic names that supplement, redefine, and speak of narrative action. Position effects, the second type, change, challenge, or reflect character roles and charatonymic development—that is, the development of individual attributes and accountabilities. The third type, object effects, operates as eponyms and emblems that violate and destablize the topic, or what Bakhtin calls the *hero*, of discourse and refocus it.[15] The fourth, which I call the *eruption of the true-real*, is deep talk at its most active.

Julia Kristeva coined the term *true-real* (*le vréel*) to describe a disruptive, iconic force that surfaces in discourse as an incarnation of what it signifies, becoming both signifier and signified.[16] I adapt the true-real in *Deep Talk* as an impossible or aberrant "truth," an idea or once foreclosed contextual aim, that reveals itself through a name's deepest levels of speech and action. The true-real grows out of a name's sustained accumulation of historical content, and its interpretation reveals an ideological message that either supports or revises surface messages. Later, I demonstrate the influence of deep talk upon the true-real as I read the names *Janie Woods* and *Vergible Woods* not only as the names of characters but as the incarnate names of gods in Hurston's *Their Eyes Were*

Watching God. In chapter 4, I discuss several names and their function as icons of the true-real, including a phrase name from Gloria Naylor's *Women of Brewster Place* (1983): *the tall yellow woman in the bloody green and black dress.* This name functions in the metatext as an incarnation of what it signifies; it is an iconic force, a *name-entity*, that obliterates the assumptions of difference and separation among women.

Issues of referential proliferation such as those that create name-entities are central to my analytic approach—an approach that departs from traditional paradigms of onomastic disclosure. The interpretive guidelines I offer constitute a transformation or reorganization of three primary theories of referential onomastics. Gottlob Frege initiated the first of these theories over a hundred years ago. The basic concepts of his sense theory originate from a belief that proper names have both connotation and denotation in the form of sense/meaning (*Bedeutung*) and reference. For Frege, sense determines reference, and nothing outside this criterion influences how a name realizes its object. The second theory, the description theory, was introduced by Bertrand Russell in 1918. Russell contends that the signs we normally consider proper names (John, Linda, Saul, Mary, etc.) are really disguised definite descriptions, truncated sets or clusters of meanings synonymous with systems of objects. In other words, proper nouns are a shorthand for descriptions and are *not* names at all.[17] The causal theory of reference is the third model. This theory was introduced in a 1970 series of lectures given by Saul Kripke at Princeton University. Kripke insists that rigid designation, fixing a referent, assures the correlation between meaning and object designation. After a referent is fixed through an initial use, that name denotes the referent in all possible worlds or situations. A causal chain of reference maintains this relationship. Kripke's referential chain does not allow new information concerning an object or a name's use (such as symbolic intent and other meanings) to affect reference as determined by its original descriptive designation.

Although I find value in Kripke's vision of a referential chain and adapt it to my own purposes, poetic names function in diverse ways and on multiple levels; therefore, I cannot define them quite so rigidly. Their ability to achieve a variety of contextual aims and support several contradictory themes gives them their discursive force as units of speech communication. It also liberates their proliferation, creating two or more parallel objects (referents and denoted name-entities or icons) whose stories develop along separate chains simultaneously. These chains of onomastic intent are not rigid but are flexible and fluid. They allow new information to enter their semiotic space, restructure meaning, and redefine both the referential foci of names and the objects denoted.

My paradigm of *Reading through Names and Naming* uses Kripke's concept of rigid designation only as a point of departure. It ignores Russell's dismissal of traditional proper nouns as names but preserves his notion of names as truncated discourses that explain the role a name plays within particular contexts. Also, it modifies Frege's sense theory by allowing images, customs, beliefs, and external signifying practices provoked by the mention of a name to influence that name's internal textual spaces as well as its external framework or chain of concrete meaning.

Throughout *Deep Talk*, I refer to this framework of meaning as a lifeworld. Poetic names, like all utterances, exist within lifeworlds. Again, I borrow from three prominent scholars—Jürgen Habermas, Linda Hutcheon, and Henry Louis Gates—only to collapse and revise their arguments.[18] Habermas defines the lifeworld (which he spells using a hyphen, *life-world*) of literary expression as one "which is culture bound, ego-centered, and pre-interpreted in the ordinary language of social groups and socialized individuals." I use the term to identify contextual environments predefined by sociolinguistic orders in which the concrete themes of certain names have value and voice while others do not. Linda Hutcheon describes something similar to onomastic lifeworlds when defining her use of the term *heterocosm* in "Metafictional Implications for Novelistic Reference." Hutcheon describes the world of literary reference as different from the referential order of everyday speech—it behaves and refers differently. For her, a literary heterocosm is "another cosmos, a second ordered referential system." In this study, the heterocosm exists but not in opposition to everyday speech. It is the product of onomastic deep talk that stands in opposition to stories and subject positions produced by the surface narrative. Henry Louis Gates describes this world of reference and rhetorical meaning as a "densely structured discursive universe, one absolutely dependent on the play of differences." This study views the sociolinguistic lifeworlds of poetic names in much the same way with only one distinguishing feature—*multiplicity*. A single text may contain several sociolinguistic lifeworlds that determine the discursive value of names and dictate what measure of resistance each name must employ when threatened by alien spheres of influence.

The authority of deep talk as the primary force of change and creativity within poetic names orders itself around a hierarchy of power. All namers do not exercise the same word force or discursive value. Those inside particular spheres, or lifeworlds, of influence speak more powerfully than those excluded from it. In some, but not all, black-authored texts this hierarchy of power is racially inflected, with white namers appearing to maintain more power and influence in the surface text than blacks, regardless of gender or class distinctions.[19] Beneath the surface, a struggle for dominance occurs that usually results in one of two events: either the resisting name reshapes defining elements within the hostile lifeworld of the surface by signifying upon its master namers and the names they control through irony, pastiche, and parody, or it is itself reshaped by hostile contact.

A name's complete concealment beneath the surface, for instance, assists it in successfully resisting the onomastic deep talk of a hostile lifeworld. In such cases, namelessness signals the "absent presence" of secret names. These are names whose existence is mentioned in dialogues, narration, and book titles without actually appearing themselves in the narrative text. Ralph Ellison's *Invisible Man* and James Weldon Johnson's *Autobiography of an Ex-Colored Man* (1912) are novels whose primary speaking subjects have secret names. One way of interpreting namelessness in these texts is as a symbolic gesture denoting the nameless characters' inability to assert themselves fully within a world that is hostile or alien to their self-image. Such a reading is supported by the surface texts of both novels; in Ellison's case the surface text excludes the invisible man as an autonomous self-defining being, and in Johnson's case the suface text allows the ex-colored man (who passes for white) only a fragmented representation of self.

When reading these texts through names and naming, character namelessness symbolizes excluded and fragmented identities only in the surface narrative. Beneath the surface, namelessness functions as pure "flesh." Because the names of the invisible man and the ex-colored man are not inscribed in the text, they are formless and elusive, able to avoid assault from alien namers whose word force dominates the surface. They are nonviolent names, so to speak, whose amorphous disobedience to narrative protocol is a form of resistance. A more intricate example of nonviolent resistance occurs in Sherley Anne Williams's *Dessa Rose* (1986), where the protagonist's "secret" name appears as the title of the novel but does not appear in "The Darky," a section of the novel controlled by slave masters as namers, or in the dialogues of any white namers. Chapter 5 provides a reading of this novel and the play of names and naming within it.

Successful resistance to the discursive force of an alien lifeworld also occurs when names enter a hostile environment and actively challenge its sociolinguistic order through deep talk. Such is the case in the *Narrative of William Wells Brown* (1847). In this narrative, competing onomastic lifeworlds grind against each other as the resistant deep talk of the name *Sandford* works havoc upon surface meaning. The demand for a name change typifies the lifeworld this name confronts. The hierarchy of the word within the sociolinguistic lifeworld of slave masters is ordered foremost by what Lacan calls the "Law of the Father" or, more precisely in Brown's autobiography, the law of white masters.

Brown's master, Dr. John Young, considers it an insult for a white child to bear the same name as a slave, a being his worldview defines as inferior. When Young's nephew also named *William* comes to live on his plantation, Young orders Brown's mother to change her son's name. In other words, Brown's master asks her to distinguish her son's identity from that of the white child through the rhetoric of naming. Young's role as master and instigator of change defines the originating contextual constraints of the new name. In the language of the master, the name assigned, no matter what it is, identifies Brown as different from the nephew. It identifies him as an inferior other whose very existence lends credibility to the nephew's assumed superiority.

Even though Brown suffers severe beatings while struggling to keep his original name, his master forces a new one upon him. This name originates within a lifeworld set apart from the master's linguistic control and communicates a deep-level message of radical difference through the letter *d*. The name Brown's mother gives him, *Sandford*, is a modified, or reconfigured, version of the Anglo name *Sanford*. The *d* empowers the new name from within, imprinting it graphically with a signifying difference that brings with it the independent voice of subversive deep talk. Similar to the resistant acts of naming often inscribed by black namers today (such as *Lisa* to *Jalisa*, *Tiara* to *Kiara*, or *James* and *Mack* to *Jamack*), change through excess and mutation builds subversive force. Regardless of whether Brown or his mother intended *Sandford* to be an act of resistance, the silent or spoken *d* can be interpreted by the reader as a site of resistance aimed against the Anglo spelling or pronunciation of *Sanford* and, therefore, against the authority of the master's word.

The *d* announces a violence within the word that undermines (or signifies upon) the master's role as unnamer. Its disruptive excess and difference speak against what Brown defines as a "cruel act" of unnaming. Brown tells the reader that he experienced the stripping away and forced replacement of his birth name as a personal assault. He writes: "This I thought to be one of the most cruel acts that could be committed upon my rights" (43). Brown's statement turns the deep talk of *Sandford* against the actions of the master who demanded his unnaming. It also extends the name's contextual constraints and its potential for meaning (its objectives as imprinted and revised through the letter *d*). The mutated name communicates a deep-level message of irony that destablizes the topic of its intended discourse. Instead of speaking of Brown's inferiority, the name's deep-level communication speaks of those who dominate the sociolinguistic order of white masters. Beneath its surface meanings and within its deep levels of discourse production, *Sandford* resists the defining elements assigned to it in the lifeworld it enters. It functions as an object effect—an emblem of black naming—that erupts in the hostile lifeworld of the master's "law" and speaks of a white man's cruelty with each enunciation.

In other words, the contextual aim and discursive task of *Sandford* split and reemerge, producing what can be read as two coexisting name functions. On one level the name is an emblem of the master's word, whose object effects express a belief in black inferiority. Alongside that name function is another, the name as an emblem of black subversive action, that challenges the master's word by speaking covertly of injustice and white cruelty. The entrance of the name *Sandford* into a hostile lifeworld (one distinct from the trace of blackness it contains) splits the concrete themes of the name, forming two streams of meaning—one operating on the surface level of interpretation to unname the protagonist and the other working in a metatext that mocks the master through an act of subversive rephrasing.

I refer to this "splitting off" of diverse meanings as *name fragmentation*. When new utterances interrupt, reform, merge with, or usurp the primary contextual aim or the dominant themes of a name, some form of fragmentation occurs—either internally (as in *Sandford*) or externally (as in Ellison's attempt to silence his middle name by reducing it to a *W*). It may also occur when stories of symbolic rebirth, death, or resurrection restructure the concrete themes of a name within the metatext.[20] In addition, any change in a character's original name, such as *William* to *Sandford*, indicates that one of three name fragmentation rituals (supranaming, unnaming, or renaming) has occurred.

The first of the three, supranaming, is simply name supplementation. It occurs when speakers use two or more names frequently and interchangeably to identify one character or when words and phrases in a surface narrative suggest alternate names that do not themselves appear in the text. In chapter 3, I offer an example of the latter form of supranaming as it operates in James Baldwin's *Go Tell It on the Mountain* (1953). In that novel, not only do the names of biblical characters emerge within a metatext, but the stories from which these names originate emerge as well.

Unnaming (which, by the way, is not always pernicious) can be represented in three ways: through namelessness, the loss of a name, or the silencing of a name's enunciative capabilities. Renaming, the third ritual, occurs when a name is redefined, reaccented, or revised as a homonym of itself; when a lost name is reclaimed; or when a new designator contains the original name as part of its graphic makeup.[21] *Sandford* unnames *William*, but an act of renaming occurs when *Sandford* is reaccented by what I describe above as rephrasing. Renaming also occurs when Brown reclaims his birth name and *William* replaces *Sandford* as an unmitigated sign of liberty.

The fragmentation of *Sandford* produces several chains or streams of meaning that operate within at least two distinct lifeworlds. The name serves as an emblem of a black signifying difference in a lifeworld that respects black human rights and autonomy—the world of black namers. In the lifeworld of the white master's word, it serves as an emblem of lost identity and inequality as well as a voice of irony and subversion. *Sandford* successfully realizes its potential for meaning. Its deep talk speaks of a slave (Brown in his youth), an act of cruelty (the stripping away of his birth name), and an idea whose trace appears in the form of the letter *d* (black human rights and autonomy). Stated another way, it functions not only as a subject persona designator but as a subject position designator (slave) and two discursive effects: a narrative effect and an object effect.

The discussions presented above outline the seven guiding principles of *Reading through Names and Naming*. By way of summary, I list them.

1. A poetic name is an action-oriented and interpretable utterance whose discursive force motivates narrative discourses beneath, but not without, the surface text.

2. Not all literary names are poetic—some are muted. The potential of their stylistic auras does not promote clearly defined and textually significant aims and themes. Therefore, their roles and enunciative desires as interpretable units of deep-level speech are frustrated and underdetermined.

3. There are two modes of reading poetic names: active and inactive.

4. Names and phrase names that enunciate subject positions have contextual aims that operate from within five interrelated and aggregating categories: cultural, ancestral, social, attitudinal, and allegorical.

5. The contextual aim of names and phrase names that motivate extralinguistic events through the proliferation of discursive value produces four types of discursive effects: narrative effects, position effects, object effects, and the eruption of the true-real.

6. Like all utterances, poetic names exist within contextual environments, sociolinguistic orders in which the concrete themes of some names have value and voice while others do not. These contextual environments are the lifeworlds of name utterances. A poetic name that successfully enters a resisting environment either reshapes defining elements within that lifeworld or is itself reshaped by oppositional contact.

7. Name fragmentation, the "splitting off" or merging of defining elements and historical content, occurs when a new utterance interrupts, reforms, or usurps the primary contextual aim or the dominant themes of a name. It may also occur when symbolic rebirth, death, or resurrection restructure the concrete themes of a name. These fragmentations appear in three ritualistic forms: supranaming, unnaming, and renaming.

Onomastic Desires

The seven guiding principles of this book offer clues for dissolving the protective core of names such as *Nunkie* and *Sandford* that embody the effects they seek to provoke, but they alone are not enough to reveal the magic of literary names and naming. Much like the reader's awareness of Hurston's nun "key," an awareness of multiple speech centers within poetic names provides the "inside scoop" on onomastic meanings, messages, and metatexts. Poetic names have several speech centers from which they perform their enunciative tasks and create their metatexts. A reader who traces these speech centers informs the process of interpretation and, if only briefly, sobers the chaotic proliferation of name-motivated discourse production.

Since Mikhail Bakhtin explores the manipulation of multiple voices within utterances, I begin my explanation of this topic with his ideas. Several critics note Bakhtin's theories as useful in the analysis of African-American literature and literary history. His concern with social dialects is a model for Mae Gwendolyn Henderson's trope of discursive diversity called *speaking in tongues*. Karla Holloway cites his concepts of *ideologija* (the socially determined, semiotic value of ideas) and dialogics when arguing the polyvocal liberation of texts and sociohistorical utterances within critical theory. His notion of double-voiced discourse informs Henry Louis Gates's theory of rhetorical revision, called *Signifyin(g)*.[22] Double-voiced discourse also informs the basic rhetorical strategies of onomastic deep talk that *Reading through Names and Naming* seeks to uncover.

Bakhtin's three categories of discourse types offer readers an organizing tool for charting the variety of voices that names contain. They are also invaluable as a model for tracing connections between the metaphoric chaos produced by names and their goal proliferation. I appropriate Bakhtin's categories and revise them so they speak specifically to issues of literary onomastics. My first and most important revision is one of renaming. Since my primary reason for discussing these categories is to provide the reader with a way to distinguish how and to whom a name desires to speak, I call them *categories of onomastic desire*.[23]

Every poetic name operates within one of three categories of onomastic desire from which it produces deep-level communications. The first of these, the referent-oriented desire, represents the monologic expression of the "real" author's authority as namer. Names in this category signify the "body" of particular characters, what I call *subject personae*, within a fictional world. They do not recognize or speak to the reader, characters, or other words outside this function. This is where the interpretation of names stops for the inactive reader or the reader who is unfamiliar with specific codes within poetic names.

Names in the second category, single-voiced objectified desire, are more vocal. Their deep talk may be sensed by the inactive reader, but it is usually omitted from the process of interpretation. For Bakhtin, objectified discourse refers to a narrator's presentation of a character's words in a manner that is characteristic or typical of a way of speaking or being. Like Bakhtin's second category, the objectified onomastic desire presents a discourse through which a name's deep talk speaks characteristically or typically of its object (titles and passing epithets fall into this category).[24] I include in this category intratextual desires that alter Bakhtin's concentration on ways of saying so that *what* the name says also becomes the object of the reader's focus. The desire of names in this category is to inform the reader of sociotypical significations or to offer truncated descriptions of narrative events and referents. They describe an extratextual referent or reveal an author's sociolinguistic revisionary action and commentary. They may also foreshadow or reflect narrative events and characterization.

Nella Larsen uses several names of this type in her novel *Passing* (1929)—each containing intratextual desire. Take, for instance, the name *Kendry*, the maiden name of the character Clare. The intratextual components of this name are "Ken" and "dry," that is, "kin dry." Because this character has decided to "pass," she disconnects or distances her *true self* from all ancestral and familial relations, including those shared with her bigoted white husband, John Bellew, and their daughter, Margery. She is indeed kin dry (or dry of kin). The intratextual components of her name give voice to this lack. They also speak of disinheritance. *Kendry* suggests that Clare's network of black community kin, including her friend Irene, either consciously or unconsciously rejects her because of her decision to cross the constructed borders of racial identity and remain there.

Like Bakhtin's objectified word, *Kendry* has only one speech center—the author's—that enters into deep-level communication with the reader. The intratextual components of names with single-voiced objectified desire constitute an utterance that reveals events and characterization without these discourses being manipulated in any way by speakers within the text, even if that speaker is the narrator. Speakers within Larsen's novel never acknowledge the allusion to lack in *Kendry* nor the suggestion of denial and doom in the name of Clare's childhood friend, Irene *Westover* Redfield.

The colorful name Irene *Westover* appears in the novel's second chapter, where two women meet inadvertently at a rooftop restaurant called the Drayton. Like Clare Kendry, Irene Westover is passing (for white) while reviving herself from the summer heat in the "whites only" restaurant. Unlike Clare, Irene plans to reclaim her racial identity the moment she leaves the Drayton. She professes disgust at the idea of passing and even denounces it when Clare questions her about it. However, both Irene's presence in the restaurant and the deep talk of her maiden name tell a different story.

Westover is an intratextual name whose metaphoric meanings proliferate aggressively to create several strings of deep talk that speak of character choices and foreshadow narrative events without moving beyond the discourse production of single-voiced desires. Throughout the novel, the West symbolizes an awareness of one's *true self* and past familial bonds, including racial and ethnic identities.[25] Because of this, the word's use as a component of Irene Redfield's maiden name, *Westover*, informs against the character and reminds the reader of Irene's chosen racial associations while a patron of the Drayton. Irene's *west* (her racial identity) is momentarily *over*—at least while she enjoys the cool breeze circulating at a "whites only" restaurant on an unusually hot summer day.

Westover also foreshadows Clare's ultimate demise and names the responsible party. The name functions within the metatext as a subject position designator and at least three discursive effects. As a subject position, *Westover* speaks of Irene's relationship to Clare. Irene represents a past, a *west*, that Clare abandons by passing permanently into a white world. As a position effect it points toward the character it denotes, Irene, identifying her as the person who ultimately causes Clare's death. As a narrative effect it foreshadows events yet to come, and as an object effect it subverts the deep-level communication of Irene's given name. Here, we find the chaotic multiplicity of onomastic deep talk at its most revealing intratextual play.

The object effects of the name *Westover* subvert the deep talk of *Irene*, which means "the personification of peace," long before the character violates the most obvious implications of this subject position through murder. Ironically, as a narrative effect *Westover* and the character's married name, *Redfield*, speak of the only method through which Irene believes peace (in her marriage) can be secured. Both names perform as "undercover" informants that foreshadow events. Irene and her actions stand as road blocks to Clare's ability to move back into the black community and recapture those things of the past for which she longs. Like a caution sign, *Westover* speaks of dangers lying ahead and announces covertly that Clare's chances to recover her "west" by seducing Irene's husband will be "over" by novel's end. *Redfield* reveals why. In a misguided attempt to maintain harmony and peace in her marriage, Irene forces the spilling of Clare's "red" blood. She pushes Clare from a window, thereby creating a "field" of red beneath it. Thus, the "undercover" informant *Redfield* foreshadows the way Clare dies and speaks, almost too graphically, of its messy results.

Distanced from these functions of *Westover* is the name's use as a description of the "strange transference of conditions" between Irene and Clare. Again, the name functions as an undercover informant. In the introduction of *An Intimation of Things Distant*, Charles Larson writes that after the murder Irene inherits Clare's life of "duplicity and isolation" (xv). Irene hopes her actions will save her disintegrating marriage, but murder only brings a realization that she has "completely lost control of [her husband's] mind and heart" (274). The poetic name *Westover*, then, informs the reader that Irene's life is one in which *her* connection to family, *her* "west" (like Clare's), is over by novel's end.

If narrators or characters use the deep talk of an objectified name like *Westover*, *Redfield*, or *Kendry* for their own purposes, the utterance contains more than one speech center and expresses onomastic desires of the third category, double-voiced signifying desires. Poetic names in this category communicate their deep talk to a variety of audiences, including characters in the text, other names, and the reader. There are three subcategories of signifying desire: single-directed double-voiced desire, multidirectional double-voiced desire, and active signifying desire. This last subcategory is the most aggressive, the one through which names create their own province, or lifeworld, of meaning and action.

The first of the three subcategories, single-directed double-voiced desire, includes stylized names; charatonymic names; and homophonic, graphic, and culturally imprinted names. These name types are single directed because they have only one denoted object and double voiced because they have at least two centers of discourse production. By this I mean that narrators, characters, other onomastic structures, and extratextual influences aggressively assist in producing what a name says without changing its denotative focus. In the *Narrative of William Wells Brown*, for instance, *Sandford* speaks from two distinct centers of discourse production: the world of black namers and the world of white masters. This stylized name signifies the idea of black communal autonomy as well as lost identity and inequality while denoting a single entity: slave.

Names in this first category of signifying desire remain single directed only if they maintain one denotative focus within one developing story (as *Sandford* does). If the name uses a metatext to develop more than one object, it becomes multidirectional. Multidirectional, double-voiced desires represent the second subcategory of signifying desire and usually speak of two or more themes and name-entities. These names are most often revisions of previously used names accented by the chiding revision of parody (such as "calling out" of one's name), the disruptive tendencies of narrator- or character-manipulated irony (or "loud talking"), and the genial revision of pastiche ("calling out to" another entity, history, memory, or name—Ralph Waldo Ellison's name is a perfect example since it "calls out to" Emerson).

In the third subcategory of signifying desire, active signifying desire, the subversive forces of poetic names work covertly to transform surface discourses and create the action of deep-level narratives. Here, the multi-directional desires of double-voiced names become agitated and expand. Not only do they develop more than one denotation, but they aggressively participate in and develop two (or more) distinct, and constantly intersecting, story lines—one in the surface text and another in the meta-text. A multidirectional name like *Ralph Waldo* can become so intimately "invested" in the development of its dual stories that at the point of intersection it "calls out to" entities or events existing within the metatext (I offer an example of this in chapter 5). This is the subcategory of onomastic desire through which name-entities and the true-real work their most aggressive, incantatory magic—a subcategory that this text spends a great deal of time exploring.

Scope of the Book

Deep Talk consists of two parts. Part 1 contains four chapters and discusses in depth the eclectic methodological foundations of *Reading through Names and Naming* outlined in this introduction. In chapter 1, I attempt to ground my use of deep talk in African philosophy through a discussion of specific similarities existing between African and African-American cultural and literary naming histories. I briefly introduce the concept *nommo* to demonstrate its usefulness in reading names in African-American literature. Some anthropologists consider the Dogon ethnographic work of Marcel Griaule (who introduced the term in 1948) to be in disrepute. I found, however, that the concepts revealed in Griaule's study are essential to reading names in canonical black texts. I demonstrate why by reading the *nommo* force of names in Toni Morrison's *Beloved* (1987) and Ralph Ellison's *Invisible Man*. In both these novels, key elements of what Griaule attributes to the Dogon philosopher Ogotemmêli appear within the deep talk of names and name calling to produce essential narrative effects.

In chapter 2, I follow this discussion with sample readings that demonstrate how the seven guiding principles of *Reading through Names and Naming* reveal name-motivated deep talk. I explore how these principles, the three categories of onomastic desire, and the reader function cooperatively to make known the deep-level meanings of names and naming in Zora Neale Hurston's *Their Eyes Were Watching God*. The poetic names of this novel create discourses that develop and refine its surface story on multiple levels simultaneously. Within each level, names act as extralinguistic actants (actors or name-entities) of the stories and events they create. A rigorous play of names and naming undergirds and undermines surface meaning throughout Hurston's text, allowing the re-creative force of onomastic deep talk to disrupt chains of reference and develop several metatexts. I envision the metatexts of *Their Eyes Were Watching God* as streamers set in motion by a zephyr of deep talk. The readings I present are only a few of these streamers.

The following chapter, chapter 3, presents in depth each of the three forms of name fragmentation and the roles they play in unpacking the voices that speak through a name. I begin by focusing on onomastic desires (more intensely than I do in chapter 2) and exploring how they expose the deep-level communications a reader unpacks. I then provide examples of each name fragmentation ritual and demonstrate how they develop brief metatexts in three novels: the renaming of *Pilate* in Toni Morrison's *Song of Solomon* (1977), the unnaming of *Tod Clifton* in Ralph Ellison's *Invisible Man*, and several supranaming events in James Baldwin's *Go Tell It on the Mountain*. In this last reading, I offer a diagram of supranaming fragmentations and follow that diagram with a description of an active reader's participation in the experience of onomastic meaning.

In chapters 3 and 4, I pay particular attention to names that intertextualize biblical stories and their socialized meanings. The development of names and themes derived from the Bible is a recurring feature of African-American literature. Therefore, my reading of biblical intertextuality continues throughout this study, where appropriate, even when biblical themes and allegories arise from the discourse production of nonbiblical names. Chapter 4, for instance, explores the relationship between onomastic resistance and the true-real in Toni Morrison's *Beloved*,

The Autobiography of Malcolm X (1965), and Gloria Naylor's *Women of Brewster Place*. My reading of Naylor's text traces a biblical allegory developed by the deep talk of several names, including the phrase name *the tall yellow woman in the bloody green and black dress*.

Part 2 opens with two chapters of application that trace extended metatexts—that is, the development of a name's deep talk throughout a novel—and closes with a discussion of race and gendered difference. I selected Sherley Anne Williams's *Dessa Rose* and Ernest J. Gaines's *A Gathering of Old Men* (1984) as my subjects for extended readings. Both are novels that actively develop extended metatexts and resistance through the manipulation of names and naming. The most obvious indication of this is that these texts announce the influencing agents of various lifeworlds by using names as section and chapter titles. I also selected these novels because they were both published in the 1980s and therefore afford an opportunity to engage a focused comparative discussion of two contemporary writers' use of names.

In these readings, I trace the development and fragmentation of the main characters' various names, epithets, nicknames, and misnomers throughout the novels to uncover what the deep talk of names and naming in these texts is really saying. I begin in chapter 5 with a discussion of *Dessa Rose* that traces the proliferation of deep talk communicated through two central female character names. I continue this discussion as I read *A Gathering* in chapter 6, commenting on a variety of differences between Williams's and Gaines's use of names. This chapter introduces names from *Dessa Rose* that raise questions of gendered difference.

Like Williams, most black women writers start with the internal definitions of self and the development of intimate interpersonal relationships before extending these definitions and relationships into the broader community and the world. In contrast, critics often consider African-American male-authored literature as one that deals foremost with the broadly representative and least with the introspective or interpersonal. My comparative reading of Gaines's and Williams's novels tests these assumptions as they relate to names and naming. These readings reveal that the discourse production of names in both novels maintains previously noted gendered differences. Gaines's *Mathu*, most consistently, signifies the development of a broadly representative idea, whereas names in *Dessa Rose* develop discourses of individual subjectivity and intimate interpersonal relations.

Since gender is often racially inflected, my comparisons of Gaines's and Williams's novels trace only the crosscurrents of gendered difference that move within the bend of race. My use of the phrase "bend of race" identifies places within a text or within the social real where gendered identity politics and socialization, as acknowledged by individuals within a particular racial category, influence aesthetic choices and moments of communal bonding. Similar to the movement of water in the bend of a river, it is the place where structures of support and new bearings change the direction of traditionally harmonic (and racially defined) ideological constructs and communal alliances—where crosscurrents of differences challenge and transform uniformity. I continue that discussion in chapter 7 while reading names that speak primarily to the difference race imposes. My subject texts are Richard Wright's *Black Boy* (1945), Toni Morrison's *Song of Solomon*, Maya Angelou's *I Know Why the Caged Bird Sings* (1970), and Alice Walker's "Everyday Use" (1967), among others. Within the bend of race, I find the strongest currents of gendered difference manifested through these authors' use of the maternal signifier.

In a section of chapter 7 titled "Don't Call Him Boy, Girlfriend," I explore how gender and race affect an author's use of name fragmentation rituals. I base my evaluations and conclusions on the fragmentations of two terms, *boy* and *girl*, used frequently as epithets, nicknames, and pet names in both literature and the social real. These words contain cultural imprints whose deep-level utterances function as resistance to racist unnaming and denigration. My discussions explain how they express their deep talk and the role that name fragmentation plays in their ability to develop utterances of resistance. My readings include a consideration of all works discussed previously as well as brief readings from two additional texts: Arna Bontemps's *Black Thunder* (1936) and James Earl Hardy's "gay hip-hop love story," *B-Boy Blues* (1994).

Deep Talk acknowledges many, but not all, interpretive possibilities and meaning experiences that literary naming offers. It celebrates the vitality and resonance of African-American literary naming practices by affirming that names in these texts are not lifeless markers of characters, void of deep-level meaning. They are elements of speech communication that perform particular contextual tasks while articulating varied themes and stories of their own. This book amplifies the matrix of literary names that develops metatexts, exposing their discursive attitudes and re-creative force. It acknowledges the onomastic strategies of discourse production by offering a discussion of the liberatory energies motivating the "flesh" of poetic names; and in the spirit of Maya Angelou's advice, it listens for the deep talk.

P A R T
O N E
The Process of Interpretation

The black Africans who survived the dreaded "Middle Passage" from the west coast of Africa to the New World did not sail alone. Violently and radically abstracted from their civilizations, these Africans nevertheless carried within them to the Western hemisphere aspects of their cultures that were meaningful, that could not be obliterated, and that they chose by acts of will not to forget.—HENRY LOUIS GATES JR., *The Signifying Monkey*

Under the recorded names were other names, just as "Macon Dead," recorded for all time in some dusty file, hid from view the real names of people, places, and things. Names that had meaning. . . . Names they got from yearnings, gestures, flaws, events, mistakes, weaknesses. Names that bore witness.—TONI MORRISON, *Song of Solomon*

1

On the N(yam)a Level

He knows my name, boy . . . he calls all colored people George.
—HENRY LOUIS GATES JR., *Loose Canons*

O, be some other name!
What's in a name? That which we call a rose
By any other word would smell as sweet.
—SHAKESPEARE, *Romeo and Juliet*

CRITICS WHO study literary names, or literary onomastics as it is better known, refer to Juliet's soliloquy so often that I hesitated before doing so in the epigraph above; but I can think of no better way to introduce this chapter than with the famous quotation and a candid question of my own. To that end, I ask: would it really? Would a rose "by any other word" really smell as sweet?

According to Juliet, it would. For her, a name is "no part" of Romeo (1005). He remains the same regardless of the name he bears; yet, for the sake of those who know nothing more of him, Juliet asks Romeo to *be* another name. The implications of Juliet's request remind us that on a deep level of understanding and signification a name bearer *is* what its name suggests, especially for those who equate the essential nature of the bearer with her or his name. If, in the eyes of those who would condemn him, Romeo can *be* or embody the attributes of some other name, maybe the unnaming of a rose can provide it with new attributes as well. Perhaps the mere suggestion of a stench produces it.

Imagine, for a moment, that the unnamed rose in Juliet's soliloquy is one transplanted nefariously from its native soil, a nurturing West African soil, to a foreign one that does not allow its unique fragrance to develop, a hostile environment. Since I am taking the liberty of creating a flower's tale, I will color this rose black—a smooth black rose from West Africa. In its native land, this flower was named for the qualities it possessed, events surrounding its birth, the day of the week it arrived, or for the joy and promise its budding aroused. These were the carefully chosen *defining elements* of its name, by which I mean the tradition- and meaning-filled essence that spoke of the flower's purpose, position, or value.

For days after sprouting its bud, the flower existed without a name so that those within its community could contemplate it and give it a desig- nation that would provide it with direction and life. During this time of contemplation, it existed in a state of liminality, considered neither fully in bloom nor completely dead. It simply existed, a shell without an es- sence, body without being. The final act of its blooming was receiving its name, an event of ceremonial glory. The flower's name, spoken by an empowered member of its community or family, gave it life. Like the nourishing West African soil through which the flower's roots spread, its name worked beneath its surface to encourage and assist it in bringing forth a unique fragrance. More than this, the name connected the flower to a community of flowers that understood the power of naming, its magic and integrity as an essential element of individual being and pur- pose. All who heard the name knew immediately the history or function of its bearer and either encouraged the named toward its goal or bowed a head of understanding and respect for its circumstances.

In the alien soil of a violent diaspora, this carefully chosen, highly valued, and powerful name is silenced and replaced by a new one. Every- one, including the flower, is forbidden to speak the original name. It be- comes a secret that, over time (three hundred years of bondage), is for- gotten. Just as receiving its birth name completed the act of being born by conjuring a spirit, the hostile stripping away of that name by the ut- terances of a hostile namer begins the act of dying. I propose that it is the stench of that death that permeates the nostrils of those who dare to un- name—for, in this place of alien unnaming, the once fragrant flower no longer bears the label *Rose* but the name *nigger*, a name change that makes all the difference.

My flower's tale suggests metaphorically that without resistance the crimes of pejorative unnaming diminish humanity and leave the indi- vidual who does not fight back "rent of spirit." The hostile unnaming of blacks during slavery and the continuing use of racist epithets today amount to crimes against their spiritual life force. "Such a crime is worse than murder, since the murdered victim can at least continue to exist as

Muntu [a human being] in the spirit form." Paul Carter Harrison, writing in the early 1970s, refers to *nommo*, a powerful cosmic force acknowledged by African-American scholars and writers for more than forty years. During the 1960s, nommo was defined by black cultural scholars and Africanists as the spiritual-physical energy of "the word" that conjures being through naming. It is the seed of word, water, and life in one that brings to the body its vital human force called the *nyama*. Nommo controls the nyama by naming and unnaming it—calling it forth. A "body" existing without the liberated life force of the nyama (what I call the "flesh") is worse than dead. It is dehumanized.[1]

French anthropologist Marcel Griaule introduced the term *nommo* in *Dieu d'eau: Entretiens avec Ogotemmêli* (1948). This book presents the creation myths Griaule collected from the Dogon philosopher Ogotemmêli in 1946. According to Griaule, Ogotemmêli's creation myth is a guide for almost all aspects of Dogon life. The validity of Griaule's Dogon ethnography has been debated among anthropologists sporadically for years. Walter E. A. van Beek, the primary investigator in a 1991 "restudy," questions whether Griaule's findings are true representations of Dogon philosophy or intercultural fictions coauthored by a European ethnographer and his creative Dogon informant. Although van Beek concedes that in current debates the centrality of speech and what he calls "the metaphoric usage of 'the word' " is not in question, he does oppose Griaule's representation of the nommo and the nyama it calls forth. Van Beek's "restudy" argues that the nommo has no creative characteristics in current Dogon thought and that the term *nyama* is from the Bambara, not the Dogon. He fails, however, to prove that this characteristic of the nommo and the belief in a vital force did not exist in the philosophy of Ogotommêli and his contemporaries.[2]

I do not present nommo in an attempt to support Griaule's ethnographic methods nor to deny his influence upon Ogotemmêli's creation myths. Such a stand would be beyond the scope of this study. Instead, I introduce the term for the benefit of its ideological familiarity among African Americans and for what it brings to the reading of names in black-authored texts. Some readers may recognize the term as the primary title of William H. Robinson's *Nommo: An Anthology of Modern Black African and Black American Literature* (1972). Readers of Toni

Morrison's fiction will recall its use as the name of a female character in *Tar Baby* (1981) whom the author describes as "word-whipping" a man in the middle of New York's Broadway and 101st Street (196). Others may be more familiar with Morrison's use of nommo's procreative powers in her fifth novel, *Beloved* (1987). This text acknowledges the incantatory power of names as nommo by emphasizing their ability to call forth conception. Ogotemmêli's claim that nommo's procreative power can "bring about the penetration of the uterus" through spoken words is useful in explaining how a ghost in *Beloved* is impregnated.[3]

In Morrison's novel a dead baby, Beloved, assumes human form and returns to the mother, Sethe, who killed it. By novel's end the incarnate ghost is pregnant and its mother languishes. The critical question in my reading of Beloved's pregnancy is: does she carry what Denver describes as the fading "flesh" (i.e., spirit) of her mother inside her womb or a ghostly "flesh" she conceives through sexual contact with Paul D? The metatext of names and naming suggests that both answers are valid. Beloved uses her name and Paul D's seed to conceive both the "flesh" of her own nyama and the body into which Sethe's spirit fades. She insists that Paul D have sex with her and that he call her by name: "I want you to touch me on the inside part and call me my name . . . You have to touch me. On the inside part. And you have to call me my name" (116–17). Beloved needs to hear her name so that she can conceive through its procreative word force. Without the incantatory effects of names as nommo, she cannot fulfill her desire to merge with her mother's spirit. Without the word-seed, this entity, which the community women call the "devil child," cannot usurp a mother's role, "eat up her life, swell with it, grow taller on it," and attempt a sinister revenge (250, 261).

Morrison's *Beloved* also relies upon the nyama (vital force) of nommo to call forth a Muntu (human spirit) as the deep talk of two names, *Sixo* and *Seven-O*, articulates a story of ancestral memory and promised freedom. Morrison begins this story by suggesting a Pan-African vitality existing within the slave community she creates. Sixo is the only Sweet Home man who remembers the language and traditions of his African past. The narrator describes him as "indigo with a flame-red tongue," suggesting the depth and purity of his ancestry, color, and African blood. Like those who came before him, Sixo has respect for the ancestral spirits represented by certain trees and dances among them at night "to keep his bloodlines open." He honors the spirit of the dead and asks their permission before entering their lodge. He is the man who stops speaking English "because there was no future in it" and executes an escape from slavery that, unfortunately, results in his death. As he strikes a final blow for freedom with the butt of a gun, Sixo sings a song in a language (African?) no one but he understands (11, 21–25).

Convinced by Sixo's song that "this one will never be suitable" for slavery, Schoolteacher decides to lynch him. The narrator tells us that as the flames "cook" Sixo's feet he laughs: "Something is funny. Paul D guesses what it is when Sixo interrupts his laughter to call out, 'Seven-O! Seven-O! . . . because his Thirty-Mile Woman got away with his blossoming seed' " (226–29). This is the calling of nyama through the deep talk and nommo force of a name. The character continues to call this name until his captors silence him with a bullet. Sixo's death scene makes a clear distinction between the captive body, which burns and dies, and the liberated "flesh," which laughs and lives on in a name; but there is more to this story.

The word Sixo shouts before his death, *Seven-O*, contains subversive nommo force and a biblical promise intertextualized through deep talk. The promise comes from the story of Nebuchadnezzar and the captured Hebrew slaves. In the Old Testament book of Jeremiah, God promises freedom to these captives after seventy (Seven-O) years in Babylon. "The Letter of Jeremiah" in the noncanonical text of this story, the Apocrypha, promises that the seventh generation will be freed from their *exile*. That text reads as follows: "You will be taken to Babylon as exiles by Nebuchadnezzar, king of the Babylonians. / Therefore when you have come to Babylon you will remain there for many years, for a long time, up to seven generations; after that I [God] will bring you away from there in peace."[4] The mention of exile in the Apocrypha brings to mind the role native Africans played in capturing, exiling, and selling into slavery members of enemy tribes. The relationship of the Apocrypha, the word *Seven-O*, and Sixo's characterization as "African" harks back to the historical circumstances of this exile. The character's name indicates that he is the sixth generation of enslaved Africans who remember and practice the traditions of their homeland but are not allowed to return to that land due to their enslavement.

Sixo is the exile in the "Babylon" of America, and Schoolteacher, a man who burns a rebellious slave, is Sweet Home's Nebuchadnezzar. The story of Nebuchadnezzar and the Hebrew slaves is a familiar one to many, and like the story of Moses, it is often compared to the captivity experienced by blacks in America. The events involving Shadrach (whose birth name was Ananias), Meshach (birth name Azarias), and Abednego (birth name Misael) are often preached in black churches. These three slaves were put in a "fiery furnace" because they refused to bow down to the golden image of King Nebuchadnezzar. Unlike Sixo, they survived their "lynching" by fire and, we assume, were brought out of exile with the others (Dan. 3:1–30).

Although Sixo's death prevents him from escaping to freedom or passing on his knowledge of African tradition, he does pass on his seed and the deep talk of his name. Like the African father who calls out his child's name while standing before a gathering of his community, this father's name calling brings with it a nommo force that awakens and summons being. Sixo's dying words announce the spiritual arrival of the seventh generation—a child who the intertextualized metatext reveals will return to Africa freed from bondage not only because its mother Patsy, the Thirty-Mile Woman, escapes but because the nommo force of the name its father calls out warrants it.

The importance of "the word" and speech in *Beloved* and other African-American literary texts makes nommo a valuable concept in the study of onomastic deep talk. I align my definitions of deep talk closely with nommo as explicated in Janheinz Jahn's *Muntu* (1958) and Harrison's *The Drama of Nommo* (1972). These studies build upon original field work done in West Africa by Griaule and others. Both Harrison and Jahn describe nommo as the agent of a primary cosmic force— the nyama of the word—appearing in various black cultures including the Dogon. Harrison examines West African philosophies in relation to black American culture, whereas Jahn draws connections among the systems of beliefs held by the Dogon, Baluba, Ruandese, Bambara, and Haitians. In spite of the present debates surrounding Griaule's ethnography, the system of beliefs supporting nommo as an incantatory word force has been and remains a powerful influence in black lives and literature. Understanding the creative, procreative, and destructive influence of the word as an agent of being (a nommo force) is therefore fundamental to exploring the magic and power of names and naming in African-American culture.

Through the manipulation and conjuring of cosmic life forces in religion, literature, music, dance, and naming, blacks as a people have survived the spiritual staining of slavery and American racism. Black naming practices are acts of resistance against ancestral loss and spiritual death. This is one reason why names and naming are so important to African Americans. It is why many blacks give their children unique names, African names, or create names using their historical memories and hopes as sources that call forth the untainted cosmic forces of resistance. Houston A. Baker comments in *Long Black Song*, "The simple English word *name* has an awesome significance for black American culture that it can never possess for another culture; the quest for being and identity that begins in a nameless and uncertain void exerts a pressure on the word *name* that can be understood only when one understands black American culture." One way of understanding naming in black culture is by reading its play of resistance in African-American literature.[5]

In the literature of black writers, we read the story of people who struggle against a legacy of unnaming and learn of their victory over its effects. In many cases the stories told repeat and revise real-world naming situations and historical events. They mirror, if you will, the re-creative power of nommo in the social real. Below I discuss a few ways that names and naming become acts of resistance in both literature and the social real, beginning with the emphatic statements of being communicated through the deep-level naming impulses of *I am*.

In an article titled "Naming, Being, and Black Experience," Michael G. Cooke contemplates the paradox of "being" presented by the philosopher Descartes, who professed, "I think, therefore I am." Cooke asks, "Who thinks?" This question immediately demands a verification of existence that identifies the essential nature of the thinker. Adding a name to the sentence eliminates its paradox: "I, Descartes, think, therefore I am." Without the name, there is no "I am" in Cooke's configuration. His answer to the question "who?"—the "I" or identity conjured through the name *Descartes*—establishes the self as an autonomous being in the world, an identifiable human presence.[6]

In literature by African-American writers, *I am* has a deeper meaning, one speaking of a cosmic link that extends beyond notions of identity or individual existence. Black authors use the naming impulses of *I am* to contemplate a connection between their characters, or themselves, and other spiritual forces both human and divine. In *Sister Outsider* (1984), for instance, Audre Lorde challenges the barriers of American racism and sexism by accepting her personal connection to the human community. In a statement of onomastic affirmation she declares, "I am who I am, doing what I came to do, acting upon you like a drug or a chisel to remind you of your me-ness, as I discover you in myself" (147). Lorde's declaration of "I am" provides her with an extension of self that gives her authority over the hostile forces of the world surrounding her by not only reminding others of her sameness but by controlling their difference as it locates itself within her.

The deep talk of the words Celie writes in Alice Walker's *The Color Purple* (1982) enunciates a similar type of cosmic expansion. "~~I am~~ I have always been a good girl," the character writes in her first letter to God (1). In the surface text, this sentence speaks of Celie's mourning for a lost state of being. On another level of meaning, it draws a graphic picture of the wounding that marks out her spirit. Careful consideration of the spiritual forces conjured through the juxtaposition of "~~I am~~" with the words that follow, "I have always been," offers another reading. Instead of marking out the character's identity or exposing a violence that erases her spirit, the metatext and renaming impulses of Celie's written words speak of an extended spirituality. This metatext corrects the discourse of the "body" (read as captivity and spiritual death) imposed by the words marked out and connects the cosmic nature of Celie's spiritual-physical being (her existence as Muntu) to what has always been—the God to whom she writes.

This spiritual extension of self is also evoked in Ralph Ellison's *Invisible Man* when the protagonist puns the name that the God of Moses claims as his own. In Exodus 3:14, God tells Moses: "I AM WHO I AM: . . . Thus you shall say to the Israelites, I AM has sent me to you." In Ellison's novel, the invisible man claims that "yams" are his birthmark (i.e., birth name); then, like Celie, he "calls out to" a cosmic connection with the ultimate Being of all creation: "I yam what I am!" (266). This statement connects the protagonist with the universal and "Almighty" in a way that identifies him as creator of not only the world of lights in which the reader first meets him but of his own true self. "Continue on the yam level," the invisible man says, "and life would be sweet" (267). On the "yam level" (the metatext), the phrase name *I am* acts as a mask for the invisible man's birth name, his true name and its *n(yam)a*. Unfortunately, the idea of openly claiming birth names in the surface text, symbolically represented as *yam*, is described as "frostbitten," and the invisible man throws it away (267). The world beyond the metatext is too cold and merciless for the survival of the idea or the spirit of freedom, the "flesh," that birth names conjure; and the appearance of namelessness again controls the surface.

While the absence of an inscribed name in the surface text displaces the invisible man's humanity (he is often described as a machine), sense of freedom, and status as an autonomous being, *I am* (introduced first in the novel's prologue, "I am an invisible man") continues to function within that discursive space to shield the invisible man's true name from alien contempt and revision. Not long after he throws away the "yam," he reclaims it. When a stranger asks his name he says, "I am who I am" (269). This act of symbolic renaming assures the reader of deep talk that the absence of a name's inscription in the surface text does not violate the "yam," or rather birth name, the invisible man bears. The text continually disavows this possibility through the mask of "I am."

The narrator's masking of the name *Jack*, used in both the prologue and the epilogue of the novel, offers another example. This name appears five paragraphs into the novel during the invisible man's comparison of himself to a bear. He writes that "a bear retires to his hole for the winter and lives until spring; then he comes strolling out like the Easter chick breaking from its shell. . . . Call me Jack-the-Bear, for I am in a state of hibernation" (6). This event of supranaming signifies upon hibernation's deep slumber while reiterating the invisible man's cosmic connection with the biblical *I AM* (through both the Easter allusion and the mask *I am*). The narrator revises the name in the epilogue by referring to the invisible man's castration nightmare as "ball the jack" (576). Neither instance of naming is sustained by the text. The name appears only twice; therefore, the use of *Jack* at the beginning of the novel and *jack* at its conclusion does not suggest that this is the invisible man's true name.

Instead, *Jack's* deep talk builds upon the thematic representation of the invisible man as "every man" and through it offers the cosmic connections implied by *I am* to all humanity.

Just as the biblical "I AM" (whose true name never appears in the written text of the Bible) functions as an absent presence in the world we occupy, the invisible man's true name functions as an absent presence in Ellison's novel. This character's true name is a "secret" that, left unrevealed, allows him to hide his spiritual life force from a world filled with people who refuse to see him except through "the construction of their inner eyes" (3). The protagonist's secret name acts as a covert discursive strategy of resistance, as an absent presence. It subverts negative constructions of his subjectivity and identity on the level of the metatext while *I am* serves as a mask that wards off potential harm in the surface text.

My reading of the role that secret naming plays in Ellison's novel is informed by the African belief in names as private sanctuaries defining and protecting one's life force. An empowered enemy or other evil entity speaking such a name can potentially transform, mutate, wound, or destroy the spirit it nurtures and protects. When unknown to these enemies, names protect the individual from such assaults and woundings. This philosophy was central to the captured African's practice of "secret" naming, a practice duplicated in the metatext of Ellison's novel.

In the public arena of white masters and white namers, captive Africans' unnaming during slavery stripped from them the proud names they were given shortly after birth (or names they assumed later in honor of self-affirming events). Except in isolated cases, empty English or Spanish names and epithets unceremoniously replaced them.[7] These names, spoken from the mouths of their enslavers, possessed a word force in conflict with that of the original names. Within the dominating master's word was an intent with the potential to dehumanize and spiritually wound the named. As a shield, captured Africans used a counterword force. Unlike Kunta Kinte in Alex Haley's *Roots*, the Africans to whom I refer did not attempt to control the master's word by offering their birth names as an open challenge. They, like Kunta, knew their original names but kept these names, and others they assumed, secret. They used them as counterwords that warded off the effects of evil covertly. This practice continued long after their descendants forgot the original name.

African Americans who mourn this forgotten word call forth its essence in a familiar phrase, *the lost African name*. This phrase name is mnemonic; it uses re-memory—a term introduced in *Beloved* that implies remembering the past and making the past become present, calling it forth—to shield those identifying with it from assault in the same way that *I am* shields the invisible man. *The lost African name* brings with it a cosmic gathering of secret names that protects the spiritual well-being of those who understand and celebrate the power of its deep talk. Instead of speaking of loss, the name covertly masks a spiritual-physical presence that speaks of belonging and of "flesh" that does not submit to pejorative unnaming. Its deep-level utterances resist namelessness and claim all African Americans who hear its voice and acknowledge its call for re-memory.

Another benefit of reading this mnemonic phrase name as re-memory is the resistance it enacts against a history of unjust laws that prohibited the legal use of surnames by slaves. A prominent aspect of that history has been the denial of secret naming in slave culture. For quite some time researchers and historians, accepting only the evidence of legally recorded first names, believed enslaved blacks never used two names; but as Herbert Gutman points out in *The Black Family in Slavery and Freedom, 1750–1925*, this is untrue. Enslaved blacks shared secret names, particularly surnames, among themselves but rarely shared them with white masters or their representatives.[8] To do so would be to endanger their physical bodies as well as their spirits.

Whites who discovered the use of surnames by slaves frequently denounced it as illegal and therefore meaningless. Gutman cites the white novelist Albion W. Tourgee, who, during an 1890 "Conference on the Negro Question," argued that blacks had been denied surnames in slavery by law. Tourgee suggested that "a name is no name unless the bearer has a legal right to it. No slave *could* have a surname because he could not have a *legal* sire" (Gutman's italics). He added that the first use of surnames among enslaved American blacks occurred after emancipation. Ex-slaves, he claimed, gave themselves surnames as an "eternal testament against injustice."[9]

Although Tourgee's hypothesis may have been true for some ex-slaves, for others emancipation was an opportunity to openly claim the names they held secretly during slavery. In both scenarios, assigning oneself a surname was a way to protect and define one's humanity, spiritual well-being, and autonomy. Regardless of the legality of names and naming subscribed by whites and their slave codes, slave surnames did exist. More than that, they existed as weapons in a complex battle for slave autonomy and life. They were secrets whose invasive force gave them the ability to function as shields protecting the named from spiritually injurious namelessness, unjust punishment, and identities antithetical to their sense of self.

This same invasive force empowers names as actors in the continuing battles of American racism—battles that are often played out on a field of pejorative unnaming and that are lost by those who do not resist, or do not know how to resist. The name *George* in this chapter's first epigraph is from a story Henry Louis Gates Jr. tells of unnaming in his 1992 book, *Loose Canons*. Gates witnessed the event as a child. According to him, his father, the only black person the owners of the local drug store allowed to sit inside and eat from "real plates with real silverware," was waiting for Gates to finish an ice cream cone when a white man, Mr. Wilson, walked by and called his father "George." Reflecting upon the incident, Gates interprets the unnaming as "one of those things that provided a glimpse, through a rent curtain, at another world that we could not affect but that affected us." [10] Given this description of the event's meaning, the name *George* is a word that rips or tears the curtain camouflaging a socially prescribed prejudice to reveal the denigration and denial inherent in American racism. The name acts. It involves itself in the creation of a discursive gesture. Its invasive energy does something.

In the metatext of Gates's written story, *George* is a name-entity whose deep talk attempts to aggressively undermine and subvert the positive utterances of a black man's "true" name. It points toward Gates's father and identifies him as a "colored man," a man without the benefits of human equality. It also points beyond itself and its referent to identify the white man as one whose hierarchical status as "master" and whose linguistic control as namer give him the power to metaphorically castrate (disempower) and dehumanize the "colored man." In Gates's recollection of the event, his father dismisses this unnaming by exposing the racist worldview from which it originates: "He calls all colored people George." This dismissal does not completely shield the young Gates from the destructive impact of the white man's hostile unnaming (as it obviously does for his father). Instead, the event and the name bring shame and spiritual wounding to the then inexperienced Gates: "I never again looked Mr. Wilson in the eye." [11]

From Middle Passage until today, African Americans have struggled with their identity as defined through names and naming. In a classic case of supplementation, several names have been used to refer to those individuals whose ancestors were removed from the shores of West Africa and brought to America as slaves. Tracing the pattern of black group naming from the 1600s to the present demonstrates how the processes of supranaming and renaming have played out: *African* (1619–1850s), *Negar* (1619), *blackamoor* (1800), *Negro* (1800–1950), *colored* (1800–1950s), *black* (1800–1900; 1960s–present), *Afro-American* (1900–1980), *African-American* (1900; 1970–present), *Afra-American* (1920–present) and *Africana* (1980–present).[12]

Joseph E. Holloway comments that the changes in group naming practices reflect the historical transformation of cultural associations and political ideologies from "strong African identification to nationalism, integration, and attempts at assimilation back to cultural identification." [13] Although I agree with Holloway's historical reading of black group names, something more arresting is at work beneath the surface of this continual performance of renaming and supranaming. Each of the names listed above represents attempts to define the being or essential nature of a people from within a structure of meaning and deep-level communication that is itself shaped by the systematic exclusion of that people.

This exclusivity is evident in the American Colonization Society's desire to send free blacks back to Africa during the 1830s. Black leaders used the name *African* in the titles of their organizations as early as 1787—the First African Baptist Church, African Dorcas Society, and the Sons of Africa, for instance. As a result of the American Colonization Society's activities, black leadership began a movement toward eliminating the name *African* from these and other titles. This movement of erasure continued through the 1860s when, increasingly, black leaders adopted the name *colored*.[14] By the turn of the century, a new, but more problematic, solution arose—the addition of the word *American* to group naming practices.

Toni Morrison points out in *Playing in the Dark* that "American means white, and Africanist people struggle to make the term applicable to themselves with ethnicity and hyphen after hyphen after hyphen." [15] Defining oneself within that which denies and excludes that self is difficult and results in continual onomastic struggle. The moment a name becomes defunct or contaminated by a history of exclusion, negative connotations, and racist stereotypes, its usefulness as a vehicle for defining group identity and socialized accountabilities disappears. The group then chooses another and yet another label, hoping with each attempt to rediscover or give voice to a long forgotten name.

During the 1950s and 1960s, members of the Nation of Islam challenged this dilemma by adding the word *so-called* to the group name *Negro* ("the so-called-Negro") and replacing their surnames with an *X*. In *The Autobiography of Malcolm X*, the narrator explains that the "Muslim's *X* symbolized the true African family name that he never could know. . . . Mr. Muhammad taught that we would keep the *X* until God Himself returned and gave us a Holy Name from His own mouth." For the Nation of Islam, not only was *X* a symbol of a lost family name; it was also a marker signifying their virtual namelessness and complete unity in a hostile environment. [16]

Booker Taliaferro Washington's autobiography, *Up from Slavery*, documents a similar mark of absence and loss in the names of newly freed slaves. According to Washington, many ex-slaves adopted a middle initial that stood "for no name, it being simply a part of what the coloured man proudly called his 'entitles.'" Both Malcolm's *X* and the proud markers of "no name" give voice to the historical loss and absence that are the progeny of racial subordination and slavery. They are also forms of resistance directed against the spiritual assaults of "entitled" and legalized ownership that dehumanize the owned. Just as the Nation of Islam's *X* symbolizes what Hortense Spillers calls "a slash mark against a first offense" that voids all claims of historical ownership, the proud markers of "no name" neutralize the cosmic effects of commodification and discounted humanity contained in slave names. [17]

Black America's historical struggle against spiritual wounding through naming does not end with these symbolic gestures and cryptic markers of resistance. Names of slaves and freed people such as *Hatcher's John* or *Miss Martha's Clare* barred the face of blackness from the human equation by speaking foremost of ownership and commodification. At the same time, degrading epithets (many still in use today) added to the dilemma of the African American's struggle against spiritual-physical forces that disrupt discourses of autonomy and render the named inhuman. Dehumanizing and degendering labels of group entitlement such as *coon, burrhead, pickaninny, shine, darky, nigger,* and *zigaboo* stripped the names African Americans were called in the public sphere of identifiable human qualities and relegated their public identities to the status of subhuman beings. These names provide "a metaphor of displacement . . . including the displacement of the genitalia" that wounds the "flesh" while metaphorically castrating the "body." [18]

Because of this type of blatant disregard for black humanity, slaves were often considered nameless after their capture and during their merchandising in America. Although Middle Passage enslaved the "body" and not the "flesh" of Africans who knew their birth names and struggled to keep them, Joseph Boskin notes that maritime regulations and the necessity for bookkeeping ignored these names. Captured Africans are listed in the ledgers of slave ships as *Negroes, Slaves,* and *heads.* The criminal practices of such record keeping inaugurated the process of African unnaming despite European knowledge of African languages and naming traditions.[19] Such crimes silence the indigenous name, erase the human face of blackness from view, and inscribe a legacy of destruction that disfigures the "flesh" each time they are revisited and left unchallenged by historiographers.

In 1860, Edward Manning, a member of the slave ship *Thomas Watson,* cited the following reason for the names he and his crew assigned to captured Africans. "I suppose they . . . all had names in their own dialect," he writes, "but the effort required to pronounce them was too much for us, so we picked out our favorites and dubbed them 'main-stay,' 'cathead,' 'Bull's eye,' 'Rope-yarn,' and various other sea phrases.[20] Names such as these reflect the condition of the slave's status as cargo, dehumanized and degendered "bodies" in the worldview of their captors. According to the standard use of the words that named them, they were not men and women but objects—things to own, use, sell, and discard. In this way, even personal names became potential vehicles for spiritual degradation. They reduced the spiritual designation of the named from *Muntu* to *kintu*, a thing. Names shared with objects and animals, on the deepest levels of discourse production, serve to remind all who use them that the bearer is not human.

The overpowering evidence of the slave name's association with negated humanity and lost identity dominates black literature. In the introduction to the 1849 narrative *The Fugitive Blacksmith*, James W. C. Pennington comments upon the pernicious dilemma facing an ex-slave who might search for a written record of his existence as a man. Pennington begins by mentioning that slave births and deaths were routinely documented in journals and other plantation records alongside livestock and pets: "Suppose insult, reproach, or slander, should render it necessary for him to appeal to the history of his family in vindication of his character, where will he find that history? He goes to his native state, to his native county, to his native town; but nowhere does he find any record of himself *as a man*. On looking at the family record of his old, kind, Christian master, there he finds his name on a catalogue with the horses, cows, hogs, and dogs" (Pennington's italics).[21] Left without any other means of locating written documentation of himself and his history, the ex-slave seeks the master's record of his name. His search does not lead to a record of human existence. Instead, it leads to a record of lost historicity, commodification, and dehumanization.

Pennington personalizes this example within his narrative as he expresses disgust for the system of slavery and those who engage in public record keeping that leads to such dilemmas. Using the metaphor of a monster, he speaks of them both. "When the monster heard that a man child was born, he laughed, and said, 'It is mine.' When I was laid in the cradle, he came and looked on my face, and wrote down my name upon his barbarous list of chattels personal, on the same list where he registered his horses, hogs, cows, sheep, and even his *dogs*! Gracious Heaven, is there no repentance for the misguided men who do these things!" (Pennington's italics).[22] There is no hint of an ancestral past, no trace of familial values, nothing resembling human expectations and obligations in the environment, or lifeworld, of his recorded name. There is no positive record of his identity; nor is there any written proof of his humanity.

The environment of his name inscribes it with nothing that resembles himself. The name he finds cannot break free from the text of its inscription; it cannot speak of a man.

Richard Wright's *Black Boy* and Toni Morrison's *Song of Solomon* offer an alternative view of written documents that consign black Americans to a fate of virtual namelessness. Wright's recitation of his grandfather's misnaming and Morrison's fictional story of Macon Dead's unique name in many ways align the history of African-American nomenclature with that of European immigrants whose names were also documented incorrectly in public records on a regular basis. These writers offer a consideration of a profound difference between the two situations, however. For African Americans the impact of incorrect name documentation binds them with a double band of historic loss and spiritual negation. Separated first from the source and knowledge of their original names and second from an American public identity, their characters' misnaming secures a menacing linguistic and identity paralysis that leads to death and obscurity. I argue later (in chapter 7) how these paths are revised by the metatexts.

An example of an enslaved African who publicly claimed the master's misnaming and reinscribed it successfully with a deep talk of her own is the eighteenth-century black poet Phillis Wheatley. In the worldview of white masters, the name she bore and the color of her skin determined the nature of her being as something other than human. Although Phillis Wheatley was reportedly loved and cherished by her white owners, her name circumscribed her subject position as nothing more than property—a subhuman *kintu* named after the slave ship *Phillis* that brought her across the treacherous waters of the Middle Passage. For her namer, the deep talk of the word *Phillis* spoke of a slave, a quaint curiosity, and a literary aberration—not the talented black woman she clearly was. Instead of submitting to the foreboding deep talk of her name as inscribed by slavery's namers, Wheatley resisted.

Unlike Frederick Douglass and other African Americans who changed their names or maintained secret names, Wheatley's act of resistance was much more covertly subversive. What we know of her worldview and self-reappropriation challenges any notion of her total interpolation by the ideologies of slavery. She resisted definitions of blacks as determined by the ruling class of slaveholders and through her writing reinscribed her humanity in the midst of a world that claimed her race and her name marked her as something less. Although she used the name *Phillis*, Wheatley considered herself fully human and proved it in a courtroom before eighteen white men who had previously seen nothing more than her race and her bondage. Because language is always a place where a struggle for dominance occurs, Wheatley's use of the name *Phillis* brings with it an inflection, or accent, of difference that challenges its negative deep talk internally. The name that emerges from this struggle for dominance is devoid of negative connotations. In other words, there are two names: one used by those who subscribe to a system of hostile unnaming and another used by Wheatley and those who acknowledge the humanity, genius, and history (the hideous crime of Middle Passage included) spoken though her self-identified name's deep talk.

Perhaps it was this name's revised invasive force that resisted the hand of Thomas Jefferson so that the attention of his racist renaming appears in the poet's surname. Jefferson wrote "Phillis Whately" (inadvertently?) instead of Phillis Wheatley in a critical commentary denouncing the writer as a poet: "Religion indeed has produced a Phillis Whately but it could not produce a poet. . . . The compositions published under her name are below the dignity of criticism." [23] Jefferson's spelling "mistake" writes over the name associated with Wheatley's white owners and their humanity, to reflect his racist worldview graphically in the name *W(hate)ly*. This case of incorrect public documentation informs against the writer, Jefferson, in ways that Pennington's, Wright's, and Morrison's texts do not. In this instance, the "record" reveals the possibility of a subconscious *hate* motivating Jefferson's criticism, a hate that appears in the deep talk of the name he inscribes. Here deep talk functions in ways similar to a Freudian slip.

Although some African Americans bought into the dehumanizing hatred implicit in the master's racist definition of blacks and suffered the broken spirits of that dehumanization, others were like Wheatley, and some were even more aggressively resistant. They rejected the dubious naming assigned to them by whites and renamed themselves. Nicknames, phrase names, and "secret" names spoken in communion with others who shared their fate or names of African origin (such as day names and phrase names) replaced the empty, objectified designations of the master's word. Sometimes mothers (or both parents) and grandmothers chose the names of slave children and empowered them with their own remembered histories. The legacy of a family presently living in Atlanta presents an interesting example of this practice and the re-memory of which it speaks.

During the years just before the end of slavery, a Georgian slave mother gave her newborn son the surname of the most prominent man in town, a white man named *Babies*. This name choice reflected the mother's hope for a safe and prosperous new beginning for her child. At least this is the story her son's namesake proudly tells. What makes me question the story's "full exposure" is the forename this slave mother assigned her son: *Loveless*. *Loveless Babies* was his name. Although Loveless Babies III admits that the story of his ancestral naming is somewhat sketchy and incomplete, the name itself reveals an implosive tale. Its deep talk speaks of two possibilities. The first tale suggests that the children of this slave mother were conceived through some type of sexual dominance or violence (such as rape) that precluded love.[24] The second suggests that the children were lost—perhaps stolen by a relentless system of slave trading, but lost nonetheless—to the love of a mother who honored them in the name of a son who would be free. For over a hundred years this name of honor, re-memory, and promise has been passed from father to son. Its deep talk speaks of a remembered past and, most importantly, designates the bodies and spirits of succeeding generations liberated and free.

Passing on the legacy of names from father to son as the Babies family does is nothing new—not even in slave communities. According to Herbert Gutman, many first-born sons of slaves bore the names of their fathers. Slave mothers, however, rarely, if ever, named their female children after themselves, preferring instead to give children the names of grandparents and other kin (male and female). Still others bore the traces of an African heritage in the misunderstood and misinterpreted beliefs embedded in their names. These fortunate few were named after deceased grandparents, siblings, and cousins. Gutman cites the *Memoir of Mrs. Chloe Spear* as an example. In that text, the narrator recalls something akin to the West African tradition of giving a child the name of a deceased relative whose spirit has returned to occupy the newborn body. The writer of Spear's narrative, "A Lady of Boston," describes the memory as "a superstitious tradition of her [Spear's] ancestors, who supposed that the first infant born in a family after the decease of a member was the same individual come back, just as they saw a young moon after the old one was gone." [25]

In another example cited by Gutman, a black woman named Sarah delayed naming her child for a month. The slave's reason was that it was "bad luck to give a name to a child before it is a month old." [26] This ominous and unidentified bad luck was probably the death of the child since West Africans did not name a child until they were sure it would survive—until they identified a spirit force to occupy the body and knew it would remain. The Yoruba, for instance, wait seven to nine days before naming a newborn. Often slave children who died before receiving a name were treated much as they were in West Africa—they were not given a name after death. Their births are recorded in plantation records as *baby*, *no name*, and *unnamed*. Each of these naming practices represents West African traditions severed from their source, traditions that lost their original meanings as a result. All that remains is the often mutated shadow of tradition. Regardless of their misreading, these practices, memories, and records signal the importance of names in defining a human presence—even within the somewhat blurred traces of African customs practiced within slave communities.

The shadow of blurred and distorted tradition in another form hovers over Gloria Naylor's *Women of Brewster Place*. In this novel, Kiswana's desire to correct the injury of displaced African names leads to a self-unnaming that her mother denounces as an assault upon family history and pride. One offense Mrs. Brown does not mention is her daughter's assault upon African ceremony and tradition. Kiswana unnames herself in an attempt to shape an identity that honors her African heritage. Like many blacks during the 1960s and 1970s, she does so by selecting a name from an "African" dictionary. This act of self-unnaming defies the traditions of the West African ancestors and spiritual forces she wishes to honor. In most African societies any change of name during adulthood occurs in honor of a momentous occasion or event that profoundly effects the individual or the community. The adult chooses a name of value not only to the individual named but also to others associated with her or him. Ann duCille comments that Africans who honor these traditions would consider the act of random choice inherent in selecting a name from an "African" dictionary "something akin to a sacrilege." [27] Kiswana's attempt to define herself through a name selected from a dictionary is a social and political statement of resistance that unfortunately violates that with which she wishes to align herself.

Her historical predecessors were more faithful to West African traditions. Many blacks celebrated the end of slavery by adopting new names. Booker T. Washington (and others) credits the many incidents of ex-slave name changes to the inappropriateness of previous names for identifying what I call the *life force of freed humanity*. P. Robert Paustian observes that the practice also indicates the retention of African traditions within the naming practices of American blacks. Surnames, such as *Freedman* and *Justice*, commemorated a major event (freedom) in the ex-slaves' life; they articulated pride in a new state of existence. Even more interesting is why Paustian believes many blacks adopted biblical names or the names of other legendary heroes. He comments that "just as Yoruba and other West Africans would derive names from legendary heroes, American blacks who wanted status and a sense of history in their name frequently chose the names of famous and important people." [28] The adoption of names associated with historical figures of revolution, such as Lincoln and George Washington, or influential biblical names were self-affirming acts of resistance poised against the memory of a captive past and against any denial of the ex-slave's right to an American heritage. In both cases, the echoes of African naming traditions persist.

As I have attempted to demonstrate throughout this chapter, African-American literature documents the search for spiritual empowerment, identity, and stories of self and community by duplicating the practices of black nomenclature found in the African and African-American social real. Along this line of thinking is the preponderance of biblical names and biblical intertextuality. African Americans' use of phrase names and story names, such as *De Word of God*, *Virgin Mary*, or *I Will Arise and Go unto My Father*, recorded by Paustian, extends the construction of names beyond the given-name/surname patterns of most white Americans. These names revive, in a distinctly black and Christian voice, traditions that originate with African phrase names such as the Ibo and

Nigerian name *Chukwueneka* ("God has dealt kindly with us"), the Nyakyusa (Tanzanian) name *Tusajigive* ("We are blessed"), or the Akan (of Ghana) name *Nyamekye* ("Gift of God").[29] Toni Morrison duplicates this pattern of naming in *Song of Solomon* through the phrase names *Magdalene called Lena Dead* and *First Corinthians Dead*. This pattern of naming through phrase names appears in other texts in less conspicuous forms such as *John, the Lord's anointed* in James Baldwin's *Go Tell It on the Mountain* and *the tall yellow woman in the bloody green and black dress* in Gloria Naylor's *Women of Brewster Place*. Names and naming patterns in black-authored texts, such as these, are part of a legacy of naming that frees, empowers, and harks back to the memory of a lost past.

It is with slave narratives, such as the *Narrative of William Wells Brown*, the *Narrative of the Life of Frederick Douglass*, and *The Life of Olaudah Equiano; or, Gustavus Vassa, the African*, that a tradition of emphasizing names and naming in African-American literature originates—but not where it ends. Defining self as well as maintaining a sense of one's humanity through a name is a dominant characteristic of contemporary short stories, autobiographies, novellas, novels, and poems written by black men and women. At least once within almost every African-American text characters or narrators foreground the power that naming has over states of being, identity, autonomy, self-respect, and freedom.

In both literature and the social real, African Americans and their African ancestors use naming as a shorthand for a wealth of discourses that resist crimes of spiritual assault and sustain human life. Black writers challenge the silencing and dehumanizing implications of being named or unnamed by an empowered, hostile, and often racist other. Like their African ancestors, the name as nommo in American black-authored literature keeps community and self in balance with the spirit forces that connect them, give them purpose, and justify kinship bonds (even bonds between strangers). The invasive force of poetic names works to silence oppression and traverse the "uncertain void" of lost names and "deflowering."

2
Reading through Names and Naming

Avenging Gods

Critics have not previously discussed . . . an extraordinarily important feature of Hurston's most widely acclaimed novel: structure, symbol, and incident replicate ancient myth.
—CYRENA PONDROM

I N "THE ROLE of Myth," Cyrena Pondrom details quite extensively Zora Neale Hurston's modernization of several ancient myths, including the Egyptian story of Isis and Osiris, the Greek story of Aphrodite and Adonis, and the Babylonian myth of Ishtar and Tammauz.[1] Although Pondrom discusses the "syncretic allusions" in *Their Eyes Were Watching God* that replicate these myths, she does not mention the meaning potential of homophonic imprints derived from the names *Virbius* and *Janus/Jana*. The birth name of the protagonist in Hurston's novel, *Janie*, is a derivative of *Janus/Jana*, the two-headed Roman god (a male/female deity also known as *Dianus/Diana*) exalted by its followers as the oldest and the holiest of deities. This two-headed god was the "Custodian of the Universe" who held the keys to paradise in one hand and a weapon in the other (usually a stick used to bludgeon spiritual foes). The female of this dyad, whom I will call *Diana*, is also associated with the second mythological figure absent from Pondrom's discussion, Virbius. Tea Cake's birth name *Vergible* (introduced when Janie first meets the character) is a derivative of *Virbius*, the divine king of the Greenwood who governed the course of nature. Like Janus/Jana, Virbius had dualistic features. He was both a man and the "deity of the oak, the thunder, and the sky." According to classical mythology, Virbius joined with Diana. Together they reigned as King and Queen of the Woods. These origins, including the image of "the Woods," define the deep talk of the characters' formal names in Hurston's text so that they speak of Janie and Tea Cake's metaphoric roles as deities. In the metatext, the name-entities *janie woods* and *vergible woods* are not only analogous to ancient gods, they *are* gods—"King and Queen of the Woods." [2] Their story is one of vengeance, fear, purification, and reincarnate power.

Pondrom cites Sir James George Frazer's *The Golden Bough* as Hurston's source of classical mythology. According to Frazer, the man-god Virbius was protector of Diana's sacred oak in Nemi at the risk of his own life. John Lowe, author of *Jump at the Sun: Zora Neale Hurston's Cosmic Comedy*, notes that Tea Cake assumes this responsibility and suffers its consequences. He comments that "Tea Cake does indeed die as a result of trying to protect Janie, who identifies with the pear tree." [3] Lowe, of course, refers to the character's struggle with a rabid dog that threatens Janie. Blinded by madness, the result of the dog's bite, Tea Cake attempts to kill Janie later in the novel. She responds by protecting herself and "accidentally" killing him instead. This is the story the surface narrative tells. If we listen for the deep talk of names in this novel, we hear another version of the events that result in Tea Cake's death.

In the metatext, Tea Cake does not die as a result of protecting Janie but suffers beneath the still hand of an avenging god. When Janie realizes the hopelessness of Tea Cake's mental deterioration, she questions God, silently asking him to save the man she loves: "She looked hard for something up there to move for a sign . . . a mutter of thunder. Her arms went up in a desperate supplication for a minute. It wasn't exactly pleading, it was asking questions." Janie does not receive the answers she wants. "The sky stayed hard looking and quiet so she went inside the house. God would do less than He had in His heart" (264). The name *God* in this quote speaks on two levels of narrative development. In the surface narrative, it refers to the omnipotent God of Christian faith; beneath the surface, it denotes a name-entity—the first avenging god of the metatext. This god, whose name derives from the deity controlling the thunder and the sky, remains quiet.

The name-entity Janie addresses is a man-god who functions in the surface text as an absent presence engaged in an internalized ethical conflict. To Virbius, the sacred tree at Nemi was Diana's "special embodiment" that he "worshipped as his goddess" and "embraced as his wife." Janie's association with the pear tree renders her body and her role as wife sacred. The narrative commentary here follows the social mandate that husbands protect and revere their wives. Tea Cake violates this mandate when his jealous fear that a light-complexioned neighbor might steal Janie's affections leads him to beat her (218). His abuse also violates the rules governing the activities of the man-god and protector that his formal name (*Vergible*) calls forth. For these violations, he suffers. The pathos of Tea Cake's insecurities, presented as jealousy and wife beating, culminates in the image of a mad man. "Whom the gods would destroy, they first made mad," Hurston claims in an essay written seven years after the novel's publication. Madness is Tea Cake's punishment for physically abusing Janie.[4]

This punishment is a determinant in the metaphorical "suicide" of a man-god dyad. The deity of this dyad, *vergible*, uses events occurring within the surface narrative to divorce himself from the man, Tea Cake, who has physically abused a sacred "tree" (i.e., a woman). As Tea Cake suffers the torment of the rabid dog's bite, "Janie [notices] a changing look come in his face. Tea Cake was gone" (269). This metaphoric death represents a split between two onomastic subject positions. One, the man whom Janie loves, disappears from the surface; the other, a mad deity (read as *angry deity*), remains. Instead of suggesting this split by supplementing the name (as in supranaming fragmentations) or foreclosing it (as in unnaming fragmentation), the narrator announces the disappearance of the original entity known as *Tea Cake* through renaming: "Tea Cake, the son of the Evening Sun, had to die" (264). Although the name and the character continue to appear in the surface text, "something else was looking out of his face" (269).

This unknown entity is hungry for murder: "The fiend in him must kill and Janie was the only thing living he saw" (273). The need to kill arises, in part, from the mythical tale of Virbius. Virbius is what the narrator of *Their Eyes* calls a "half god" (216). His association and sacred union with Diana confer his full divinity and secure his position as a king. According to Frazer's *Golden Bough*, because of this the King of the Woods was constantly in battle for his life against enemies who hoped to dethrone him. He carried a weapon to protect himself and murdered all but the strongest challenger. In the metatext of Janie and Tea

Cake's story, *janie*, a name-entity whose deep talk calls forth the uncompromising divinity of both Janus and the goddess Diana (or Jana), becomes that challenger: "Janie was the only thing living he saw" (273). Unlike *vergible*, who banishes Tea Cake through a "suffering mind" and thereby avenges a physical wrong, the name-entity *janie* avenges the spiritual injuries the protagonist suffers due to the betrayal of a sacred trust (278). Because "real gods require blood," death, in this case, is not metaphorical but terrifyingly real (216).

Both avenging gods, *vergible* and *janie*, manipulate the surface conflict through an image of fear. The narrator comments that "fear is the most divine emotion" (215). For Tea Cake, fear overcomes him twice: first when he strikes Janie because "it relieved that awful fear inside him" and again just after Janie's silent prayer: "A great fear had took hold of him. What was this thing that set his brains afire?" (219, 264). Fear of Janie's "potential" infidelity causes Tea Cake to brandish a pistol in her direction until she notices a "ferocious look" in his eyes. Then, she also experiences fear. The text describes her as "mad with fear" and "frenzied" by a "desperate fear for her life" (272–73). In the metatext, Janie's fear, like Tea Cake's, signals the deep-level activities of a divine presence. These interpretive "hints" suggest that because of the divine presence of fear, *vergible* is just as responsible for violating the sacred charge of protection his subject position demands as the man Tea Cake (no matter how minutely). In retaliation for this betrayal, the fully divine name-entity *janie* secures a rifle to avenge what it considers an assault against its spirit. Thus, we find the King of the Woods and two "real" gods, the Custodian of the Universe (who kills its spiritual foes) and the Queen of the Woods (who has been betrayed), standing face to face in armed battle.

Identity confirmation of these avenging gods emerges in the surface narrative through a statement that again renames Tea Cake: "We find the death of Vergible Woods to be entirely accidental and justifiable, and that no blame should rest upon the defendant Janie Woods" (279). I call moments of confirmation such as this the *eruption of the true-real*, which is the message of an onomastic event produced when foreclosed utterances resurface (or surface) dramatically within alien contextual environments. In this instance, name-entities that were once foreclosed to surface representation emerge and confirm the identity of the "something else" that was looking out of Tea Cake's face, *vergible woods*, as well as the name of the god who kills it, *janie woods*.

The verdict also reveals that the novel's all-white jury considers murder "justifiable" and "accidental." Since the metatext develops a story in which murder is purposely committed, its description as "accidental" cannot easily exist in that discursive space. This is a point of contradiction that appears solvable only through the reading given to us by the nameless voices of front porch gossips presented in the surface text: "She didn't kill no white man, did she? Well, long as she don't shoot no white man she kin kill jus' as many niggers as she please" (280). Although the gossips read the verdict correctly, the paradox of the jury's statement does serve a purpose beyond its racist implications. It is a moment of convergence through which the jury addresses the actions of both the surface and deep-level stories. In the surface story, murder is "accidental"; in the metatext, it is "justifiable."

Because *Vergible Woods* and *Tea Cake* are each part of a single subject persona (character), it appears that they both die as a result of this "accidental and justifiable" homicide. This occurs only in the surface text. In the metatext—the place where death purges, cleanses, and prepares the character's primary name for an existence beyond the surface— "Tea Cake with the sun for a shawl" survives (286).[5] This phrase name's presence in the surface narrative assists in foreclosing any further use of the character's formal name, *Vergible Woods*. The appearance of *Tea Cake with the sun for a shawl* in the last paragraph of the novel constitutes name fragmentation through unnaming, a final onomastic event informing the reader that death cleanses *Tea Cake*. He survives as a subject position purged of all "sin" and as an extralinguistic actor of the novel's deep-level story. *Tea Cake* lives, but, ironically, so does the symbolic god-figure *vergible woods*.

Virbius is a reincarnate deity. According to beliefs, rituals, and mythologies recorded in *The Golden Bough*, the soul of a slain man-god is reincarnated in his slayer, who then succeeds him as an image of the divine.[6] "Of course he wasn't dead," Hurston's narrator informs us. "He could never die until she [Janie] herself had finished feeling and thinking" (286). Janie Woods is heir to the divine incarnate spirit of *vergible woods* and more. Her forename still associates her with the male figure of a male/female deity, Janus, "Custodian of the Universe." This gender-based name inversion is essential to understanding the events recorded in the novel's final paragraph. When Janie Woods returns to Eatonville, she has power over nature (as Virbius) and the universe (as Janus). Thus empowered, she adorns herself in the horizon, pulls "it from around the waist of the world and drap[es] it over her shoulder. So much life in its meshes! She called in her soul to come and see" (286). The mention of "her soul" emphasizes that both parts of Janie, the divine and the human, share the fullness of life her new status provides.

John Lowe finds Hurston's gender inversion of names an "intrigue" and concludes that the gender switch in Janie's naming indicates that Pheoby, the friend to whom Janie tells her story, plays the role of a "maternal, moon associated" figure. Although this is perhaps a very viable assumption, I contend that the mythological association of the name's homophonic imprint stems from *Phoebus*, Diana's brother and a second name for Apollo, Roman god of the sun (this association connects Pheoby to "Tea Cake, with the sun for a shawl"). Pheoby's name also replicates the West African female day name *Pheba* or *Phibbi* (meaning Friday), which experienced what J. L. Dillard calls *historical change* or mutations in spelling during slavery. The new name appears in estate records as *Pheoby*.[7]

I read the African day name and the name's association with Phoebus foremost as an indication of the adopted kinship bonds between Janie and Pheoby. Janie does not tell just anybody her story; she tells someone she trusts, someone with whom she has a kinship bond. Both women have mythologically male-derived names to accentuate their position as their own "best thing" (to borrow from Toni Morrison) and to emphasize their potential as gods and goddesses in the story of the metatext. In this novel, divinity is something transferable; thus, by sharing her story, *janie* shares her reincarnate and divine spirit. Pheoby's association with the sun god (and Tea Cake) alludes to the freedom and strength she gains from hearing Janie's story. Like the sun god, she "cut[s] the darkness in flight" toward a new beginning: "Ah done growed ten feet higher from jus' listenin' tuh you. . . . Ah means tuh make Sam take me fishin' wid him after this" (284).

More essential to this reading, Hurston gives Janie a name derived from a male/female god to reveal a "truth" not mentioned but alluded to in the second paragraph of the novel: "Now, women forget all those things they don't want to remember, and remember everything they don't want to forget. *The dream is the truth.* Then they act and do things accordingly" (9, emphasis added). Janie forgets Tea Cake's abuse and remembers the dreams and joys they shared. Through her name's magical, metaphoric, or "dream" role as a god/goddess, she then proceeds to act as his avenger against a god who denied him life and as her own protector. Her actions and her name work in concert to produce at least two ideological messages: women must depend upon themselves for protection, just as Janie does; and, like Janie, women must realize that they too are reflections of god on earth. In other words, women should follow the advice given decades later by Alice Walker's Shug Avery: "git man off your eyeball" (*The Color Purple*, 204).

Unleashing the Fires of Onomastic Desire

Perhaps this is the prime usefulness of literary criticism—it helps to make conscious those aspects of the text which would otherwise remain concealed in the subconscious.
—WOLFGANG ISER, *The Implied Reader*

The re-creative fires that forge the discourse production of poetic names are often quenched by surface events and stories that dominate the reader's attention. These events and the stories they tell conceal the discursive actions of the metatext. To unleash the re-creative force of poetic names, one must hollow out the transparently meaningful and reveal the treasures of onomastic desires existing beneath it. This means exposing and analyzing what might otherwise be ignored or devalued. The seven guiding principles I explore below assist readers in achieving this task. They reveal the meaning potential of poetic names and liberate the flames of internalized signifying systems that give names discursive and invasive force. Instead of highlighting one or two poetic names as I do in the readings above, I draw connections between several so that each principle can be explored fully.

The first of the seven principles defines poetic names like *Janie* and *Vergible Woods* as action-oriented and interpretable utterances communicating ideas and developing narrative events beneath the surface text. This principle grounds my understanding of literary nomenclature as a strategy of discourse production. Proper names such as *Janie* and *Vergible*, phrase names such as *son of the Evening Sun*, markers such as *X*, epithets like *nigger*, nicknames like *Tea Cake*, and titles such as *Masa* and *Mistress* are all rhetorical figurations of naming and can be classified as poetic names. Only two conditions exist: poetic names must have literary subjects, character roles, or an event of charatonymic, thematic, or perceptual change as their referents, and they must perform as an utterance with a fully developed contextual aim or task.

The name *Janie*, for instance, associates Hurston's protagonist metaphorically with the Roman god (Janus) of classical mythology who possessed the keys to paradise. Several times in the novel, Tea Cake tells Janie that she possesses "de keys tuh de kingdom" (181). This information magnifies the meaning potential of the name's deep talk and supports the reader's interpretation of it as a name-entity (one of the most active forms of onomastic desire). It is important to note here a point that is vital to avoiding misreading while expanding the parameters of interpretive play. *Context supports the deep-level discourses produced* by this name. Names with discourse-producing potential appear occasionally within a text without this type of contextual support and encouragement. This observation leads to the second principle of reading poetic names.

Simply stated, all personal names and phrase names are not poetic. The absence of narrative development silences names such as Shelby, Eleanor, Oscar Scott, and Jeff Bruce in Hurston's text. These names appear only once, and we learn almost nothing of the characters, circumstances, or actions they designate. Any desire for deep-level communications these names possess remains hidden from the reader. The dual-sex name *Shelby*, for instance, can denote either a male or a female. In Hurston's novel, it identifies a white male character, the oldest grandchild of the Washburn family. The potential for meaning exists within this name because of its socially defined duality. The text does not develop this potential, however. After its initial appearance, both the name and any themes it suggests disappear from the text. Hence, the potential utterances of its deep talk fall silent. The result is a flat, nonpoetic name.

The third principle of reading through names and naming reminds us that there are two modes of reading, active and inactive. It implies that readers should take note of anything strange or unusual they sense when reading a name. Readers perceive the meaning potential of poetic names on a preconscious level of processing before conscious interpretation ever begins. The criteria for all conscious representation of information and sensory inflow, according to psychologists, are applied at a level beyond consciousness—the preconscious or supraliminal level of analysis. In *Preconscious Processing*, Norman Dixon reasons that if the acceptance of information inflow is determined preconsciously, then meaning must also be "discriminated preconsciously."[8] The cumulative effects of what is perceived operate as supraliminal interpretive stimuli that, when accepted by a reader, can be read as utterances within a metatext. This does not mean that all readers consciously interpret a story's metatext. Through selective attention a reader can ignore the perceptions received from supraliminal stimuli by choosing preconsciously not to be aware of their meaning potential. Even if a reader does choose to acknowledge the stimuli consciously, he or she may still choose to ignore the discursive potential of the name. In both cases, the name sending the information is read inactively, and the reader ignores the desire of onomastic deep talk as it might relate to an interpretive moment within the text.

Actively tracing the social, cultural, historical, allegorical, and intertextual accents of names, as I do in the introductory reading of this chapter, is active reading. This mode of analytical involvement focuses on how the speaking discourses of names chaotically fold into each other, constructing onomastic desires that transpose interpretive deep talk in multiple ways and on multiple levels of meaning simultaneously. When employing an inactive mode of reading, poetic names like *Vergible Woods* and *Janie Woods* are interesting but silent. Active reading moves beyond this narrow understanding of names and investigates them as utterances. This is the mode of reading that "opens" the metatext and reveals the deep talk of poetic names. It provides the reader with an active understanding of the roles names play as subject position designators and as motivators of (and actants within) extralinguistic events.

The fourth principle categorizes thematically the contextual aims of names and phrase names functioning as subject position designators. An awareness of a poetic name's cultural, ancestral, social, attitudinal, or allegorical thematic orientation helps the active reader decipher deep-level discourses and expose a variety of character roles. All poetic names contain these themes and name tasks, with some names containing aspects of two or more of them. The phrase name *Mouth-Almighty*, used by Janie, for instance, designates a community custom of front porch gossiping and storytelling. The name has a cultural contextual aim— name tasks that organize and associate the bearer with specific customs and rituals of community-focused or group identity.[9] It also contains an attitudinal contextual aim that reflects Janie's perception of the characters designated by the name. Instead of reflecting cultural identities or community rituals, attitudinal name tasks announce the bearer's personal reputation, the speaker's attitude and personal feelings toward the bearer, and, in many cases, the bearer's self-image. Their appearance (or disappearance) in the text may also inform the reader of a character's growth or changing belief systems.

Such is the case when Amos Hicks introduces himself to Janie and Joe Starks in chapter 5 of the novel. "Hicks is the name. Guv'nor Amos Hicks from Buford, South Carolina. Free, single, disengaged" (57). The title *Guv'nor* is no title at all; it communicates a position of pseudo-influence and stature the character *believes* he possesses in situations of courtship and wooing. This attitudinal discourse develops later through another self-imposed name. "Ah'm uh bitch's baby round lady people" (59). Both names, *bitch's baby* and *Guv'nor*, communicate the same idea concerning the character's belief system and self-image: charisma. Names such as these disappear from the text after Janie's reproof. Amos grows (or rather his attitude changes) immediately following his realization that he is not the "lady killer" he believes himself to be.

Often name-focused transformations effect onomastic desires without affecting the characters designated. The phrase name *Mouth-Almighty* is an example. This name is introduced early in the novel and sets up the theme of "mouths" that gather on front porches to gossip or tell stories. It primarily announces a community ritual that appears repeatedly throughout the novel and Janie's flippant attitude toward gossips. In this context, the name achieves a charatonymic desire by subordinating individuality to a one-dimensional, single-focused utterance of group identity and role designation. Its thematic presence in the novel claims a community of people extending from Eatonville to the Florida mucks with

Joe Starks being its biggest conquest. In the metatext, *Mouth-Almighty* functions as an absent presence whose onomastic desire is stylized by Joe's perception of himself as a "big voice" (74). Read through the name *Mouth-Almighty*, Joe is a "mouth" who thinks itself a god, an almighty. (I develop this reading later.) Joe's characterization adds a condition to the name's previous onomastic tasks. As a result, the name changes so that it speaks of a community of characters in the surface text and a name-entity (a god) in the metatext.

Unlike *Mouth-Almighty*, names with ancestral contextual aims relate the bearer to a particular family, race, geographic identity, or history. In its most meager expressions of deep talk, Hurston's use of *Washburn* creates a word with tasks of this type. "They was quality white folks up dere in West Florida. Named Washburn" (20). The name speaks of a white family from a particular geographic location with a history distinct from the African-American community surrounding them. The absence of given names for the adult members of the Washburn family accentuates the ancestral contextual aim of the family name, making it the primary focus of the word, its dominant theme.

This primacy does not prevent other themes from entering the name, influencing its internal framework of meaning, and fragmenting it. Hurston links the defining elements of an attitudinal contextual aim with the name's dominant ancestral utterances through Janie's description of the Washburn family: "They was quality white folks." Because ancestral thematic aims dominate the deep talk of this name, the idea of "quality" and all other utterances and themes present within it function only as supplements to the name's ancestral utterances—at least, in the surface text. In the metatext, the word takes on the flavor of irony as its multiple levels of supplemental discourses interact to produce a name-entity.

The importance of supplemental discourses to the development of metatexts should not be ignored or glossed over. They offer poetic names, like *Washburn*, a variety of linked, and often conflicting, contextual aims, thereby increasing their value as catalysts for the playfulness enacted within and among liminal actants. These actants are action-oriented utterances that assume the behavior of liminal name-entities. Here, I align the poetic name with Victor Turner's description of liminal personae or "threshold people" existing within circumscribed cultural spaces. In doing so, I push forward, or prioritize, the "living" word in order to read its discursive activities. Turner defines liminal entities as "neither here nor there; they are betwixt and between the positions assigned and arrayed by law, custom, convention, and ceremonial. . . . It is as though they are being reduced or ground down to a uniform condition [one center of power] to be fashioned anew and endowed with additional powers." [10]

Much like the "threshold people" described in Turner's *Ritual Process*, the discourse production of a border-crossing name actant like *Washburn* exists "betwixt and between" presence and absence. In my reading of *Vergible Woods* and *Janie Woods* (and in my discussion of *Mouth-Almighty*), I identified these actants as name-entities. As we read, name-entities vacillate between surface and deep-level action, collecting information until they can express themselves in the surface fully. Meaning is "ground down," truncated, within the name, providing it with the energy of several narrative events. On the surface, border-crossing name actants signify various characters' roles; in the metatext, they homogenize diverse characterizations and events in order to become them. In other words, they rely upon the qualities they share with other discourses within the text to produce meaning. These names enter into a "conversation" with discourses that gives voice to their onomastic desires and makes clear their contextual constraints.

The border-crosser *Washburn* internalizes the voices of multiple themes, descriptions, and actions that develop a complex undergirding of intratextual utterances within a multilayered deep-level discourse. The life story of Janie's grandmother, Nanny, provides the space of liminality through which this name first moves (it later moves within the story of Janie and Joe Starks's first meeting). As Nanny tells her story, we learn that Janie's mother is half white, the product of Marse Robert's lasciviousness. We also learn that the wife of Nanny's master reacts violently to the child's birth and physical appearance. " 'Nigger, whut's yo' baby doin' wid gray eyes and yaller hair?' " she says and began "tuh slap mah jaws ever which a'way. Ah never felt the fust ones 'cause Ah wuz too busy gittin' de kivver back over mah chile. But dem last lick burnt me lak fire. . . . she kept on astin me how come mah baby look white." Not getting the answer she wants, the mistress finally resolves to have Nanny whipped, promising to watch " 'till de blood run down to yo' heels.' "

Nanny eludes this final punishment by escaping into the swamp "by de river" (33–35).

Nanny's recitation of her interactions with whites while a slave illuminates the border-crossing performance of *Washburn*. Unlike the Washburn family, the text does not assign her former master, *Marse Robert*, nor his family a formal last name. This is a site of conversion that assists readers in reconceptualizing and extending their interpretation of the deep-level discourse speaking through *Washburn*. As an ancestral family name, *Washburn* is genealogical probing and double voiced. It denotes all individuals within a particular racial family—namely, Caucasians—as well as characters with kinship ties. This association of the name with white characters sharpens our awareness of it as a poetic word whose deep talk homogenizes and describes the attitudes, values, and actions of particular types of people or groups.

Nanny's memories also reveal diachronic thematic links that merge the defining elements of the name utterance *Washburn* with actions that preceded her contact with it historically. The discourse produced is both recursive (the term, meaning complex textual layering, is Karla Holloway's) and reflective, adding to the name a third level of deep talk that speaks constantly of the events revealed in Nanny's remembered story.[11] Within the metatext, the intratextual components of *Washburn*, *wash* and *burn*, relativize familial associations and reinstall the name as a description of at least four previous actions: Nanny's child is white*washed*, her features and hair lightened by paternal genetic influence; the mistress promises to watch as Nanny's blood *washes* over her body; during Nanny's escape both she and the child are *washed* in the water of the swamp; and the burning indicated by *Washburn* recalls the slaps that burnt Nanny's face like fire.

Echoes of these utterances contained within *Washburn* delimit the name's use as one designating a particular family and allow its dual function as both a reflective and a self-projecting narrative effect. The use of the name to identify a family of well-intentioned whites, in the surface text, assigns responsibility to that family for the past crimes of those whose race they share. Although no one within the Washburn family assaults or legally enslaves and sexually abuses Nanny, the name designating them behaves as an "undercover" informant whose deep talk speaks to the reader of these memories and activities reflectively. This onomastic desire renders the idea of "quality" speaking through the name ironic in force and intent. At this point in the novel, each of these meanings remains hidden from the characters who use the name. They remain "undercover." Even the narrator does not acknowledge the informant's intratextual desires. Instead, the deep-level communications produced by *Washburn* establish a dialogue between the author or writing subject and the reader only. Later, I explain how the name abandons its "undercover" status through a different type of discursive action.

Hurston uses no other names to distinguish between husband and wife except the titles they bear—*Mr. Washburn* and *Mis'* (sometimes *Mrs.*) *Washburn*. The addition of titles to the name further modifies its contextual aim, adding to it utterances that speak of *social* relations. Social contextual aims, such as those operating within titles, are the fourth category of intent emphasized by subject position designators. They associate the bearer with a particular economic status, with certain sociopolitical expectations, ethics, responsibilities, interpersonal behaviors, gender distinctions, and power relations. Epithets like *nigger* and *darky* and titles like *Madam* and *Mayor* each contain social contextual aims that express the imperatives of externally mandated social roles and behavioral standards. Utterances of names that diminish and disavow the value of female subjectivity such as *Mrs. Mayor Starks* and *Mrs. Mayor*, for example, clearly announce social status and structure hierarchical power relations. They identify the named as property, the mayor's property. Titles accompanying other names like *Rev. Pearson* and *Brother Killicks* speak of social relations informed by ethical and spiritual connotations. Even *Washburn* contains socially defined utterances.

Like *Mouth-Almighty*, names that function as subject position designators often collapse and internalize a variety of contextual aims. This deep talk provides them with the ability to structure social discourses that are either self-affirming or deprecating, manipulating or disciplinary, presumptuous or officious, amalgamating or estranging. Joe's use of the name *Mrs. Mayor Starks* meshes attitudinal, social, and ancestral themes to produce a desired effect: "You'se Mrs. Mayor Starks, Janie. I god, Ah can't see what uh woman uh yo' sability would want tuh be treasurin' all dat gum-grease from folks dat don' even own de house dey sleep in"

(85). Here, Joe attempts to separate his wife from the community and its ritualistic "porch talk" by reminding her of what he (a self-declared god, a *"Mouth-Almighty"*) believes the entity called *Janie* should represent. "You'se Mrs. Mayor Starks, Janie. I god." This string of names alone deprecates Janie's communal associations, disciplines her behavior, presumes Joe's superiority, and estranges Janie from those around her.

Although Joe manipulates his wife primarily through the social themes of *Mrs. Mayor Starks*, he also manipulates her through the deep-level communications established by the concrete themes of another name in the quote. A transition in meaning determined by the structural relations and proximity of words in Joe's statement occurs that affects the theme of a non-onomastic unit of speech. Just as none of the preceding thematic categories are mutually exclusive and unyielding, none of them are the sole property of proper names and epithets either. In Joe's statement, their incantatory force organizes the concrete theme of an interjection and transforms it.

After identifying Janie's subject position, Joe goes on to identify himself. "I god," he says. The sequential positioning of these words behind the names *Mrs. Mayor Starks* and *Janie* aligns its contextual aims with those of a descriptive subject position designating Joe Starks as a god. The interjection "I god" (repeated often in this text) refines Joe's role as one of supreme power—at least in Eatonville—and further distinguishes Janie from the people surrounding her. The social and attitudinal utterances within Joe's statement transform "I god" into a descriptive phrase name with allegorical contextual aims (name tasks that develop a story through the agency of connotative and denotative transposition—intertextuality). This use of the phrase expands its deep talk, giving it hidden onomastic meanings that function throughout the metatext of Joe and Janie's story. It points to Joe as the god whom everyone watches, and it relegates Janie, the wife of a god, to the role of an icon, or idol, symbolizing Joe's supreme power.

A name empowered by thematic links such as this can contribute to events in each of the four categories of discursive effects constituting principle five of *Reading through Names and Naming*: narrative effects, position effects, object effects, and the eruption of the true-real. Names with narrative effects are influencing agents or extralinguistic actors whose task is to manipulate various aspects of discourse production through brief and extended narrative action. If the deep-level discourse of a name supplementing and redefining narrative action develops throughout a text, the narrative effects of its deep talk creates an extended metatext. This occurs through the deep talk of *Mouth-Almighty*. Although the name appears only in the first chapter of the novel, it is linked thematically to the names of all characters who gather on front porches, telling jokes and gossiping. In the metatext of Joe Starks's story, the name fragments through unnaming and becomes "I god" and a "big voice."

If deep-level discourses develop within a word, sentence, paragraph, or a few chapters only, they create brief narrative action like that of the diachronic name *Washburn*. Such names reflect or foreshadow narrative events and function as truncated utterances of values, interests, actions, narrative themes, and various other concepts. Hurston's text contains several names whose contextual aims achieve this type of discursive effect. *Beef Stew*, for instance, functions as a truncated description of a character's special interest in food. The character comments at one point in the novel, "dey got beef stew, so you *know* Ah'd be heah" (222). This name and others such as *Sop-de-Bottom*, *Coker*, *Hambo*, and even *Tea Cake* add humor while developing the novel's celebratory (and name-focused) theme of food and eating.

In contrast, names such as *Janie Mae Killicks*, *Who Flung*, and *Logan Killicks* read like sentences or phrases that foreshadow narrative events (they speak through intratextual onomastic desires). The deep talk of the protagonist's name informs the reader that "Janie May Kill" long before she embarrasses Joe to death (almost literally) or shoots Tea Cake. The name *Who Flung* reveals the actions of a man who throws away love for money. Logan Kill-*icks* suggests the disgust Janie eventually feels for her first husband's odor and, perhaps, even her disappointment in his sexual performance (his Lo-*gun*): "Ah'd ruther be shot wid tacks than tuh turn over in de bed and stir up de air whilst he is in dere" (42). The name even foreshadows the character's defenselessness against Janie's abandonment and infidelity. Unlike Tea Cake, who raises a pistol against this possibility, Logan (i.e., *low gun*) does not. Each of these names contains within themselves brief narrative effects.

The second type of discursive effect, position effects, delimits the constraints of a name's contextual aims, allowing it to project its meaning potential beyond its primary object. Like ripples in a pond, meaning may be projected forward to the character bearing the name or beyond that character to another simultaneously. When Janie first meets Joe Starks, the narrator employs the position effects of a single name, *Mr. Washburn*, to invoke images and connotations of interracial intimacy and ancestral coupling as well as behavior. "He was a seal-brown color but he acted like Mr. Washburn or somebody like that to Janie" (47). The juxtaposition of Joe's color with an utterance defining white ancestral relationships empowers the name's ability to act. Subsequently, its position effects perform tasks beyond their original intent. The deep talk of *Mr. Washburn* is projected beyond the characters originally denoted toward Joe. Therein, the position effects of the name credit Joe Starks with the same attitudes, mannerisms, responsibilities, and ancestral relations as the novel's white characters.

In this example, *Washburn*, a name that functions first as an "undercover" informant, mutates or fragments. The narrator's conscious manipulation of the name transforms it into an active sideward glance (a signifying desire) whose deep talk signifies upon Joe Starks's racial heritage and ancestry. Position effects such as these influence change or reflect charatonymic development (that is, the development of individual attributes and accountability) by modifying the reader's interpretation of a character's personality traits or by highlighting specific physical, moral, and ethical transformations and ideas. The name *Mr. Washburn* infiltrates Joe's initial characterization by aligning his subject position with that of the novel's white ruling class—as his story develops we understand why. Similar to the white masters of the ancestral world denoted by *Washburn*, Joe Starks wields an "outstretched hand of power" in Eatonville. He allows no one but himself to sit in "de rulin' chair," issuing orders for the blacks in *his* town to follow (134).

Another example occurs earlier in the text as a name, originally introduced because of its social contextual aims and value, meets such violent attitudinal hostility that an epithet replaces it. In this example, meaning is projected forward as the position effects of an epithet open the discourses of characterization and accountability to the influences of a new discursive space. The subject at issue in the scene of the name's first appearance is Janie's need to marry a financially stable and morally decent man (even if she does not love him). To encourage Janie, Nanny uses a name that speaks of esteemed social status and community acceptance—a name with a social contextual aim: "Brother Logan Killicks. He's a good man, too" (28). Although the women's conversation has nothing to do with religion, the idea of religious piety and spiritual bonding speaks through the word *Brother* and expresses the position effects of a behavioral expectation (an accountability). The association of the name with Nanny's opinion of the character's "goodness" reinforces this subject position and identifies her use of the name as one expressing positive attitudinal aims.

This name changes when Nanny suspects that Logan's behavior is something different from her expectations, something other than good. Three months after entering a loveless marriage, Janie visits her grandmother. "You and Logan been fussin,'" Nanny asks, "Lawd, Ah Know dat *grass-gut, liver-lipped nigger* ain't done took and beat mah baby already!" (40, emphasis added). In her anger, Nanny not only violates the positive social components of the character's original subject position, but she replaces these utterances with a derogatory phrase name that reflects a dramatically different attitudinal view. Religious piety, respect, spiritual bonding, esteemed social status, and community acceptance all disappear in the wake of the epithet's position effects.

Position effects, such as these, influence, reconfigure, and challenge hierarchical and interpersonal relations among the novel's characters. Their primary task is to generate change in the ancestral, cultural, social, or attitudinal worldviews of both the name bearer and others who come into contact with the name bearer. These effects are often brief and undermining. They initiate conflict and create moments of contradiction, irony, paradox, and foreclosure. Near the end of Hurston's novel, the deep talk of a position effect challenges Tea Cake's self-concept and provokes an immediate response from him that forecloses any further use of the offending name.

The incident occurs after a hurricane hits the Everglades, where Tea Cake and Janie live. Two armed guards, seeking unemployed men to bury the dead, address Tea Cake as they do all black men; they call him *Jim* (as in Jim Crow, a gesture of the author's sociotypical commentary). "'Hello, there, Jim,' the tallest one called out. 'We been lookin' for you.'" According to the worldview advocated by these men, all blacks are the same. The speaker's use of the name *Jim* collapses individuality into a category of group entitlement much like a passing epithet. Tea Cake rejects this blind and objectifying categorization by correcting the man, "Mah name ain't no Jim" (251). His response forecloses the name's deprecating contextual aims and the word *Jim* disappears from the text.

Before moving forward in this discussion to the third discursive effect (the object effect), it is necessary to take a brief excursion into the sixth principle, which addresses the activities of name utterances like *Tea Cake* and *Jim* whose sociolinguistic environments collide. It also provides definitions for a few terms and explanations of name-motivated events essential to the discussions that follow. This unavoidable violation of sequence is a consequence of these principles' interdependent nature and of the natural sequential displacement and resistance to order provoked by poetic names themselves. Even a reordering of the guiding principles would not constrict the chaotic energy germane to the onomastic discourse production of poetic names.

Like all utterances, poetic names exist within contextual environments, sociolinguistic orders in which some names have value while others do not. These contextual environments are the lifeworlds of name utterances, their spheres of influence. A poetic name that successfully enters a resisting environment either reshapes defining elements within that lifeworld or is itself reshaped by hostile contact. The utterances spoken through the names *Jim* and *Tea Cake* originate from within two separate sociolinguistic environments. Both the naming traditions and the structure of racial relationships within the social lifeworld of the white guards support the word *Jim* as a perfectly acceptable one to use when addressing a black man. Tea Cake, on the other hand, interprets the name as an insult. The naming traditions within his sociolinguistic worldview inform him that the word *Jim* (as used by the white guards) has no value or meanings he wishes to associate with himself. He acknowledges only two names as his own, *Vergible Woods* and *Tea Cake*. Ironically, these names also function within distinct and separate spheres of influence.

They first appear in chapter 10. "De name mah mamma gimme is Vergible Woods. Dey calls me Tea Cake for short" (149). In the sociolinguistic lifeworld of their origin, *Tea Cake* (a name that speaks of something sweet and leisurely) has value and promotes intimate interpersonal relationships that the more formal and maternally assigned name, *Vergible Woods*, does not. Just as Joe silences Janie's voice earlier in the text, Tea Cake silences the utterance of a name identified with maternal naming. After its initial introduction, *Vergible Woods* disappears from the surface text, leaving behind only *Tea Cake*. The foreclosed name reappears within the scene containing Janie's vindication from murder. Note that the language used in the sentence containing the name's reinstatement is quite different from that used when foreclosing it: "We find the death of Vergible Woods to be entirely accidental and justifiable, and that no blame should rest upon the defendant Janie Woods" (279). This change in idiolects (an individual speaker's use of linguistic patterns, a dialect) indicates that the speaker exists not only within an alien geographic environment but also in an alien sociolinguistic environment—a lifeworld beyond the muck and its community of blacks in which Tea Cake as a namer has no power.

Poetic names like *Tea Cake* "remember" previous tasks and contexts. These defining elements are the historical content of names or phrase names that give them voice and determine their dominant themes, whether foreclosed or explicit, within all contextual environments (alien and familiar). The memory of intimate community bonding and male self-naming privilege guides the ability of *Tea Cake* to function as an object effect. This third type of discursive effect results from the role a name plays as an emblem and motivator of onomastic themes in conflict. A reader's ability to detect these effects relies heavily upon an awareness of a poetic name's ability to respond when entering an alien sphere of influence. Without an object of conflict, however, this ability means nothing.

A name that successfully achieves an object effect (or becomes the emblem of one) enters into a dialogic relationship with the defining elements of names, or other utterances, that stand in diametrical opposition to its own historical content. The idea of maternal naming and formal sociolinguistic structures contained within the utterance *Vergible Woods* presents a perfect opportunity for developing discourses of hostility, disagreement, and foreclosure in relation to *Tea Cake*. When such interactions and exchanges occur, the dominant utterance either redefines elements in the opposing name that violently conflict with its onomastic intent or eliminates from the text the names containing the offending utterances.

Tea Cake asserts itself this way in both examples presented above. Although the character does not mention his preferred name when speaking with the guards, and the jury does not mention it within the courtroom scene, the continual use of the name within the narration challenges conflicting discourses and eliminates them. " 'Mah name ain't no Jim,' Tea Cake said watchfully" (251). Here, as in the example of the interjection "I god," proximity empowers a name's use as a strategy of discourse production. In this case, however, the contextual "memories" and primary themes within *Tea Cake* challenge the deep talk of *Jim* and replace that utterance within the text.

A similar event occurs after the name *Vergible Woods* reappears, establishes its dominance in the formal lifeworld beyond the muck, and briefly reaffirms black maternal naming (as well as the identity of an avenging god). The reappearance of *Tea Cake* a few lines later produces object effects that foreclose the defining elements of *Vergible Woods*'s conflicting deep talk. It eliminates the reaffirmation of both formal names and the maternal namer by replacing the word speaking these discourses. After this last collision, *Vergible Woods* does not appear within the surface text again. *Tea Cake*, the character's preferred name, replaces it and serves as the emblem of an object effect that privileges black communal idiolects over white formal discourses and maternal namers. This object effect is forged further by the onomastic desires of the phrase name *Tea Cake with the sun for a shawl*, a name that purges and resolves all conflicts. Because it is assigned to the character through "the song of the sigh" Janie imagines, maternal naming concludes the text (286).

The possibility for privileging communal idiolects over maternal naming ends when Janie kills Tea Cake. Janie is the ultimate namer in Hurston's novel, whose ability to forestall the influence of communal namers, specifically those that are male determined, begins when she insults Joe's manhood, describing his genitals as "de change uh life" (123). This ability is refined through her interaction with another male character and his name's object effects (123). The discursive play enacted among the various names denoting Joe's delivery boy projects a theme of maternal naming into the word *Janie*. This deep talk runs parallel to *Janie's* other (many other) name-oriented meanings and tasks. Although all the delivery boy's names involve themselves in creating this discourse, the one most central to Janie's ability to forestall the idiolects of male-defined communal naming is *Hezekiah*. The conflict it generates develops a story of struggle between female and male namers that begins when Janie calls Joe "out of his name" and continues within the metatext until Tea Cake's death leaves Janie the novel's *only* surviving namer of the surface narrative.

Following the development of *Hezekiah* reveals how this name assigns *Janie* new contextual aims and how its development of a brief metatext supports these aims. The name's function in the scenes of interest to this discussion is four-fold. It functions as a character's subject position, a position effect, a narrative effect, and (after assisting the development of contextual themes within not one but two other names, *Tea Cake* and *Janie*) an object effect symbolizing an event of maternal naming. The name changes (or mutates) three times indicating three fragmentations. In the lifeworld controlled by Joe Starks, it appears as *Hezekiah Potts*. When Janie becomes owner of Joe's store, the character's name changes to *Hezekiah*. Once Tea Cake assumes the role of namer, the character receives a third name, *'Kiah*. The brief metatext these names develop subverts a preponderance of male naming influence and gives Janie, a symbolic maternal namer, "the last word" in a story developed through metatextual layering.

A series of name-centered conflicts installs her symbolic role as namer. They begin when the delivery boy assumes the subject position of a little Joe—"the best imitation of Joe that his seventeen years could make" (141). Janie finds the boy's role as a "little Joe" humorous and harmless; but in the multilayered, metatext of discourses produced by names, three not-so-harmless conflicts emerge. First, the description of the character as an "imitation of Joe" adds historical content to his name that mutates it from within, reducing it graphically and phonemically from *Hezekiah* to *'Kiah*, a name that highlights the character's subject position as a teenager, not quite a grown man.

On one level of discourse production, this name change assaults the boy's self-image. It imposes an externally conceived perception dictated by defining elements within the social lifeworld of the adults Tea Cake and Janie. On another level the name change embodies a reflective action that reshapes the subject position of Tea Cake (a name, by the way, that already suggests the idea of something little and childlike). Because Tea Cake uses the diminutive first, his linguistic control as namer creates discursive action that usurps Hezekiah's subject position as a "little Joe," a "little namer," and assigns that role, briefly, to the name *Tea Cake*.

Although both Janie and Tea Cake use the name *'Kiah*, the original name continues to appear in the narration, indicating the development of a second conflict. The poetic name's allegorical contextual aims act as a vehicle for this conflict. An external collision of connotative meaning and denotation transposes the meaning potential of *Hezekiah*. Derived from the Bible, *Hezekiah* speaks allegorically of a father-son relationship. The biblical Hezekiah, however, is nothing like his father Ahaz, the king who surrendered Judah to idolatry. Instead, Hezekiah frees the land from his father's restrictions, opening the temple his father once closed.[12] This discourse contradicts the idea of the character as an "imitation of Joe" while also developing the idea of Hezekiah as a symbolic son.

The name's primary use in the metatext remains true to the biblical story it interpolates. There, the delivery boy "delivers" Janie from her imposed status as an object of idolatry by telling her the one thing she desires to hear most—that Tea Cake is unmarried. " 'What's de matter wid Tea Cake, 'Kiah? . . . is he got uh wife or something lak dat?' She held her breath for the answer." " 'No'm,' " the boy answers, "and nobody wouldn't marry Tea Cake tuh starve tuh death lessen it's somebody jes lak him—ain't use to nothing" (155–66). Janie responds by reinstalling the character's original name, *Hezekiah*; in doing so, she forecloses the nickname *'Kiah*: "Oh, dat's all right, Hezekiah. Thank yuh mighty much" (156).

Janie interprets Hezekiah's answer differently than he expects. To Janie, his denunciation of Tea Cake offers her a freedom that she desires and eagerly anticipates, a freedom she is not "use to." In this way, Hezekiah's answer completes the allegorical development of events within the brief metatext that symbolically redefines Janie's subject position. Like his biblical namesake, Hezekiah frees the community of idol worship and opens the doors his "father" closed. His words free Janie from her role as a community "idol," representing Joe's power and godlike reputation, and open the doors Joe closed against her will to speak as one of the folk. From this moment on Janie speaks without censure or regret.

Her renaming of the delivery boy and the biblical allegory of the metatext function together to identify her as a symbolic maternal namer.

The third conflict in this series results from the collision between the dominant subject positions designated by the delivery boy's two names, *Hezekiah* and *'Kiah*. The presence of these names in the surface text metaphorically places Janie as namer in opposition to Tea Cake as namer. The conflict ends when Janie realizes that the allegorical son serves her better than the idea of a "little Joe." Her use of *Hezekiah*, in response to the boy's condemnation of Tea Cake (his unwelcomed namer) not only validates the character's self-image but forecloses any further use of the name speaking the conflicting discourse. In this example, *Hezekiah* functions as an emblematic object effect representing an event of maternal naming.

The fourth and final name-focused discursive effect, the true-real, emerges briefly during this event but fails to maintain a concrete presence within the surface text. *Hezekiah*, the name through which it speaks, disappears. Unfortunately, we never again hear of the character Hezekiah nor his subject position (as one who frees). Instead of developing a sustained discursive position that creates a concrete presence and discourse of its own (like *Vergible Woods* in the story of avenging gods), the brief emergence of the true-real through the name *Hezekiah* repositions Janie as a maternal namer and then falls silent. The true-real emerges through the name only to produce an object effect. It neither creates a name-entity nor offers a sustained message.

The seventh principle, name fragmentation, defines the splitting off or merging of discursive value through three ritualistic forms: renaming, unnaming, and supranaming. *Their Eyes Were Watching God* benefits from a rigorous play of name fragmentation that undergirds and undermines surface meaning constantly. It is through unnaming that *Vergible* becomes *Tea Cake* and *Tea Cake* becomes *Jim*, and through renaming that Tea Cake reclaims his preferred name (*Jim* becomes *Tea Cake*). Through supranaming the character introduced first as *Janie Starks* becomes *Janie May Killicks* and *Janie Woods*. Each of these fragmentations leaves behind a trail of onomastic deep talk that not only develops the novel's primary story but often informs against it. Name-motivated discourses extending from these fragmentations create moments of meta-phoric chaos within the text that disrupt reference, communicate deep-level stories, and build textual layering.

As reading Hurston's novel through names and naming demonstrates, the layering effects of onomastic discourse production are limited only by the constraints of context (what the text allows a name to say) and the name's functions (what a name is able to say). These covert operatives enter into a deep-level communication that ultimately moves the discursive force of naming toward a desired goal: an expression of meaning that is at once explosive and re-creative. Like flint against flint, the onomastic desires of poetic names grind against imposed constraints to generate the igniting sparks of metaphoric chaos and thematic proliferation. Once denied entrance to the surface text, these sparks of potential meaning subsist in the metatext, where they are nurtured into flames. Only then can readers hear the crackling of onomastic deep talk and expose the cache of treasures its fires forge.

3
Unpacking, Categorizing, and Interpreting Treasures

MILKMAN'S JOURNEY of self-discovery in Toni Morrison's *Song of Solomon* begins with a sack he is sure contains a treasure of gold. With great anticipation, he unpacks the stolen sack only to discover that it contains nothing more than his grandfather's bones. Although this might appear to be a failed quest, the unpacking of the sack is the first step on a journey that leads the character to an understanding of his own true name. Unpacking poetic names is very much like this step in Milkman's journey. It begins the reader's journey toward understanding the deep-level communications and discursive strategies of names and naming. The reader's next acts on this journey are categorizing and interpreting the treasures that unpacking reveals.

Categorizing discourse types assists readers in interpreting a poetic name's strategic posture and meaning interpolation. It also assists readers in identifying the effects of textual layering produced by multiple name fragmentations and the onomastic desires that forge their deep talk. There are three broad categories of onomastic desire through which a name's discursive movements achieve a multitude of deep-level communications: referent-oriented desire; single-voiced, objectified desire; and double-voiced, signifying desire. The list below includes several, but not all, varieties of each. Like Mikhail Bakhtin's discourse types, mine is not an exhaustive list; it is, however, an adequate one for the purposes of this study.[1]

Categories of Onomastic Desire

I. *Referent-oriented desire* is a monologic expression of the author's authority as namer. The goal of desires in this category is to identify a character, object, or place within a text.

II. *Single-voiced, objectified desire* transmits information from author to the reader. Characters within the text remain unaware of this system of deep-level communications and do not acknowledge the name's onomastic intent.

   A. Intratextual (foreshadows or reflects narrative events and characterization)

      1. "Undercover" informant

   B. Picturesque (describes an extratextual referent)

   C. Sociotypical (reveals an author's sociolinguistic revisionary action or commentary)

III. *Double-voiced, signifying desire* communicates to and interacts with various audiences, including the reader, characters, and other names.

   A. Single-directed, double-voiced desire (develops one referent within a surface-level story)

      1. Charatonymic (speaks of its textual referent implicitly)

      2. Imprinted (speaks of its textual referent explicitly)

         a. Homophonic imprint

         b. Graphic imprint

         c. Cultural imprint

      3. Stylized (adds a thematic condition to previous onomastic tasks)

   B. Multidirectional, double-voiced desire (repetitions accented by oppositional contextual aims)

      1. Calling out of one's name

         a. Parody (chiding revision)

      2. Calling out to another entity, history, event, idea, or name

         a. Pastiche (genial revision)

      3. Loud talking

         a. Irony (sardonic or contradictory revision)

C. Active signifying desire (develops primary and deep-level story lines through discourse transformation and onomastic action)
   1. The sideward glance (may be "undercover")
   2. The eruption of the true-real
      a. Name-entities
      b. Active mnemonic names
      c. Ideological messengers

Although these are all categories of deep talk, I do not identify them as utterances in this list. The title "Categories of Onomastic Desire" speaks to a lack within the act of listing itself. It represents the discursive attitudes of only two active participants in a three-pronged relationship—the hypothesized author and the name. The absence of an active (or even imagined) addressee who unpacks the name renders deep talk nothing more than desired dialogue (what a name wants to say) and muted utterances. The discussions below reflect the addition of a third participant, the reader. My role as an interpreter who unpacks and reads the onomastic desires I intuit renders each of them fully expressed utterances.

To unpack a name is to evaluate and record the events involved in constructing its discursive attitude. Interpreting what is unpacked means determining how a name utterance reacts to or interacts with other elements of a text, including other names associated with the character denoted. This means tracing mutations and shifts in accent that result from name fragmentation: renaming, unnaming, and supranaming. If we follow a character's name from its inception within a novel or short story throughout the text, we discover that, in many cases, the name changes. As the story progresses, the interpretive function and onomastic desires of the original name shifts, or the name itself graphically or graphemically mutates (renaming); a new name replaces the original, or events in the text usurp its ability to speak (unnaming); a second name supplements the original, or the metatext produces names that supplement the original (supranaming). These are the concrete traces of name fragmentation that appear in the surface text. Noting their creative force, categorizing their onomastic desires, and analyzing their discursive impact are central to understanding the interplay of a name's enunciative variety and deep talk.

Renaming

Perhaps the most difficult fragmentation to identify and interpret is renaming. In most cases of renaming, the interpretive function of a name changes while the name remains graphically the same. Because the fragmented name internalizes its thematic shifts, its appearance within the surface remains unaffected. Bakhtin identifies this as *inner dialogization*, which he defines as "a disintegration of double-voiced discourse into two discourses, into two isolated independent voices."[2] When a name splits in accent only, its homonym works beneath the surface to achieve distinct and often diverse goals within that alternate space. These names are two *different* words: one appearing within the dialogues and descriptions of the main story as a character designator and the second accompanying it as an invasive and subversive name-entity (or icon) that acts out its contextual aims within the metatext. In extreme cases, the second name moves parallel to the first like a shadow, developing a story of its own. In these instances, the enunciative acts of aggressive onomastic desire not only develop surface meaning but also inform, challenge, transform, and contradict characterization and narrative events as defined within the surface.

The name *Pilate*, in Morrison's novel, fragments through this type of renaming. Its concrete themes and functions shift, giving the name an interpretative force that tells a deep-level story quite different from that told on the surface. Because diverse onomastic desires manipulate this name, the development of deep talk within it becomes internally undecided and proliferates, fragmenting the name from within. *Pilate* emerges in the text as an utterance with multiple functions and homonyms, each operating on different levels of textual meaning and narrative development. A few of this name's symbolic associations are easy to uncover—the name's association with flight (as in airplane pilot), travel (as in riverboat pilot), lynching (its description as a tree *hanging* above a group of

85

smaller trees), and religion (Pilate of the Bible), for instance. Although easy to identify as symbolic associations, the onomastic desires these symbols develop fragment the name in ways not immediately recognizable. Because of its depth and multiplicity as an enunciative act, I have chosen to unpack this name below.

It is almost impossible to render a focused and coherent reading of a name with several independent centers of meaning such as *Pilate* without specific questions in mind. This is an essential step in identifying the variety of onomastic desires speaking through a name. After choosing a name to trace, the reader must ask how that name communicates as an utterance. The point here is to reveal the name's dominant themes. The process of unpacking a name demands that a reader become involved with its deep talk by exploring why the name is being used and how it has been used previously, evaluating these findings and determining their function and constraints. Has any mutation of the graphemic or graphic makeup of the name occurred? Has any fragmentation (either internally or externally) occurred, and if so, why? What influences the fragmentation and how does this shift in accent affect other signifying structures? Does the fragmented name speak? If so, what voices speak through it, and what do they say? Questions such as these allow the reader to evaluate the name in its totality. They also assist in determining how various accents reshape or influence the relationships between the name and other elements of the text.

A controlling question should guide these inquiries. The controlling question of an analysis provides the focus of evaluation and serves as a guide for future questions and responses. In my reading of "Avenging Gods," my controlling question asked how *Their Eyes Were Watching God* transposes signifying systems from classical mythology and how the deep talk of those transposed systems performs within the novel's metatext. The questions governing the following analysis address the most obvious thematic concerns of the name I have chosen to unpack in this reading and ask foremost: how does *Song of Solomon* transpose signifying systems from the Bible, and what does reading the deep-level communication of *Pilate* disclose?

Since a reader's interpretation of onomastic desires transforms them into utterances, my controlling questions limit only my *reading* of *Pi-*

late—not its meaning potential. Controlling questions guide the choices I make as a reader as well as my understanding of what I hear as an interpreter. All deep-level communications outside the realm of my controlling questions or beyond the scope of my search remain in the name as desires. Like the inactive reader, I sense the intertextualized voices of other words, texts, or characters within the name and their potential meanings but read them inactively.

In its simplest form, *Pilate* refers to a character. To avoid confusion as this reading progresses, I identify this utterance as *Pilate I*. Literary names in their simplest forms are always referent oriented. Similar to Bakhtin's first word type, this name allows nothing outside its referent-oriented intent to influence it in any way. All utterances or intentions foreign to the authoritative voice of the author remain outside it. Names like *Pilate I* serve as ladders leading to a basement of treasures. Although their function as character designators is vital to the descent and must be considered, this level of meaning and reference is not the treasure.[3]

We discover the first treasure shortly after the name's introduction. The narrator tells us that the character's illiterate father, Jake, honored a family tradition by selecting his newborn's name from the Bible and writing it down "as illiterate people do, every curlicue, arch, and bend in the letters" (18). The mention of this practice within the text adds historical content and value to the name Jake selects. The word that results contains a sociotypical utterance referring to a fictional and a real-world historical past. Through this event, Morrison repeats her own family history. Her grandfather named her mother *Rahmah* by selecting it from the Bible without considering its context.[4] Morrison revises or rewrites this history by choosing for her character (her metaphoric child) a name from the Bible. Her revision fragments the original word to produce *Pilate II*, a sociotypical utterance that informs the reader of the author's revisionary action.

Morrison comments that she uses biblical names in *Song of Solomon* "to show the impact of the Bible on the lives of black people, their awe of it and respect for it coupled with their ability to distort it for their own purposes."[5] The third poetic name, *Pilate III*, results from such a distortion. Like Morrison, Jake does not select the name *Pilate* blindly. He selects it over any other because its letters "seemed to him strong and handsome; [he] saw in them a large figure that looked like a tree hanging in some princely but protective way over a row of smaller trees" (18). Jake's description of the name revises and fragments it—separating *Pilate II*, a historical mode of naming, from *Pilate III*, a picturesque name (also of the second desire category).

The words *tree, prince, hanging*, and *protective* used in Jake's description provide clues as to the hidden desires operating within *Pilate III*. To interpret these clues we must visit the source of Jake's selection. Several times the Bible uses the word *tree* as a synonym for the cross on which Jesus died. First Peter 2:24 provides a good example. In this verse, the author explains that Jesus "bore our sins in his body *on the tree*" (emphasis added). The word *tree* also serves as a metaphoric description of human beings. Concerning false prophets, for example, Matthew 7:19 states that "every tree that does not bear good fruit is cut down and thrown into the fire." Psalm 1:3 uses the word as a simile referring to all who abide by the laws of God: "They are like *trees* planted by streams of water." The word *tree* conjures images of Christ, humanity, reward, and sacrifice. *Prince, hanging*, and *protective* also conjure images of a biblical archetype. Considered together, these intertextual clues reveal the picturesque deep talk of *Pilate III* to describe Christ, the *protecting* *"Prince* of Peace" who *hung* upon a *tree* and sacrificed his life for humanity's reward.

Later in the same scene, the midwife installs the biblical meaning of the name—implicitly calling the newborn out of her name: "It's a man's name. . . . Like a Christ-killing Pilate. You can't get much worse than that for a name. And a baby girl at that" (19). The midwife's discourse parodies the picturesque utterances of *Pilate III*. Her description intensifies and stratifies the internal discourse of the name and fragments it again. When a narrative agent (a character or narrator) uses a name defined previously in the text, but does so with a different purpose or meaning installed into the name, dual themes emerge. In this instance, parody decenters Jake's descriptive revisions to make room for its own goals. The phrase "like a Christ-killing Pilate" juxtaposes images of Christ and the Roman procurator of Judea who sentenced him to death, creating a phrase name, *Christ-killing Pilate*, that speaks of the original word's biblical referent and context.

Jake expunges the name of its true biblical meaning immediately after discovering it. He recalls that the night of Pilate's birth, he pleaded with Jesus to spare his wife's life. The answer to his prayer was *no*, and his wife (named Sing) dies. Jake responds to the indifference and rejection he feels Jesus showed his prayers by denying the biblical history of the name he chooses for his baby girl.[6] Instead of rejecting the name, he places it inside the Bible. With this act, he confines the name's reference to a Christ killer inside the text of its origin: "It come from the Bible. It stays in the Bible" (19). That nothing in the characterization of Pilate, the woman, re-creates the story of Pilate the "Christ killer" confirms this conclusion.

Jake's actions stylize his initial reading of the name. If the dual themes of a name develop without suffering a collision of contextual aims, they stylize the name, and a single-directed, double-voiced discourse results.[7] The deep talk of the name Jake places in the Bible follows the direction or intent of his original impressions while his hostility makes that direction conditional. The revised name, *Pilate IV*, speaks of Jake's rejection and revision of its biblical meanings. The name is single directed in its role as a subject position designator (a "strong and handsome" picture of trees) and double voiced because it contains a condition that acknowledges the Bible only to deny its linguistic control.

Jane Stryz notes that Jake's decision to place the name between the pages of the Bible is inconsistent with his almost blasphemous indifference to Jesus' authority as "Savior." Jake honors family tradition over the authority of Christ by giving his daughter the name "where [his] finger went down" (19). At the same time, he pays homage to the text that records Christ's authority by placing the name of his child inside it. Stryz concludes that Jake's contradictory act, in part, identifies the name as a "physical entity and not just either sign or symbol."[8] Although I agree with Stryz that Jake's actions create a physical entity, I do not read the name he places in the Bible as the same name his daughter bears. There are four names at play here—one whose referent is a character in Morrison's text (*Pilate I*), another validating family history (*Pilate II*), a third denoting a pictorial image of Christ, humanity, sacrifice, and salvation (*Pilate III*), and a fourth that includes the third as a condition of its deep talk (*Pilate IV*). This fourth name speaks of and parodies its biblical source. Whereas Stryz reads this as an unresolved paradox, I read it as a moment of narrative dissonance through which an icon of the true-real, a name-entity, is born.

As the product of extreme internal dialogization, *Pilate IV* not only speaks of and metonymically refers to Christ but contains onomastic desires that transform events within the surface text. When the twelve-year-old Pilate retrieves the piece of paper containing the picture of trees Jake copied so painstakingly, puts it inside her mother's snuffbox, and wears it as an earring, only the name's picturesque deep talk (the *protecting* "*Prince* of Peace" who *hung* upon a *tree* and sacrificed his life for humanity's reward) accompanies it. As Jake commanded, the name referring to a "Christ killer" came from the Bible and remains there. Much like Jesus, who began his ministry at the age of twelve, this name-entity becomes active twelve years after its birth (Luke 2:42–49). By novel's end, it experiences an allegorical story of sacrifice, resurrection, and ascension.

After burying his grandfather's bones, Pilate's nephew, Milkman, asks her if they should mark the grave with a rock or a cross. "Pilate shook her head. She reached up and yanked her earring from her ear, splitting the lobe. Then she made a little hole with her fingers and placed in it Sing's snuffbox with the single word Jake ever wrote" (339). In the surface text, respect and honor accompany this burial rite; it marks the importance of the earring as a symbol of love and familial, historical value. Also, when the protagonist refuses to mark her father's grave with a religious emblem, she honors Jake's rejection of the Bible's linguistic control over his act of naming. Ironically, her actions work within the metatext to parallel the biblical story of covenant history and covenant love. In the metatext, it signals the development of a story of sacrifice, a story demanded by the biblical analogy. Through this story, the name-entity contained within the snuffbox experiences a death and resurrection similar to the biblical Jesus.

Matthew 27:51 tells us that when Christ died, "the curtain of the temple was torn in two from top to bottom." The splitting of Pilate's earlobe reenacts this event in miniature. Biblically, the ripping of the curtain symbolizes the end of humanity's separation from God as a result of Jesus' death, the fulfilled promise of his covenant. The symbolic repetition of this act in *Song of Solomon* signals to the reader the development of an analogous story within the novel. The splitting of the protagonist's earlobe (from top to bottom) represents the death of a name-entity and the end of a confused and fragmented oral history—a separation between self and the ancestors ends. Milkman has discovered his true history and his true name by this point in the novel, and with these discoveries confusion ends. Also like Jesus, *Pilate* experiences a resurrection and ascension. After being placed lovingly inside a grave, the name-entity leaves its "tomb" and takes flight in the beak of a bird. The narrator comments that "without ever leaving the ground she could fly" (340). The "she" referred to here is not *Pilate I*, the woman (who does not leave the ground), but *Pilate IV*, the name-entity and metonymic icon of the story's allegorical metatext.

Critics often argue that Morrison's novel is not a revision of the biblical *Song of Solomon* and disregard the deep talk of the names she uses because of it. This is a mistake. Like the book of the Bible from which its name originates, Morrison's novel can be read symbolically and literally. Read literally, the biblical *Song of Solomon* is an expression of romantic love between a man and a woman; symbolically, the book speaks of the love of God for the nation of Israel. In other words, the reader of the Bible interprets the love between Shulamite and King Solomon as a symbolic representation of the love of God for humanity. The characters of Morrison's novel experience a similar type of agape love.

Morrison's *Song of Solomon* is literally a story of cultural, historical, and personal discovery; but symbolically, it is the discovery of "a love so supreme" that one is "willing to sacrifice" one's own life to its power and beauty.[9] When Milkman understands the messages and secret meanings of the true-real contained within the deep-level story of *Pilate IV*, he learns that to gain love one must sacrifice oneself to love. "You want my life?" he says to Guitar, a friend hunting to kill him. Standing on the edge of a high cliff, he decides to give his friend what he needs: " 'You need it? Here.' Without wiping away the tears, taking a deep breath, or even bending his knees—he leaped. . . . For now he knew what Shalimar knew; if you surrendered to the air you could ride it" (341).

Unnaming

An underlying motivation of Ralph Ellison's *Invisible Man* is the protagonist's search for a way to define his true self. An important element in his search is his consideration of names. As the invisible man contemplates the similarities between himself and Frederick Douglass, he wonders what Douglass's "true name" had been and concludes: "Whatever it was, it was as *Douglass* that he became himself, defined himself. . . . Perhaps the sense of magic lay in the unexpected transformations. 'You start Saul, and end up Paul,' my grandfather had often said. 'When you a youngun, you Saul, but let life whup your head a bit and you starts to trying to be Paul—though you still Saul around on the side'" (381). The invisible man understands the key to reading names: identifying the magic of unexpected transformations.

In *Song of Solomon* these transformations are cyclic, forming patterns of life, death, and renewal through renaming. In *Invisible Man*, patterns of naming move linearly from rebirth, through death, into silence. This type of linearity I call *unnaming*. Unnaming occurs when a name phrase, name, or nickname *replaces* the original designator, forcing it from the text entirely; when an epithet, or another pejorative name, functions as the primary signifier for a character; or when a sense of namelessness, nullification, or a loss of historicity dominates either a name's deep talk or a character's subject position within a text. Unnaming fragmentations may even result from narrative actions that strip a name of its governing defining elements, leaving it void of empowered meaning and therefore incapable of meaningful deep-level signification. The deep talk of these names vanishes and, sometimes, the names do, too.

Names experiencing this type of transformation usually disappear from the text and do not reappear—at least not with the same onomastic desires. Because of their weakened internal structure, they no longer possess discursive force; they are impotent and void, nonpoetic like *Clifton* in Ellison's novel. Unlike *Pilate*, whose fragmentation involves a series of renaming fragmentations, *Tod Clifton* fragments only twice, once by way of renaming and once through unnaming. Unnaming occurs when a lexical meaning of the word *Tod* (*death* in German) "calls out to" and ultimately usurps the contextual aim of the name. Prior to this silencing,

Tod Clifton is a vehicle of the true-real that reminds both the reader and the invisible man where the defining elements of one's true self can be found.

As a result of Tod Clifton's "unexpected transformations," we discover that in the invisible man's world the only method for defining a true self is in resisting *Paul* while discovering *Saul*. The biblical allusion to Saul's transformation into the apostle Paul guides our interpretations. Saul was a Roman citizen born "of Hebrews . . . a Pharisee" who strictly adhered to Jewish law and persecuted the newly formed Christian church. Saul was transformed dramatically by a vision of Christ while on the road to Damascus. He then assumed his Roman name *Paul* and "suffered the loss of all things" he had known before. Although the biblical Paul regards his losses as "rubbish," Ellison's text does not duplicate this sentiment (Phil. 3:3–8). Instead, it celebrates the memory of a resisting Saul. In Ellison's novel, *Saul*'s poetic deep talk speaks of the black community and its struggle to maintain its historical definitions of self.

Tod Clifton and *Saul* are subject positions existing beyond what the novel's hegemonic lifeworld of white male society calls *history*. As subject positions they offer the novel's black characters individuality and a chance for resisting imposed identities and lost historicity. *Tod Clifton* develops a discursive effect that achieves the latter tasks fully. The fragmentation of this name results from the manipulation of its interpolated historical content. Before the name disappears from the text, it suffers an internal collision of meaning that ultimately situates it as an utterance of rejection—an utterance that subverts the dominant ideological constructs defining social significance, human value, and language within the surface text.

The name first appears in chapter 17. As a subject persona designator, *Tod Clifton* refers to the black Harlem youth leader appointed by the white-organized and -controlled Brotherhood. The character is a staunch supporter of the Brotherhood's ideals, and his characterization as one of its best black members remains constant until chapter 19. At the end of that chapter, he disappears. When the invisible man finds him selling dancing Sambo dolls, he describes his friend's unexplained actions as a betrayal: "Why should a man deliberately plunge outside of history and peddle an obscenity. . . . Why should he choose to disarm himself, give up his voice and leave the only organization offering him a chance to 'define' himself? . . . Why did he choose to plunge into nothingness, into the void of faceless faces, of soundless voices, lying outside history?" (438, 439).

Instead of plunging outside history, as the invisible man contends, Tod Clifton's strange behavior is a plunge deeper *into* history as defined by the dominant white society, including the communist Brotherhood. In other words, it is a plunge deeper into what the novel defines as *Paul*. According to the invisible man, the lifeworld of the white, male-governed Brotherhood refers to anyone whose self-concept lies outside their scientifically orchestrated history as "disarmed," "void," "soundless voices." The Brotherhood advocates a "scientific approach to society," an approach of experimentation that disavows arguments of sentimentality and racial inequality (350). Its white membership subordinates issues of race to a focus on class and the social relations that maintain it. Under the guise of science, discipline, and equality, Tod Clifton and the invisible man become pawns and puppets of the Brotherhood. Because they are controlled by the organization's invisible strings, they are much like "Sambo, the dancing doll" (431).

Before his disappearance, Brother Tod Clifton is a resistive, violent force within the organization. Unfortunately, this violence and resistance are focused inward toward a history he denies, toward the very source of his true name. While in the lifeworld of the white brotherhood, *Tod Clifton* internalizes the definitions of history as articulated by that organization. Their definitions become a part of the name's defining elements, its truncated discourse. Already present within that name is a previous history, a foreclosed history, one that gives the character a "Negro stride" and "chiseled black-marble features." This denied history gives Tod Clifton the peculiar look of "a hipster, a zoot suiter, a sharpie" (363, 366). His attempt to keep that history denigrated forces him to strike Ras the Exhorter after listening to the man proclaim black brotherhood as a power deserving of respect and support. These two definitions of history occupy the internal, textual spaces of the same name. Because one forecloses the other, the reader does not become fully aware of the name's multiplicity and metatextual functions until the invisible man eulogizes his murdered comrade.

In chapter 21, we discover that *Tod Clifton* is more than the signifier of a martyred character, a political symbol; it is also an icon of the true-real, an utterance that subverts the defining elements of the name as understood within the story's dominant lifeworld. During the invisible man's speech, renaming occurs, and the onomastic desires of *Tod Clifton* double, which enables it to enter the metatext as an invasive force, a mnemonic name, whose presence contradicts the original word's dominant utterances. The eruption of the true-real in this chapter strips the controlling lifeworld of its ability to limit meaning and discipline the deep talk of a socially (and politically) marginalized discourse. A series of events signals this eruption.

First, in this novel, an old man's song opens the surface text to a moment of iconic emergence (the eruption of the true-real). "It was not the words, for they were all the same old slave-borne words; it was as though he'd changed the emotion beneath the words while yet the old longing, resigned, transcendent emotion still sounded above, now deepened by that something for which the theory of Brotherhood had given me no name" (453). Trying to "contain" this nameless "something" and maintain its foreclosure results in a memory lapse. "All that I could remember was the sound of his [Tod Clifton's] name" (454). This memory lapse is the second event signaling the eruption of the true-real. Through it the sound of a name merges with memories of the nameless something at the core of the old man's song, and the name becomes mnemonic. When the song ends, the invisible man drifts into a daydream depicting a peanut vendor being devoured by "feasting birds." This third event brings the action of the true-real into the surface text: "The song had ended. Now the top of the little mountain bristled with banners, horns and uplifted faces. I could look straight down Fifth Avenue to 125th Street, where policemen were lined behind an array of hot-dog wagons and Good Humor carts; and among the carts I saw a peanut vendor standing beneath a street lamp upon which pigeons were gathered, and now I saw him stretch out his arms with his palms turned upward, and suddenly he was covered, head, shoulders and outflung arms, with fluttering, feasting birds. Someone nudged me and I started. It was time for final words. But I had no words" (454).

Alan Nadel interprets this scene as an image of crucifixion suggesting "a spiritual reading of the text that reveals the ascension of Clifton's soul." [10] My problem with this reading is that nothing ascends in this scene. The birds descend and then they devour—but devour what? This event symbolizes the plucking away and devouring of surface meanings that mask the true-real. It is the plucking away of the "body" of surface discourses so that the liberated "flesh" of a mnemonic name's deep talk can reveal itself. The vision removes the name's reference to a character and baptizes its onomastic deep talk so that when the invisible man awakens from his daydream, nothing more exists.

The only thing remaining to tell the awaiting crowd is a name. "What are you waiting for, when all I can tell you is his name?" the protagonist asks in desperation (455). With the language of the story's dominant life-world exposed as insufficient and inadequate, the invisible man enters into a monologue about the only thing his delusional experience leaves him, the name *Tod Clifton*. Building a speech around the sentimental memories evoked by an individual's name violates the laws that define the politics of the Brotherhood completely. "It wasn't the way I wanted it to go, it wasn't political. Brother Jack probably wouldn't approve of it at all" (457). Tod Clifton's name appears twenty-one times in the speech. Much as repetitive action reshapes the potter's clay, the repetition of the name transforms it into a new word, a homonym of the subject persona designator. The new name functions as a subject position representing the voices of those "outside history" and an icon of the true-real whose narrative effects reshape surface discourses.

The eruption of once foreclosed meanings restructures the invisible man's speech so that it becomes a listing of the once foreclosed defining elements, the historical content, of Clifton's name. As the invisible man speaks a new definition of *Tod Clifton* into being, we discover that it is a name "full of illusion"—forgotten history, time, places, and manhood. It speaks of poverty in overcrowded dwellings and the aroused yet unfulfilled hope of Brotherhood (458, 459, 467). The deep talk of this name is not political; it is apolitical, humanizing, and subversive. Its utterances relativize the meaning of history installed into the name's textual spaces by the scientific laws of the Brotherhood, making those laws subordinate and silent. A poetic word results that not only names a martyred black man but symbolizes *Saul*—that which was forgotten, a loss considered "rubbish" by the communist Brotherhood—"a whole unrecorded history" of southern blacks in transition (471).

This new name, with its new implications, cannot enter the lifeworld of the word as spoken by Brother Jack and the other members of the Brotherhood. That world denies the new utterances of *Tod Clifton*. For the Brotherhood, remembering and empowering the forgotten black masses is unimportant. The only valid reason for fraternization with blacks is to build a new political party (American communism); therefore, those within this lifeworld cannot hear the revised deep talk of *Tod Clifton*. For Jack, Clifton is "a traitorous merchant of vile instruments of anti-Negro, anti-minority racist bigotry [who] has received a hero's funeral" (466). The members of the Brotherhood refuse to see that, like the man, the name *Tod Clifton* is "jam-full of contradictions" (467). They refuse to acknowledge the true-real because they are afraid to see the truth as the "real," afraid to see truths they consider impossible—themselves as martinets pulling the strings of the dancing Sambos they create.

"The dolls are nothing," the invisible man explains in an attempt to ease their fears. "Nothing," Brother Jack replies, "that nothing that might explode in our face" (468). Jack is afraid of being exposed as a fraud and a manipulator of blacks for reasons other than those he professes. As a result of these fears, the newly empowered name *Tod Clifton* with its new contextual aims remains outside Brother Jack's language. Only in the discourses of those occupying the margins can it speak its illusions and contradictions—only the worldview of the invisible man and other blacks in the novel allows its discursive effects to subvert meaning as defined by the dominant sociolinguistic lifeworld. Only there is it sprawled across banners and written on signs as an icon of memory and hope.

The name loses this power as the novel continues, and we learn that the mnemonic name revealed to us through the invisible man's speech dies. "Tod Clifton was underground," dead and buried. When the invisible man buys into the Brotherhood's denial of the invasive power within the redefined name, the name suffers the same fate. It experiences "Tod

Clifton's *Tod*" (460). By the end of his meeting with Brother Jack, the invisible man accepts the notion that a name standing outside the dominant society's discourse is powerless and can never be heard. "I looked at him [Brother Jack] . . . with the feeling that I was just awakening from a dream," the invisible man tells the reader (476). The first delusional experience mentioned in this analysis fragments and redefines *Tod Clifton*. As a result of a second experience, it fragments again. This time unnaming silences the name that speaks of the forgotten, leaving behind only its trace—*Clifton*—a word "as dead and as meaningless as Clifton," the man (478).

Unlike *Pilate IV*, a name-entity that remains an empowered presence in Toni Morrison's *Song of Solomon* until novel's end, *Tod Clifton* loses its influence as an active mnemonic name—an icon of the true-real that remembers the forgotten and provides an opportunity for blacks to affirm themselves (469). After this chapter (chapter 22), it is not mentioned again. The name *Clifton* replaces it within the surface narrative, where it functions as a subject persona designator only. In Ellison's novel, names like this one provide neither redemption nor a permanent space of self-affirmation—at least not for those who play *Paul* when they should be celebrating and living the resistance of *Saul*.

Supranaming

Neither of his sons was here tonight, had ever cried on the threshing-floor. One had been dead for nearly fourteen years—dead in a Chicago tavern, a knife kicking in his throat. And the living son, the child, Roy, was headlong already, and hardhearted: he lay at home, silent now, and bitter against his father, a bandage on his forehead. They were not here. Only the son of the bondwoman stood where the rightful heir should stand.—(113–14)

This excerpt from "Gabriel's Prayer" in James Baldwin's *Go Tell It on the Mountain* offers an excellent opportunity for reading the rigorous textual layering of supranaming. This type of fragmentation relies heavily upon renaming and unnaming to maintain its invasive force. Supranaming occurs when new designations supplement a character's primary name without foreclosing it. Instead of disappearing from the surface, the primary name functions in concert with its supplements. *Janie* in Zora Neale Hurston's *Their Eyes Were Watching God* experiences this type of supranaming when the character it designates marries (without divorcing) and becomes Janie Starks. Supranaming also occurs when onomastic desires and the reader act as a re-creative team that excises embedded names, phrases, and allusions to expose their deep-level onomastic play. Through this team effort the "flesh" of alternate names and intertextualized stories emerge in the metatext and chaotically intertwine. In this manner, the paragraph quoted above develops a series of layered metatexts that interpolates biblical stories. I diagram these stories in this reading to demonstrate how the deep talk forged in the fires of active signifying desires chaotically enfolds.

Baldwin begins this paragraph after explaining in previous chapters that Gabriel and his wife, Elizabeth, have two sons: the fourteen-year-old John and his younger brother, Roy. Gabriel favors Roy but beats him. The couple also have two daughters, Sarah and Ruth. Deborah, who is now dead, was Gabriel's first wife. The protagonist, John, believes her death is the reason he lives and the key to his unanswered questions. "If she had lived, John thought, then he would never have been born; his father would never have come North and met his mother. And this shadowy woman, dead so many years, whose name he knew had been Deborah, held in the fastness of her tomb, it seemed to John, the key to all those mysteries he so longed to unlock" (29). Through a letter written years before her death, the reader discovers at least one of those mysteries. Deborah suspects Gabriel has an illegitimate son. We know little about this son except what we learn from Deborah's letter: his mother died, unwed, during childbirth. I refer to him in the diagram as the *nameless child*.

"Gabriel's Prayer" takes place in a church the evening of John's birthday. The characters present are John, his mother, Elizabeth, his father, Gabriel, and the piano player Elisha among others whose names are not pertinent to this reading. Roy is at home nursing a wound he received earlier that afternoon (he was stabbed in a gang fight). Everyone is praying, or at least they pretend to pray. Gabriel, for instance, thinks of the past and the son he hopes will be heir to the "royal" line of "the holy and faithful," a line of which he claims to be the first patriarch.

In this novel, Baldwin, the stepson of an itinerant preacher, continually compares Gabriel's quest for an heir to that of the biblical patriarch Abraham. In fact, from its title to its last page, *Go Tell It on the Mountain* is filled with biblical names that enter the metatext, develop distinct onomastic desires, and disrupt surface discourses. The novel's constantly shifting point of view, played out in the surface text, increases the activities of this narrative dissonance. These shifts occur so frequently that readers are often unaware whose thoughts they are reading until they are a few words or sentences into a paragraph. This sense of ambiguity generates interpretive misjudgments, reassessments, and confusion that further proliferate names and layer the reader's meaning experience.

My subject paragraph uses multiple supranaming events—generated by confusion—to develop its layered metatext. For this reason, my synopsis reveals only the skeletal facts of the narrative preceding the subject paragraph and none that follow it. Similarly, my diagram of the paragraph and my descriptive reading reveal events, step by step, as they would occur during an initial encounter with the novel (see table 1). In other words, I attempt to duplicate the reader's experience of and interaction with onomastic desires without in-depth analysis. To borrow from Stanley Fish, my reading "will be a description of a moving field of concerns, at once wholly present (not waiting for meaning but constituting meaning) and continually in the act of constituting itself." [11] Therefore, familial relationships, belief systems, and naming events are clarified in the order in which they appear in the original text. Readers unfamiliar with the novel will experience my diagram differently than those who know the full genealogy of this fictional family or those who have studied the metaphors of naming that this novel contains. For them, the disruptive feeling of metaphoric chaos might have less impact, rendering the meaning experience of onomastic deep talk, its rhapsody and playfulness, its chaotic displacement and recuperation, less vigorous.

Table 1 replicates the onomastic layering created by several supranaming events. It is a journey into the lifeworld of the metatext that demonstrates how onomastic deep talk develops within that discursive space before entering the surface. I open each section of the diagram with

TABLE 1: Metatextual Layering in Baldwin's *Go Tell It on the Mountain*

1	"Neither of his sons"		
	Gabriel's sons	*God's sons*	ABRAHAM'S SONS
	John and	*John the Baptist and*	ISHMAEL AND
	Roy	*Christ*	ISAAC
5		*the archangel*	
	"was here tonight,"		
	Roy and the nameless		
	child are not there.		
	"had ever cried"		
10		*John the*	
		voice of	ISHMAEL CRIES
		one crying	
	"on the threshing-floor."		
		in the	IN THE
15		*wilderness.*	WILDERNESS.
			THE WILDERNESS
			WHERE HAGAR
			NAMES THE ANGEL
			WHO HELPS HER
20	"One"		
	either Roy		EL-ROI
			THE WELL HAGAR
			NAMES BEÉR-
	(ROI)		LAHAI'-ROI
25	or the		WHICH MEANS
	nameless child		THE LIVING ONE
			WHO SEES ME
	"had been dead"		
			SARAI'S WOMB
30	the nameless	**John's dead*	HAD BEEN DEAD
	child		
	"for nearly fourteen years"		
	John is fourteen		FOR FOURTEEN
	years old		YEARS AFTER
35			ISHMAEL'S
			BIRTH THEN
			(continued)

TABLE 1: *Continued*

		but Herod thought	
		*John was risen	
		from the dead when	
40		*Christ began his*	THE PROMISED
		Galilean ministry.	SON WAS BORN
	"—dead in a Chicago tavern,"		
	the nameless	*John*	ISHMAEL DYING
	child		
45		*in Herod's*	IN THE
		prison,	WILDERNESS
	"a knife kicking in his throat."		
			FROM THIRST.
	*the nameless	**John, who*	
50	child's		
	throat was	*was*	
	slashed.	*decapitated.*	
	"And the living son,"		
	**John	***Christ,*	ISAAC (John),
55	son of	*Son of God,*	SON OF (son of)
	Gabriel		ABRAHAM (Gabriel),
	(the nameless child)		
	"the child, Roy,"		
	(ROI)		
60	"was headlong already"		
		hung his head	
	"and hardhearted: he lay at home"		
			STAYED AT HOME.
	"silent now"		
65		*and said not a word.*	
	"and bitter against his father,"		
	Roy's father		EL-ROI'S FATHER
	Gabriel	*the archangel Michael*	GOD
		(ROI)	
70		*" 'E'loi,*	
		E'loi, lema'	
		sabach'thani?'	
		which means,	

TABLE 1: Continued

75		'My God, my God, why have you forsaken me?' "	
	"a bandage"		
			FREED FROM
	Roy was		BONDAGE
80	cut	*thorns*	
	"on his forehead"		
		in the place of the skull (in Golgotha)	
85	Roy (ROI)	*Christ*	
	wore a scar	*wore thorns*	
	on his forehead	*for a crown.*	
	"They"		
	Roy (ROI)	*God, the Father*	
90	and	*and*	
	the nameless	*the Holy Spirit*	
	child		
	(John)		
	"were not here."		
95		*were not there.*	
	"Only the son of the bondwoman"		
	John (nameless child),		ISHMAEL,
	son of		SON OF
	Elizabeth	*John, the Baptist*	HAGAR.
100		*son of Elizabeth and forerunner of*	
	"stood where the rightful heir"		
		Christ	ISAAC
	John	*(John)*	(John)
105	(the living son)	*the living son*	THE PROMISED SON
	(the nameless child)		
	"should stand."		

quoted material from the subject paragraph (within quotation marks). Below the quoted text I outline the deep-level supranaming events it generates. If the three columns of the table are read vertically, they reveal portions of several deep-level stories. Printed in plain text, the first column outlines a story I call "Gabriel and the Bondwoman's Child." It records the deep-level meanings an active reader might experience during a first reading. The second column, printed in *italics*, reveals the interpolated events from the biblical stories of *John the Baptist and Christ* that an active reader may intuit. The final deep-level story, printed in SMALL CAPS, appears in the third column. It provides examples of an active reader's sense of discourse-producing events that re-create the biblical stories of Abraham, Sarai, and Hagar. Read horizontally (left to right), table 1 traces supranaming fragmentations and word manipulations occurring beneath the surface. Each horizontal column contains some names written in parentheses. These are homonyms, shadows, signifying doubles of names that appear in the surface text (*Roy* and *roi*, for instance). Because of their close association with surface names, these supranaming events move from the deepest levels of the metatext toward the surface level of interpretation. In other words, they follow their doubles like a shadow. Some names and phrases are preceded by asterisks (single and double) indicating supranaming events I analyze in the discussion that follows the table.

Mistaken identity begins the process of name proliferation in this diagram—not a mistake made by a character, but one made by readers. The narrator's previous references to Gabriel's sons, John and Roy, and the lack of information concerning the (briefly mentioned) nameless child lead readers to interpret the opening sentence in multiple ways. A sense of ambiguity and name supplementation dominates our word-by-word interpretation of the sentence until the narrator clarifies surface meanings. Even then, the biblical connotations and allusions suggested by the words *his* and *sons* continue to encourage a proliferation of names and stories that supply the metatext with its supplemental actors and deep-level action.

The quoted material following the introduction of supplemental actors clarifies the narrator's intent: "Neither of his sons *was here tonight.*" The only sons not present at the church are Roy and the son we suspect

Gabriel has, the nameless child. This clarification does not negate the discourses already established in the metatext. As a result, the metatext and the active reader continue to develop these names, multiplying the meaning of almost every word quoted. The words "threshing floor," for instance, speak of the church and the wilderness (lines 13–15). In the layered metatext, this doubling is multidirectional. It speaks of John the Baptist and Ishmael's wilderness experiences as well as the wilderness experience of Hagar.

The paragraph's next sentence contains three supranaming events that the active reader recognizes as valuable to the development of the metatext. That sentence reads: "One had been dead for nearly fourteen years—dead in a Chicago tavern, a knife kicking in his throat." First, the word *one* calls forth a name whose homophonic imprint duplicates (in miniature) two names appearing in the story of Hagar's wilderness experience. The Bible tells us that Hagar escapes into the wilderness after a dispute with her mistress, Sarai. An "angel of the Lord" finds her and advises her to return. Hagar mistakes this angel for God: "You are El-roi [God is seeing]; for she said, 'Have I really seen God and remained alive after seeing him?' / Therefore the well was called Be'ér-la'hai'-roi," which means "the living *one* who sees me" (Gen. 16:7, 13). The reader realizes the connection between the word opening the sentence ("one") and its duplicate appearing in the name of the well. This leads the reader to a second connection. The homophonic imprint of ROI contains onomastic desires that rename Roy. In the metatext this renaming produces a name-entity with several aliases: EL-ROI, ROI, and THE LIVING ONE WHO SEES ME (lines 21–27). These aliases, when parenthesized in table 1, follow the name *Roy* like a shadow, speaking of vision, living, and rescue each time it appears, while the word *one* serves as the icon of these events in the surface.

The next supranaming event occurs when the story of John the Baptist merges with surface discourses to produce a second name-entity. In the paragraph's metatext, death and resurrection constitute moments of deep-level, iconic emergence through which one name speaks of two or more individuals and stories simultaneously. The death and resurrection of *John* mentioned in the italicized metatext (marked with asterisks, lines 30 and 38) transform it into a border-crossing name-entity. As *John* moves through the surface and deep-level stories, it gathers details about itself using as its informants non-onomastic units of speech as well as name utterances.

This border-crossing name-entity gathers its most valuable information from the phrase "fourteen years" (quoted text, line 32). Fourteen is the verse number of two scriptures in the book of Mark concerning Herod, John the Baptist, and Christ.[12] The information given in these verses is central to decoding the masked action of the metatext (lines 30–41, read vertically). In Mark 1:14, Jesus begins his Galilean ministry; in Mark 6:14, Herod mistakes Jesus for a resurrected John the Baptist. The number also reminds the reader of John's present age and the fourteen years Sarai remained childless after Hagar gave birth to Ishmael (line 29–41, read vertically).

The final supranaming event in this sentence combines the story of Sarai and Abraham's promised son with surface discourses to reveal that Gabriel's choice for an heir (Roy) is not God's choice. This fragmentation uses the word *dead* to record Gabriel's error and destroy his hopes. Reading the metatext of Sarai's story (line 41) and the surface text (line 42) as a continuous thought, we find that the promise is broken: THE PROMISED SON WAS BORN / "dead." In other words, not only is Gabriel's nameless child dead, but his hope for a promised son, a "holy" heir, is also dead. Reading the text this way also reveals a second level of metatextual discourse communicating through the same words. This discourse speaks of John and the nameless child in a manner that reinstalls Gabriel's hope—but not his choice. John's age, fourteen, informs the reader that the nameless child dies in the same year John was born. This discourse suggests that as one promised son dies another is born as his substitute. It is, therefore, John whom this second level of metatextual discourse identifies as the promised son born; and, of course, it is the nameless child whom it describes as "dead."

The next sentence opens with double-voiced deep talk that challenges its own assertions through a phrase name: "And the living son, the child, Roy" (line 53, 58). John and Roy's surface-level subject positions as Gabriel's living sons are both present within the deep talk of "the living son." The name-entities these subject positions create, however, battle to dominate the speaking discourses of this phrase name. This is a point of contradiction and conflict resolved by *Roy's* deep-level identity as ROI. Since the metatext describes ROI as THE LIVING ONE WHO SEES ME and not as "the living son," only John, Gabriel's oldest living son, can assume that subject position—at least within the metatext. More significantly, the deep-talk speaking of a "living son" dissociates John's multi-directional name from a "dying" ISHMAEL—who, by the way, was a substitute for the son that God promised to give Abraham (line 43). As a result, any deep talk speaking of John as a substitute for God's promise splits off—dies. John is no longer a substitute; he *is* the promised child. Each time *Isaac*—the primary name representing this promise in the metatext—appears, *John*, written in parentheses to indicate its role as a shadow name or metaphor for God's promise, follows it (line 54).

In the next section of the diagram, *John* assumes a shadow relationship with the name *Christ* through their shared subject position as "the living son" (line 54, double asterisks). This shared subject position causes the names to interpolate deep talk from each other. *John* shares a similar relationship with the nameless child through images of death (line 49, single asterisks, read vertically). The story of John the Baptist's decapitation repeats the experience of Gabriel's dead son, although with more dramatic effects. The deep-level actions resulting from this repetition sever the name-entity's relationship with the story of John, the forerunner of Christ, and its discourse of substitution (lines 37–41, italic text, read vertically). This metaphoric death leaves *John* with primary utterances associated with ISAAC (the promised son), *Christ* (the living son), and Gabriel's dead son (the nameless child). These relationships create shadows or echoes within the metatext. For instance, each time either son, John or the nameless child, appears in the metatext, the name of the other and its deep talk follow it (lines 57, 93, 97, 104–6).

The name *Roy*, on the other hand, appears and disappears continually in the form of EL-ROI, BEÉR-LAHAI'-ROI (THE LIVING ONE WHO SEES ME), or simply ROI. When sensed by the reader, the shadowing effects of ROI assign new onomastic desires to the discourse-producing abilities of *Roy* each time it appears in the surface narrative. The subject persona, Roy "sees" the *true* image of his father—his anger, his abuse, his evil—and reacts to it. The narrator, speaking from Gabriel's viewpoint, describes Roy's reactions as unrestrained and merciless. "The child, Roy, was headlong already, and hardhearted: he lay at home, silent now, and bitter against his father." Instead of being silent, as the surface text suggests, the deep-level utterances of ROI speak: " 'E'loi, E'loi, lema' sabach'-thani?' which means, 'My God, my God, why have you forsaken me?' " (lines 70–76).

Here, the narrative effects of several name fragmentations merge the words of Jesus with the defining elements of ROI, giving ROI a new inflection—a distinct voice. In the diagramed passage, this merging occurs immediately after the words *his father* summon and juxtapose three biblical subject positions (line 66). The first, EL-ROI, is one of three angels that the Bible mentions by name (or misnomer). The second is the archangel Gabriel, who shares his name with this novel's patriarch. The name of the third angel appears as a fragmentation of *Gabriel* (line 68, read horizontally). In the metatext, the position effects of *Gabriel*, the archangel, call out to and repeat a real-world unnaming event. Christ, whom the Bible never clearly identifies as an angel, is often thought of as the chief angel—"the great prince" and archangel Michael (Dan. 12:1). The narrative effects of juxtaposing ROI (the angel) with Christ (the chief angel) and Gabriel (the archangel) result in a metatextual merging of three stories. Within that narrative space, ROI speaks to both God and the patriarch Gabriel while Christ/Michael calls out to his father: "My God, my God, why have you forsaken me?" This discourse informs against the surface by redefining as impassioned and forsaken the character described in the surface text as "hardhearted" and "bitter against his father."

Throughout this reading the name-entity *John* experiences several metaphorical deaths that silence elements of its deep talk. In the last sentence of the paragraph *John* regains everything its death experiences foreclose. In the italicized crucifixion story, *John* looses its association with *Christ*, "the living son," and reclaims it when *Christ* appears as a resurrected name and "rightful heir" in the metatext (line 102). *John* also realigns itself with the biblical allusions of a phrase name, "the son of the bondwoman." This phrase name contains metonymic deep talk that directs the reader's attention toward the story of HAGAR AND ISHMAEL. Its goal is to align John, "the son of the bondwoman," with Ishmael, who is also the son of a bondwoman, thereby reestablishing the former shadow relationship of their names.[13]

The word *bondwoman* functions in the surface text as an icon of two other events that reestablish links between the name *John* and its previously silenced desire to speak of John the Baptist. *Bondwoman* refers not only to Hagar but also to Elizabeth, the mother of the novel's protagonist—and Elizabeth, the mother of John the Baptist (lines 96–100). The reader recognizes *bondwoman* as a culturally imprinted name whose multiple connotations and deep-level stories merge.

This merging of deep talk presents readers with name-motivated contradictions that the paragraph does not clearly resolve, leaving the reader with at least three interpretive choices. A reader who chooses to interpret the most obvious metatextual discourses of the diagramed paragraph without considering its multiple deep-level communications disinherits John by calling him out of his name—by calling him ISHMAEL, the "son of the bondwoman." Looking deeper into the multileveled discourse production of the metatext reveals deep talk that speaks of the forerunner of God's "living son" in addition to a substitute awaiting the arrival of a promised son. On this level of interpretation, John of the novel stands "where the rightful heir should stand," just as John the Baptist stood as God's heir until Christ arrived and Ishmael served as a substitute for Isaac. If the reader unpacks the phrase "rightful heir" further, John inherits all. His name becomes a metonymic icon for both ISAAC, the "rightful heir" and promised son, and Christ, the living son and divine heir of God (lines 102–5).

The three paragraphs immediately following my subject passage provide information that clarifies ambiguities, resolves contradictions, and asks readers to reassess their interpretations. In these "follow-up" paragraphs name-entities and deep-level onomastic desires break free of the metatext to make brief appearances in the surface text. Once installed as surface discourses, they continue to assist the reader's manipulation of meaning but do so within the constraints of the surface text only. By this I mean they no longer speak openly of the stories developed within the metatext. The stories of Abraham, Hagar, Sarai, Jesus, John the Baptist, Isaac, and Ishmael as written in table 1 remain beneath the surface as inspirations for the allegorical development of surface events.

The first of the three paragraphs merges the names *John* and *Elisha*. The narrator tells us that the pianist Elisha cries out and falls in spiritual ecstasy. Gabriel contemplates going to comfort and pray with him but remains still while listening from his place on the mourners' bench: "Each cry that came from the fallen Elisha tore through him. He heard the cry of his dead son and his living son" (114). From our reading of the previous paragraph, we assume that the "living son" Gabriel imagines he hears crying out is *John*. The deep talk of *John* merges with the biblical story of *Elisha*. Just as in previous incidents of discourse interpolation, the multidirectional name-entity *John* assumes this biblical character's subject position and, in this case, speaks of a prophet who worked in harmony with the established government of Israel. In the surface narrative this deep talk refers to white American government (or society) and John's future role within it.

The second paragraph reveals that Royal is the name of Gabriel's dead son, the son called the *nameless child* in table 1. We do not know how the discourse production of *Royal* affects John's subject position as the *nameless child* or Roy's position as ROI until a transference of roles becomes clear. As the passage proceeds, we surmise that *Royal* is also the given name of Roy and that the phrase *nameless child* is more than a shadow alias for the name-entity *John*:

> [A mother's] curse had devoured the first Royal; he had been begotten in sin, and he had perished in sin; it was God's punishment, and it was just. But Roy had been begotten in the marriage bed. . . . It was to him the Kingdom had been promised. It could not be that the living son was cursed for the sins of his father. . . . And yet, it came to him [Gabriel] that this *living son*, this headlong, *living Royal*, might be cursed for the sin of his mother, whose sin had never been truly repented; for that *the living proof* of her sin, he who knelt tonight, a very interloper among the saints, stood between her soul and God.
>
> Yes, she was hardhearted . . . this Elizabeth whom he had married . . . years ago, when the Lord had moved in his heart to lift her up, she and her *nameless child, who bore his name today*. (114–15, emphasis added)

This passage, excerpted from the second and third paragraphs, provides new information about the protagonist: John is not Gabriel's biological son. In the surface narrative, John bears the family name of his stepfather, Grimes. This information explains why Gabriel's hope for a promised son (biological heir) must die. Roy, Gabriel's biological son, has no interest in being an heir to holiness. This new information does not, however, negate the deep talk that *John*, the name-entity, expresses in its role as the *nameless child*.

Instead, it provides the name-entity with the contradictory deep talk it uses to confer upon itself not only Gabriel's surname but Royal's name as well. In the metatext the phrase "who bore his name today" is ambiguous. Whose name does *John*, the "nameless child" and "interloper among the saints," bear? The surface eruption of shadow names previously associated with *John* provides two answers. He bears the names of the *living son* and the *nameless child*. As the *nameless child*, John assumes the subject position of Royal, and as the *living son*, he becomes the *living Royal*—a living heir and nameless child born illegitimately.

John's revised subject position as *Royal* brings with it onomastic deep talk that conflicts with surface narration. The narrator identifies Roy (ROI) as the *living Royal*, but unlike the confirming deep talk of *John*, the utterances of ROI stylize this association by amending it. A meaning of the biblical name *Beér-lahai'-roi* not mentioned previously in this reading is "the well of living after seeing." [14] This sense of the name is revealing in its promises of hope for Roy's future. Roy, Gabriel's preferred son and a name that at once speaks of death *within* the living and living after seeing death, inherits the assurance of rebirth and vision. The association of his name with EL-ROI (literally, God is seeing) suggests that God protects Roy through these gifts. Although Roy experiences several metaphorical deaths (through visions and deep-level name play), his name's association with BEÉR-LAHAI'-ROI suggests that he survives through continual rebirth. John's subject position as the *living Royal* (the living ROI) suggests that he too sees his stepfather's evil and survives his abuse through continual rebirth.

In *Go Tell It on the Mountain*, the names *Roy* and *John* function as foreshadowing devices. Within a few paragraphs, their deep talk informs us of future events that the surface does not address openly. The stability and immovability indicated by the well image suggest that Roy never moves beyond the streets of the black community, a place Baldwin's novel describes as one of racial segregation and bondage; but John, the *living Royal*, is ambulatory. His metaphorical subject position as *Elisha*, a man who functions successfully within the established government, stylizes the deep talk of immovability that the well image brings to the utterances of his name. From the discourse production of names in Baldwin's novel, we can assume that its protagonist will one day move from the confines of bondage and oppressive communal relationships (for John this means his stepfather, Gabriel, specifically) into the promises of the world beyond community and family. This expansion of personal power and space is evident in the universal, all-encompassing nature of the deep talk of *John*.

The product of this word's supranaming fragmentation is a metatext through which the hypothesized author communicates the victory of the disinherited over all others. *John*'s deep talk speaks of the protagonist's and other African Americans' futures as individuals freed from the burdens of the past: "No matter what happens to me, where I go, what folks say about me, no matter what *any*body says, you remember—please remember—I was saved" (220, Baldwin's italics). In his role as the "rightful heir" of a saving grace, as a *Christ*-figure, *John* the name-entity offers a legacy of salvation. It speaks for "the lowest among the lowly" and serves as the subject position of those who suffer lost individual awareness, a lost nation, a lost inheritance, and a loss of influence in the world beyond community (202). As the benefactors of the legacy of *John*, African Americans are inheritors in each of these areas.

Teasing out the deep talk of a name—coring its external frame—is essential to determining its objectives, constraints, functions, and goals as a strategy of discourse production. To read these discourses fully, one must unpack the poetic name, identify its signifying desires, and interpret the treasures uncovered. This is discursive archaeology. Julia Kristeva alludes to an analogy similar to this when discussing D. P. Schreber's *Memorabilia of a Nerve Patient*: "Beneath the plausibility of Schreber's narrative lies the 'core' of a truth: the enunciative archaeology of the proper name as a strategy of discourse." [15]

Although Kristeva's comment refers to the discourse of the neurotic and the semiotic structures supporting it, I see her insights as valuable to any discussion of literary names and naming. Her use of the term *enunciative archaeology* is particularly insightful. *Enunciative* emphasizes that a wide variety of expressions, gestures, words, phrases, activities, texts, and voices make up the utterances of poetic names. *Archeology* addresses the role of the reader in the production of onomastic deep talk. It brings to mind the act of digging, unearthing, and hollowing out the obvious while making connections that unpack what lies beneath. In the three novels this chapter examines, what lies beneath is a series of stories and deep talk created, revised, and colored through the enunciative archeology of onomastic play.

4

Onomastic Resistance and the True-Real

QUESTION:
"Do you know what white racists call black Ph.D.'s?"

ANSWER:
"Nigger!"

—*The Autobiography of Malcolm X*

NAMES ACCRUE meaning continually. From the place of their original use through each articulation, source and context transform or
illuminate the nature of their discursive impulses and social accents. The
utterance that surfaces from the cache of narratives and counternarratives
contained within names depends, in part, upon the lifeworld of their
fragmentation and the speaking subject's worldview. This chapter's epigraph, from *The Autobiography of Malcolm X*, demonstrates the effects
of worldview and source upon deep-level communication. While speaking at a historically white university, Malcolm X received intense heck-
ling from a professor he describes as the "university's 'token-integrated'
black Ph.D. associate professor." Like others before him, this professor
calls Malcolm out of his name: "He was ranting about what a 'divisive
demagogue' and what a 'reverse racist' I was. I was racking my head, to
spear that fool" (284). Nothing Malcolm says "spears" its target until
he questions the professor and follows that question with a name that
shames.

Malcolm's use of the epithet *nigger* stands at a crossroad of onomastic
intent with the double edges of its deep talk sharpened and exposed. On
the surface, it is a violent act, an attempt to deflate and quiet an oppo-
nent. The question and its answer propose that in the eyes of a racist all
blacks are "niggers," no matter how educated or distinguished by class.
The racist sees "Ph.D." but reads "NIG." On the level of onomastic deep
talk, however, Malcolm's use of the passing epithet *nigger* dissolves discourses of difference and separation by renouncing them, collapsing

them upon themselves, dismissing them, and speaking the true-real—an extratextual, ideological message of what was once foreclosed.

Beneath the surface of linguistic battling and animosity, an entire history of "a nation dispossessed" speaks and claims the professor as one of its own, the denigrated and denied of a racist society.[1] The epithet producing this discourse functions as a bonding ritual that consummates discourses of the true-real. In this way, *nigger* speaks of racism but not from a racist worldview. Instead, it speaks from the worldview of the dispossessed, the angry, the humiliated, the sullen, and the banished. Moreover, it speaks of the familiarity assumed by a bonded fate that, in this instance, shames and silences while, at the same time, unifying the futures of Malcolm and his hostile "brother." Even though Malcolm resorts to humor and sarcasm to communicate what his earnest elocution does not, his use of unnaming is a serious affair that the "brother" who hears it understands.

The anonymous protagonist of James Weldon Johnson's *Autobiography of an Ex-Colored Man* comments on the use of the word *nigger* as a linguistic bonding ritual. His discussion of the term highlights elements of discourse production that exclude by ethnicity and race. Johnson writes, " 'I noticed that among this class of colored man the word 'nigger' was freely used in about the same sense as the word 'fellow,' and sometimes as a term of almost endearment: but I soon learned that its use was positively and absolutely prohibited to white men" (67). Johnson does not claim that the term speaks of endearment only between New York's Sixth and Seventh Avenues (where he hears the name used); he says that only ethnicity and race as indicators of a shared cultural language limit this sense of the word. Like any word, the name *nigger* in *The Autobiography of Malcolm X* and in Johnson's text functions within conceptual fields of language, not geography, that exclude and bond through an understanding of cultural and linguistic deep talk.

Some onomastic theorists call these *idiolects*. Gayatri Chakravorty Spivak calls them worlds; Henry Louis Gates calls them *discursive universes*—I call them *contextual environments* or *lifeworlds*.[2] This term refers to both the conceptual fields of language as a referential order and the worldviews it articulates, creates, and organizes—its sociolinguistic order. Malcolm's use of the term *nigger* stands between two lifeworlds, the world of white racism and the black world of communal bonding and support. The epithet's deep talk means two very different things in each. By using the name *nigger* while in the presence of a white audience and by framing the name within the context of white racism, Malcolm merges both discourses to create an utterance that renounces pretense and class difference while calling forth the true-real—a racial bond, a "brotherhood" of shared fate.

My focus in this chapter is the discourse-producing activities of the true-real as determined by worldviews and sociolinguistic lifeworlds in conflict. A poetic name's border-crossing experiences within and between narrative lifeworlds—its intersection, negotiation, disagreement, and agreement with one or more alien worldviews—stratifies it and enriches its performance as a force of onomastic resistance. As in the example above, these internally stratified names act within chains of referential, denotative, and connotative force that multiply their meaning potential and communicate the often disruptive impulses of the true-real.

Julia Kristeva coined the term *true-real* to describe an "obsessive fear" of the truth as the "real." This idea of the real should not be misconstrued as a substantial reality but as the implausible intuitive value of the signifier itself. In other words, values existing outside dominant socialized meanings are made incarnate in the signifier, thereby replacing the signified (not the referent) with the real. The word *real* is used here in the Lacanian sense to denote the denied, disavowed, or denigrated residue of intuitive experience situated between the imaginary and the symbolic as categories of perception. For Lacan, the real emerges when the imaginary (the perceived or imagined) and the symbolic give way to that which is considered the impossible.[3]

Kristeva elaborates on these concepts by describing the "*true*-real" as "an area of risk and salvation for the speaking being." For her, the "impossible" implied by Lacan's use of the word *real* becomes possible, if only briefly, in the form of icons that defy nonexistence and deny death. These icons of meaning emerge paradoxically within the framework of the imaginary and function as an incarnation of what they signify, becoming signifier and signified. Kristeva uses an example from a psychological case study to demonstrate. In her example, a patient experiences the word *green* as an undefined vision or sensation of the color green.

Kristeva describes the patient's hallucination as a "blinding moment that corresponded to no object, not even to the word green itself ('it's too simple, too weak, it's not that')." This vision of something *green-but-not-green* marks a place of being or experience before contamination by the socially bound naming practices of the Other (in this case, the order of the paternal signifier). It is a pure intuitive designator, an icon of the true-real, foreclosed previously and thereby left unblemished by the imposing laws of symbolic order and socialization.[4]

As I define it, the term *true-real* is an extension and modification of Kristeva's word. Here the true-real is an impossible or aberrant ideological "truth" or discursive action revealed through a name's deep-level communications. It is the name's cunning tenacity as an utterance to denigrate imposed meanings so that it can negotiate and play out denied discourses. Once charged with discursive force, these discourses resurrect and transform the "body" of words, markers, and phrase names (the name as image) through the liberation of their "flesh" (aberrant impulses). This transformed and liberated "flesh" coalesces perceptions and concepts that are implausible within and denied by a text's dominant laws of socialization, narrative development, structure, and ordered signifying conceits until they erupt on the surface as name-entities, ideological messengers, and icons of deep-level meanings. I call this iconic emergence the *eruption of the true-real*.

I use the term *eruption* instead of Kristeva's "irruption" because of the nature and activities of the event as I see it. It is the violent emerging of names and phrase names as icons of meaning that signals the arrival of a vigorously active creative force. In literature, the true-real does not merely *irrupt*. It disturbs, disassembles, and reassembles primary signifying structures, causing moments of mistaken identity, epiphany, dreaming, role-playing, phantasma, delusion, psychosis, and narrative dissonance (i.e., ambiguity, paradox, contradiction, or name fluctuations). Narrative events such as these signal the arrival of aberrant voices or foreclosed onomastic tasks that affect meaning and language within the surface text. They are moments through which names reveal their most impossible functions and speak their most radical ideological messages.

Names that result from an eruption of the true-real fill a gap between the object of naming and original names, wherein it reorders meaning and exposes the foreclosed elements of discourse production. Ultimately, it gives a name the ability to enact and announce (to be and speak) its most impossible desires. One of the most well known icons of black nomenclature appearing in literature is the Nation of Islam's X. When the names *Little* and X meet in *The Autobiography of Malcolm X*, a collision of opposing worldviews and subject positions occurs that opens the text to radical interpretive possibilities. Since any name change (name fluctuation) is an opportunity for the eruption of the true-real, reading the X in Malcolm's autobiography reveals the surprising effects of the true-real upon the discourse production of names in this text.

The collision between *Little* and the worldview of the Nation of Islam separates the name from its previously established function. Malcolm's surname, *Little*, identifies him as a member of a family. Its deep talk speaks of the history and struggles of that family and the person Malcolm has become. Malcolm spends a great deal of time in the autobiography installing this history, calling the names of his parents as well as his own names and nicknames. In sum, *Little* speaks of a criminal and of men and women struggling to define themselves within a world that is itself defined by their exclusion. In the worldview of the black Muslims, *Little* speaks of a slave. It represents itself as a name "some blue-eyed devil named Little had imposed upon [Malcolm's] paternal forebears" (199). It is not the true name of Malcolm's family, and its deep talk does not speak of the Muslim Malcolm becomes. As a subject position designator, *Little* restricts discourses concerning Malcolm's (African) historical past and lies about his status as a man. In the worldview of Black Muslims, the deep-level communication of *Little* speaks of an injustice that bars a black man from his humanity and his potential, a sin imposed by a "devil."

This collision doubles the meaning potential of *Little* and creates a gap between it and its object (in this case, a member of the Nation of Islam). A new name, X, fills this gap, and with it the true-real emerges. This new name brings with it truncated discourses and name tasks that challenge and negate the value of *Little* as an appropriate name for Malcolm's newly discovered identity. The surface text of the autobiography informs the reader that the contextual aim of the poetic name X is symbolic. It symbolizes the true African family name that Malcolm could never know (199). Its utterances speak of a lost history, a hostile environment, a new identity, and a mandate to wait for God's renaming. Like his West African ancestors, Malcolm changes his name in honor of an event that shapes his new identity. The name he selects, *X*, classifies all members of the Nation of Islam as one in discipline and solidarity. It bonds them through kinship ties that speak through a shared name.

In the autobiography's metatext, the *X* Malcolm bears is both signified and signifier of an action that unnames. Instead of recording an event of personal change, the name *becomes* an event of change through which the true-real emerges. In other words, it speaks of unnaming as it unnames. While offering Malcolm the defining elements of black solidarity and discipline within the surface text, the deep talk of the true-real emerges within that space to negate and mark out the history of slavery and dehumanization that the name *Little* calls forth repeatedly. In addition, the *X* functions as an ideological messenger—a mark that actively bars intrusion from outsiders and serves as a warning that those who tread upon the name it protects (*Malcolm*) may themselves be marked out. Surprisingly, it also suggests the possibility of a double cross revealed fully when Malcolm changes his name to El-Hajj Malik El-Shabazz. Such a reading magnifies the function of *X* as a word that unifies a small group of African Americans while denying the possibility of unity between them and the multiethnic and international community of Muslims that Malcolm later discovers.

As this reading of *X* demonstrates, the eruption of the true-real creates multiple meanings and various types of utterances. In such cases, the type of utterance that determines the textual reading of onomastic deep talk depends upon two things, the success or failure of the true-real in entering an alien contextual environment and its ability to establish a concrete connotative and denotative function within that lifeworld. During Malcolm's visit to Mecca the deep talk of *X* fails to maintain value as an icon of surface or deep-level meanings. Through unnaming, *El-Hajj Malik El-Shabazz* denies discourses speaking of ethnic exclusion and hostile warnings; its deep talk allows only a renewed and expanded sense of solidarity, discipline, and historical belonging to remain.

One of the most dramatic examples of how the true-real influences surface discourses is in Toni Morrison's *Beloved*. In this text the true-real appears in the flesh when an incarnate ghost emerges from water, enters the lives of Sethe, Denver, and Paul D, and spells her name "slowly as though the letters were being formed as she spoke them. . . . Paul D smiled. He recognized the careful enunciation of letters by those, like himself who could not read but had memorized the letters of their name" (52). Because Beloved spells her name, Paul D's memories flow to a time four years before her appearance. "Odd clusters and strays of Negroes wandered the back roads and cowpaths from Schenectady to Jackson" (52). Paul D's reaction to the spelling of a name sets up a pattern of name-invoked re-memory that the text repeats several times. Beloved's name functions mnemonically; it ignites, or resurrects, memory and self-recognition.

Beloved, the ghost, is the incarnate body of onomastic "flesh," the body of "flesh" that revises discourses of the past. Karla Holloway describes her this way: "Because origin and source are thematic issues in this novel, we must acknowledge the interpretive significance of Beloved as not only Sethe's dead daughter returned, but the return of all the (African) faces, all the drowned, (re)membered faces of mothers and their children who lost their being because of the force of Euro-American slave history. Beloved becomes a cultural mooring place, a moment for reclamation and for naming." As a mnemonic icon of the true-real, the name *Beloved* gives the past living form and validates experiences that were once denied expression. Adam McKible describes the name as "a container of uncontainable incongruities . . . that shatters the truth-value of Schoolteacher's method of historiography."[5] This is the true-real, grinding against the alien discourse of established historical "truths" and revising them.

The presence of the true-real also breaks and revises the rules of grammar and composition within the surface text of Morrison's novel. Verbs and punctuation disappear, prose merges with poetry, and voices merge, giving marginalized linguistic subjects control over the internal structures of an alien grammar: "Beloved, she my daughter. She me. See. . . . In the beginning I could see her   I could not help her because the clouds were in the way   in the beginning I could see her   the shining in her

ears   she does not like the circle around her neck   I know this. . . .
Beloved / You are my sister / you are my daughter / You are my Beloved /
You are mine / You are mine / You are mine" (201, 211, 216, Morrison's
spacing). Cixous calls this type of text *writing the body*.[6] I call it *writing
the liberated flesh of the true-real*.

Moments of iconic emergence, such as that quoted above, unfold dramatically within the text, imposing themselves upon the surface narrative's ordered social and historical definitions of character identity, narrative action, and narrative structure. Marginal discourses such as those
expressed by the true-real break *free* of stagnation and foreclosure and
establish themselves as absent, yet ambiguously present and disruptive,
forces within a text. They assume the role of icons that invade the surface text and cunningly open it to unforeseen, judicious, and radical interpretive possibilities. In Morrison's *Beloved*, the action of "breaking
through" the surface is graphically drawn—especially during moments
when spaces between sentences and thoughts replace punctuation. Both
the referent (the character) and her name (*Beloved*) exist within the text
as icons of a remembered past. As an icon of the true-real, *Beloved*, in
the end, performs an additional interpretable act—it serves as both signified and signifier of self-affirmation, historical reclamation, and linguistic control (or ownership). All three women in this novel—Sethe,
Denver, and the ghost—affirm, "I AM BELOVED and she is mine"
(210, 214). In other words, I am the past and it is mine.

The most dramatic revelations of the true-real are those that provide
a message of truth to the reader by revealing a name's manipulation of
intertextual and, sometimes, extratextual associations.[7] Below I read the
discourse production of *Lorraine* from Gloria Naylor's *Women of Brewster Place*. This novel intertextualizes a biblical archetype to develop the
story of its metatext. This metatext describes a name-entity who suffers
a death and resurrection that breaks down barriers of difference. Just as
the name *X* merges the identities of Malcolm and those African Americans who share his faith and *Beloved* merges the present (Sethe), past
(Beloved), and future (Denver) in Morrison's text, a phrase name in
Brewster Place merges the identities of those who share its gendered
identity. Moments of iconic emergence develop discourses of history,

social difference, and bonded fate through the phrase name *the tall yellow woman in the bloody green and black dress*, which communicates an experience of bonding that the women of Brewster Place cannot escape. Similar to Beloved, this name-entity haunts those it wishes to claim as "mine."

I Would Die for You

Gloria Naylor's *Women of Brewster Place* depicts the character Lorraine, a lesbian, as an outcast of both society and the community in which she lives. Various names denote her—"Miss Innocent," "butch," "dyke," "lesbo," "freak," "cunt," and finally "a tall yellow woman in a bloody green and black dress" (145, 162, 170, 173). Her status as outsider ends with a rape that breaks the barriers of difference separating her from the community of women in which she lives. Through a strategic manipulation of the names, epithets, and phrase names associated with Lorraine, a multiplicity of meanings and discursive effects emerges. Her name is at once a subject position, designating the character as the archetypal symbol of hope for all of Brewster Place's women, and the signifying space through which multiple discursive effects do their work. The name's final fragmentation speaks from the margins of the narrative's primary lifeworld to announce and enact an obliteration of female difference. In this reading, I address two of this character's name fragmentations and one of another character whose name plays a pivotal role within the metatext.

Lorraine's transformation into a symbol of hope begins with a name fluctuation. Another female character, named Sophie, shows her objection to Lorraine's presence during a tenants' meeting by calling her something other than her name. Sophie raises a statue the text describes as being "like a crucifix" and points it toward Lorraine. "Don't stand there like you a Miss Innocent," Sophie says as she points the statue (145). By suggesting that Lorraine might assume the role of a "Miss Innocent," not only does Sophie signify upon Lorraine's lack of (sexual) innocence, but her violent tone demonstrates the hostility confronting Lorraine and her name in this environment. This indirect name calling foreshadows the character's ultimate subject position as a community scapegoat. Like a scapegoat, Lorraine becomes the outcast member of a community who suffers for the wrongs of others but is personally innocent of those wrongs herself (in this case, the wrong is separation, discrimination, and hate based on sexual identity).

As an onomastic event, Sophie's indirect name calling juxtaposed with the narrator's description of the statue as a crucifix (the Christian symbol of sacrifice and personal suffering, the crucifix of innocence) splits *Miss Innocent* into two separate words. One designates the character of the surface text. The other acts as a border-crossing name-entity that coalesces aberrant surface discourses and, with the assistance of an active reader, creates an allegorical metatext. Reading the projective intent and duality of *Miss Innocent* brings to light the many parallels between the character's plight and the religious archetype. Like Jesus, Lorraine is misunderstood and rejected by her own people, an outcast who becomes a sacrifice for the promise of hope.

Woven into Lorraine's story is a metatext that tells of a name-entity's birth, sacrifice, death, and resurrection. The development of this deep-level discourse depends upon several additional name fragmentations that are linked clandestinely to *Miss Innocent*. The first fragmentation occurs in Ben's name. Ben is the janitor and building handyman who develops a transformative father/daughter relationship with Lorraine. After Sophie's rebuff, Lorraine, feeling despondent and alienated, visits Ben's basement apartment and continues to visit him regularly. During these visits, Ben nurtures and "re-creates" Lorraine until her "fading spirit" revives. Tee, Lorraine's lover and partner, acknowledges this change when she notices that there was a "firmness in her [Lorraine's] spirit that hadn't been there before" (145, 155). This event stylizes Ben's name and situates him as the agent of spiritual renewal.

Ben's new role is a condition of his name's descriptive discourse, its deep talk. Whenever the name appears, the reader of the novel's archetypal religious inflections gathers information about a developing deep-level story. Within the metatext, the name *Ben* functions as a god figure who brings spirit to the body of innocence that Sophie installed earlier. (Before moving forward in this reading, I must emphasize that Ben is not himself a symbol of god; only his name as an extralinguistic actor in the novel's metatext serves in this capacity.) The metatext uses Ben's basement apartment as the metaphoric "womb" of a new creation. In this lifeworld, a god "nurtures" and develops the "spirit" of the name-entity *Miss Innocent* so that it becomes, in part, *Ben's* creation. This event replicates the virgin birth of the biblical story by metaphorically presenting a name-entity whose body (*Miss Innocent*) is born of a woman but whose spirit comes from a god.

This deep talk replaces the discourses of difference speaking through names identifying the character Lorraine after another fragmentation, proceeded and followed by several incidents of iconic emergence. After Lorraine's brutal rape, the narrator describes her as "a tall yellow woman in a bloody green and black dress"; then the character and her name disappear from the text (173). In the surface text, the phrase name replaces *Lorraine* as a subject persona designator, filling the gap unnaming creates. Within the metatext, it replaces *Miss Innocent* and serves as a metonymic incarnation of the Christian archetype presented throughout Lorraine's story. It is through the experience of this name that all the women on Brewster Place comprehend and remember the true-real.

The surface text renders the story of Lorraine's sacrifice as rape. After her assaulters "had finished and stopped holding her up, her body fell over like an unstringed puppet . . . Lorraine lay pushed up against the wall on the cold ground with her eyes staring straight up into the sky" (171). The use of the words "body," "unstringed puppet," and "cold ground" suggests the departure of spirit from the body. In other words, it suggests lifelessness. Symbolically, Lorraine's battered body and distorted mind mirror the pain, mental impairment, and spiritual decay that all of Brewster Place's women have suffered at some point within the novel. As she lies in the alley, silenced by a dirty bag the men jammed into her mouth and bloodied by the brutality of their physical abuse, she pays the price of silent, personal sacrifice demanded by her role as community scapegoat.

In the metatext, this scene develops the allegorical story. Although the biblical Christ is not raped, his body is penetrated by the "spears" of men's brutality and hate. The metatext, then, uses Lorraine's rape to symbolize the undesirable wounding of the body experienced by the biblical archetype. Similar to Christ, Lorraine's physical being rises from its stillness after hours of suffering a deathlike paralysis. Unlike Christ, Lorraine kills her creator. This break with the religious archetype results in a distorted version of the murder of the Father.

Ben's murder occurs during a moment of iconic emergence (in this case, a mistaken identity caused by Lorraine's hysteria). In the description of this delusional experience, Ben's name changes. The narrator refers to him as "the movement by the wall" and "the movement on Brewster Place." In the surface text, it is the movement that was "almost in perfect unison with the sawing pain that kept moving inside of her" (the dehumanized residue of rape) that Lorraine attacks (172). Beneath the surface, something more occurs. Both phrase names result from a supranaming event that adds defining elements to Ben's original name designation. The iconic representation of the true-real, appearing here as the indefinable movement of God, refines the name's function as an actor within a deep-level narrative event.

The eruption of the true-real through the name *Ben* interrupts the development of the novel's allegorical story for a reason. To maintain the narrative theme of a healing community that is woman centered, Naylor's characters must reject the male image of healing and spiritual renewal (because it is male). Lorraine's actions strike out female dependence upon men and kill its representative in this text. The message here is not that women must kill men to survive, but that they must not depend upon them for healing and spiritual renewal.

The name *Ben* appears once more after Lorraine's attack: "Rain. It began the afternoon of Ben's death and came down day and night for an entire week, so Brewster Place wasn't able to congregate around the wall and keep up a requiem of the whys and hows of his dying" (175). As a result of its last fragmentation, *Ben* reads differently in the metatext. There it confirms the absence of a god's presence on Brewster Place: *Rain. It began the afternoon when the indefinable movement of god died and came down day and night for an entire week, so Brewster Place wasn't able to congregate around the wall and keep up a requiem of the whys and hows of god's dying.* This sentence reinstalls the allegorical enactment of the biblical story by demonstrating the stillness of God's influence in human affairs during the days before Christ's resurrection.

A second break between the biblical Jesus and Lorraine exists in the vehicle and purpose of their resurrection visits. This deviation from the allegorical development of the story marks the second successful eruption of the true-real, an eruption that affects the discourse production of the name designating the character Lorraine. As a result of her spiritual death, all the women and female children on Brewster Place receive visits from (or are haunted) the spirit of "the tall yellow woman in the bloody green and black dress . . . [who] came to them in the midst of the cold sweat of a nightmare, or had hung around the edges of fitful sleep" (175–76). These dreams represent a shared delusional experience among all of Brewster Place's women, an experience of the true-real.

The phrase name *the tall yellow woman in the bloody green and black dress* serves as both signified and signifier of obliterated difference. The name's function triples. It denotes the subject persona, an iconic analogy of the Christian archetype of hope (a subject position), and an event through which delusional experiences destroy imposed boundaries of difference (a position effect). The haunting image of Lorraine's *disembodied spirit* indicts the women's prejudices as partially responsible for her pain; moreover, it identifies them as the community for whom she suffers and survives. Because a shared experience is necessary to install the novel's underlying promise of hope, all of Brewster Place's women must suffer and acknowledge their guilt.

As the women and girls of Brewster Place dream, they experience Lorraine's pain. It "spreads" and becomes their pain, and her creator's blood merges with their blood. Note how Naylor describes Kiswana's reaction to one of the bloodstained bricks ripped from the wall where Ben was killed and Lorraine was beaten and raped: "Kiswana looked down at the wet stone and her rain-soaked braids leaked onto the surface, spreading the dark stain. She wept and ran to throw the brick spotted with *her blood* out into the avenue" (187, emphasis added). This quote describes one character's experience (Mattie) of the dream delusion. Mattie dreams about all the women on Brewster Place, and subsequently her identity merges with theirs. The phrase "her blood" is ambiguous and indicates a point of narrative dissonance through which this merging occurs. Whose blood is on the brick? In Mattie's nightmare, the blood on the brick is both Kiswana's and Lorraine's blood and by extension Mattie's blood. "It's spreading all over," she says (187).

The text tells us that every woman on Brewster Place experiences dream-visits from this apparition. They all find their identities meshed with Lorraine's. They all share the experiences of "the tall yellow woman in the bloody green and black dress." Each of them suffers from the eruption of the true-real—perceptions they "knew, and yet didn't know," desires, instincts, and values once foreclosed and considered implausible (176). The phrase name speaks of this meshing of identities. Its deep talk does not highlight Lorraine's sexual identity, her difference. It merely speaks of a woman, a "tall yellow woman" in a "bloody green and black dress."

The deep talk of this phrase name highlights racial unity through its cultural imprints. During the Black Power movement of the 1960s and 1970s, the colors red (bloody dress), black, and green symbolized African-American unity. This coding mechanism extends itself beyond America through the color yellow, an addition that includes African unity as well. The message of the true-real, then, is that Lorraine, regardless of her sexual identity, is a woman—a black woman whose biological vulnerabilities are the same as every other woman on Brewster Place and beyond. Her name's discursive effects force both the reader and the characters to recognize a very important ideological message: "regardless of social status, regardless of sexual preference, the commonalty is the female experience. When you reduce that down in this society even to something as abysmal as rape, there is no difference between women." [8]

The discourses produced by names in this chapter resist worldviews that demand separation and difference. The deep talk of the epithet *nigger*, the iconic marker *X*, the mnemonic name *Beloved*, and the phrase name *the tall yellow woman in the bloody green and black dress* each use race as a bonding agent communicated through the true-real. These poetic names denounce division even as a history of pretentious class differences, a memory of infanticide, and a tradition of repressive sexual mores threaten to destroy communal unity. The discourses of the true-real in each case communicate messages of resistance that bridge the possibilities of renewal in defiance of the impossibilities that oppression and prejudice impose. In this way, onomastic resistance announces itself as a primary force in identity politics, purification, and historical reclamation that allows characters to break free of boundaries that deny, denigrate, and exclude them.

PART
TWO
Reading the Extended Metatext

We are rooted in language, wedded, have our being in words.
Language is also a place of struggle.
The oppressed struggle in language to recover ourselves—
to rewrite, to reconcile, to renew.
Our words are not without meaning.
They are an action—a resistance.
—BELL HOOKS, *Talking Back*

Let us make up our faces before the world,
and our names shall sound throughout the land with honor!
For we ourselves are our true names, not their epithets.
—RALPH ELLISON, *Shadow and Act*

Don't call me out my name!
—Traditional

5

"Callin' Her Out Her Name": The Lifeworlds of *Dessa Rose*

I N NOVEMBER OF 1829, five black men were hanged for leading an uprising of a slave coffle bound for sale in the Deep South. The coffle, resulting from the purchase of slaves in Maryland, consisted of ninety women, children, and men. On the morning of the uprising, the group of slaves traveled from Greenup to Vanceburg, Kentucky. In the confusion of rebellion, two white men were killed and a third wounded. The wounded man, assisted by a pregnant female slave, escaped and informed others of the incident. The slaves were recaptured and the pregnant woman jailed until the birth of her child. On 25 May 1830 she was hanged. Her name was Dinah.[1]

Sherley Anne Williams's *Dessa Rose* fictionalizes this event and changes its ending. That Williams was aware of the woman's name is doubtful, since she does not refer to her by name anywhere in the novel or its "Author's Note." She does, however, suggest that this information was missing in the sources she documents by her preoccupation with and probing manipulation of names within the novel. Mary Kemp Davis notes this probability and comments that "*Dessa Rose* is a stinging rebuke of historians and other commentators who have either failed to note or to name the female slave resistor or, even worse, who have called the female slave out of her name."[2] Reading resistance in this novel's naming practices, then, begins with the words that unname Dinah; it begins with the name *Dessa Rose*.

This name speaks of resistance in the face of tremendous obstacles. Unlike Dinah, Dessa rose. She lifted herself up and succeeded against all odds. The story of her rise is not only a rebuke of Dinah's historical namelessness but a rebuke of broken promises, false security, and celebrated misnamings. Dessa's escape from death leads her to a world that offers a false promise of equality and security. Although she enters this world powerless, sick, and poor, Dessa moves forward until she controls her own destiny and defines her own modes of being. In the face of constant racist unnaming and renaming, Dessa maintains a secret name and, through it, the power to rise. In this chapter, I chart her rise from captive "body" to liberated "flesh" by reading the discourses of resistance that various names, including Dessa's secret one, create throughout the novel.

Williams organizes the three major sections of *Dessa Rose* under headings designated by names: "The Darky," "The Wench," and "The Negress." Each of these epithets defines the various interpersonal subject positions the main character assumes while on her journey toward the hope of egalitarian relationships. They also suggest the dominant social attitudes and onomastic desires defining each lifeworld of the surface text. The worldview or agency of onomastic discourse production within each section creates hostile language environments that foreclose the use of names whose contextual aims contradict their own. Narrative voice and character voice within each section maintain the prejudices, oppressions, and exclusions commensurate with the discursive attitudes of slave masters in "The Darky," pseudoliberators in "The Wench," and racial stratification in "The Negress." The surface narrative forecloses any challenge to these worldviews immediately, forcing conflicting onomastic desires, as well as the stories and discursive actions accompanying them, beneath the surface or into italicized dream sequences and monologues.

Such is the case when we first meet the novel's protagonist in the italicized portion of the prologue. The italics indicate that the words presented are reflections and images from the world of Dessa's thoughts and dreams. This italicized dream-lifeworld is one of memory existing outside the restrictive lifeworld of "The Darky." It is a world that the discursive force of the slavemaster's word cannot invade nor penetrate through craft or manipulation. In this lifeworld, the name *Dessa* speaks to the protagonist with the ease and fluidity of unencumbered love and poetry; it flows *"high and clear as running water over a settled stream bed, swooping to her, through her*" (11, Williams's italics). This description of the name's movement through speech draws an image of peacefulness existing within the subject position it names and the entity its deep talk creates.

Through *dessa* our protagonist is able to define herself.[3] Since a poetic name's deep talk is informed first by the meanings it inherits from within the lifeworld of its initial use, *dessa* expresses the liberated "flesh" of the protagonist's self-knowledge and self-esteem. This subject position obscures and forecloses the woman's role as a slave while the italicized prologue conceals slavery's impact upon her ability to know her true self. Both the character and the name-entity, *dessa*, remain unbound by restrictions that gauge, monitor, and determine their ability to express love, to move, to live. Although the protagonist's freedom is not of the standard variety (she is a slave), Dessa expresses every aspect of her humanity, involving herself in sensual relationships and community bonding without restrictions or hesitation. She loves a man called Kaine, and together they enjoy the fellowship of family and friends.

In Dessa's dream-lifeworld, power is memory, intuition, and imagination. The protagonist's imagination offers an intuitive knowledge and remembered sensation of her true name and identity: "*She had felt herself with him [Kaine], knew herself among Carrie and them*" (14, Williams's italics). The character's unfettered community interactions secure her name's affiliation with a self-perception that is spiritually, emotionally, and sensually free. Throughout the italicized portion of the prologue, the protagonist maintains this sense of spiritual liberation, and her name maintains its original onomastic desires. The identities derived through the remembered and imagined intuitive deep talk of *dessa*, the beauty and power of its original force, guide both.

The first fragmentation of *Dessa* occurs within the italicized prologue when Kaine calls the protagonist *Dess*. *Dess* is a sensual pet name whose deep talk speaks of sexual intimacy and desire. "*Thighs spreading for him, hips moving for him. Lawd, this man sho know how to love*" (14, Williams's italics). The activities of this name-entity are short-lived. The world beyond Dessa's imagination interrupts her experience of *dess's* sensuality as the ugliness of slavery rips the veil of her memory, suspending the beautiful world of her dreams. The italics fall away, and the nonitalicized section of the prologue forecloses the position effects of the poetic names *Dessa* and *Dess*. With it the protagonist's freedom ("Chains rasped, rubbed hatefully at her ankles") and her erotic passions sputter away: "Desire flowered briefly, fled in dry spasm, gone as suddenly as the dream had come" (14). Foreclosed by the intrusion of "The Darky," neither *Dess* nor its action-oriented position effects appear again until the novel's second major section. Although Dessa continues to dream and remember, she does so through the subject position *dessa*. Behind closed eyes *dessa's* dream-lifeworld lives, and the protagonist experiences its secret memories and communal longings:

> Kaine's eyes had been the color of lemon tea and honey. Even now against closed eyelids, she could see them— Kaine's eyes, Carrie's smile . . .
>
> I sent my Dessa a message
>
> Dessa mouthed the words
>
> > Chilly Winds took it,
> > Blowed it everywhere.
>
> and heard his voice in her ear
>
> > Hey, hey Dessa da'lin,
> > This Kaine calling, calling . . .
> > (14, Williams's ellipses and spacing)

The ellipses in the final line of the prologue's dream sequence serve a dual purpose. On the surface, they give the impression of words and actions drifting away. In the metatext, they function as a bridge linking fragments of surface events, sentences, and words with the discourses of memory and internal monologues within the novel's dream-lifeworld. In both instances, they connect the sentence preceding them to whatever follows. This bridging technique leads the reader's eye to the title of the novel's first major section. We read "The Darky" printed in bold and dramatic fashion. These words, read in succession with those preceding the ellipses, reveal the traces of a deep-level story. In the metatext, the name-entity *kaine* calls out to a part of Dessa that the invasive force of a hostile lifeworld mutates and redefines as *the darky*. The agency of deep talk controlling "The Darky" fragments the protagonist's name through supranaming. "Hey, hey, Dessa da'lin, / This Kaine calling, calling ***The Darky***."

This calling constitutes the first name fragmentation associated with slavery and denied freedom (the captive "body"). The values, expectations, and obligations informing the historical content of the word *darky* arise from commodification, ownership, restricted mobility, and the inhumanity associated with slaves in the worldview of their enslavers. Throughout the first major section of this novel, chains restrict the protagonist's mobility. Her characterization as a slave and an animal redefine her subject position. In this lifeworld and in the worldview of her captors, the protagonist is a dangerous, yet valuable, possession.

The epigraph of "The Darky" hints at this transformation of worldview and characterization. Quoted from Frederick Douglass's 1845 *Narrative of the Life of Frederick Douglass*, it reads: "You have seen how a man was made a slave" (Williams, 15). Douglass's narrative continues, "You shall see how a slave was made a man" (77). Williams's use of this statement as an epigraph for "The Darky" highlights her novel's inversion of the male slave narrative's journey motif (from slavery to freedom). Instead of showing how a slave gains freedom and manhood, "The Darky" transforms a woman's previous experience of spiritual freedom into an experience of physical and mental bondage. "You have seen how a man was made a slave"; now you shall see how a woman was made one.

Immediately following the prologue, we read the story of a runaway slave captured and bound with chains. Darkness surrounds her, emphasizing the complete control of the epithet *darky* over the conditions of this lifeworld. No light (no hope, no love) can reach the protagonist in this hostile environment. The section opens with Dessa's report that Masa (Terrell Vaugham) hit Kaine. Dessa continues in monologue to inform the reader of her life as a slave. She recalls stories of breeding, meeting and falling in love with Kaine, becoming pregnant with his child, and discussing escape with him. She speaks of Kaine's home-made banjo and the freedom and self-validation it represented, Masa's destruction of that banjo, Kaine's retaliation by attacking Vaugham, and Vaugham's subsequent murder of Kaine.

Many of the words we read are not the direct speech of Dessa but her words as recorded by Adam Nehemiah, a white researcher who inter-views her concerning the ordeal that led her to the dark cellar. Nehemiah is researching his second book, *The Roots of Rebellion in the Slave Popu-lation and Some Means of Eradicating Them.* As he records her story, we learn of Dessa's escape and capture. Through an interplay of Dessa's monologues, Nehemiah's written notes, and narration, we discover that Dessa attacked her mistress and was sold into a coffle. On their journey toward the Deep South the slaves in the coffle attempt an escape that results in the murder of five white guards and thirty-one slaves. Because she is pregnant, Dessa cannot escape. The slave trader, Wilson, recap-tures her and arranges to keep her alive until the birth of her child. As this first major section of the novel draws to an end, Dessa escapes. She is a runaway, but she is free from the physical bondage of "The Darky's" lifeworld.

This is the story as told in the surface text. Reading through names and naming reveals a second story, the deep-level story of Dessa's resis-tance against white namers and her search for an identity that she con-trols and defines. By the end of the first section, she faces a choice of three subject positions revealed to her through the play of names and naming.

The Darky

The attitudes and cultural languages of southern slavery, a world con-trolled by white masters and white namers, dominate the lifeworld of "The Darky." Utterances that challenge the exclusive nature of that in-tent remain separated from this lifeworld through characters' inability to "hear" as well as the narrative's use of irony, internal or spoken mono-logues, and italicized dream sequences. When Dessa questions the ubiq-uitous power of the master, for instance, all of these distancing devices work in concert to hide the meaning of her question: "thank it be a place without no whites?" (41). This question originates from a cultural language and attitude contrary to the intent of "The Darky." As a result, the question and the role reversal it generates meet resistance.

The double negative "without no" emphasizes the possibility of a place without whites. The phrase can also be read as self-negating. This type of reading renders meanings that are just the opposite of Dessa's intent. This ironic turn represents one of three distancing devices used in the quote. Irony subsumes the intent of the question, using its own construction to undermine its meaning. Furthermore, Nehemiah does not understand her question, or perhaps he merely refuses to believe what he hears. In either case, his inability to hear is the second indication that the discourse of Dessa's question meets resistance in the lifeworld of "The Darky." Furthermore, Dessa and her interviewer are not engaged in conversation when she asks this question—at least not in the way one normally defines conversation. As she does in many speeches in "The Darky," Dessa talks as if she is barely aware of Nehemiah's presence. She speaks in a monologue. "She continued to herself, in a deeper dialect than she had heretofore used, really almost a mumble, something about Emmalina's Joe Big telling Kaine something and going, but where [Nehemiah] could not make out" (41).

Just as Nehemiah cannot understand or hear Dessa's question, he cannot hear the name of the place she mentions. "What?" he asks, but receives no answer. Instead of repeating the name, Dessa masks her thoughts by retreating deeper into her own psychical space: "the blank look returned to her face; the humming started again" (41). The discursive effects of the name *Darky*, the definer and controller of this lifeworld, let nothing foreign to its defining elements enter the surface. "The Darky" silences Dessa's story and forecloses the name of the place without "white folks." Neither the reader nor Nehemiah learn of it.

Dessa's retreat into monologues represents the third, and most important, distancing device used to separate the lifeworld of Dessa's words from the lifeworld of the master. Set apart from the world of primary action, they organize a second world of action, a dream-lifeworld of communities existing within distinct social spaces. Dessa's dream-lifeworld, as well as the monologues and actions its discourses develop, floats around, above, or through the dominant lifeworld of each titled section without becoming a part of them. Although Dessa's physical body exists within the same geographical site as Adam Nehemiah, her words (and her name) originate from a place beyond it—a place of dreams, memories, and events that are not a part of his world.

Earlier in "The Darky," an italicized dream interrupts the main action of the story as Dessa's memories drift to a hot day and a conversation between two slaves. Note the description of Dessa's physical relationship to the action of the memory: " '*Sho was hot out there today,*' " one slave says. The second slave responds, " '*Yeah, look like it fixin to be a hot, hot summer.' The desultory conversation eddied around Dessa*" (32, Williams's italics). Distancing such as this prevents Dessa's monologues, the activities of her dream-lifeworld, and the poetic names she calls from being "contaminated" by the transformative potential of a hostile environment. Her monologues acknowledge the existence of the subtitle's designated lifeworld by intermittently commenting upon events, characters, situations, and social constructions within that lifeworld, but as events of consciousness and memory they remain distanced from each.

Through monologues Dessa is able to subvert the master's use of names and claim her own subjectivity. The presence of a dream-lifeworld and the monologues within it produce parodies, ironies, and other chaotic discourses through which we learn of hierarchical constructions functioning beneath the surface—constructions that challenge the validity of events, ideologies, and even names that dominate the primary lifeworld.

In the section's first chapter, the narrator describes Dessa crawling about the cellar floor "like a wild and timorous animal finally brought to bay, moving quickly and clumsily" (22–23). Her body, appropriated by the institution of slavery, is a reproductive machine that the slave trader, Wilson, wishes to keep functioning. He is "obsessed with seeing, and selling, the kid she carried" (22). Because of her violent behavior when attempting escape from the coffle, she is called the "fiend," the "treacherous nigger bitch," and the "devil woman," among other centered epithets (21, 22). These epithets represent one of the three subject positions from which the protagonist must choose.

Dessa inherits one of these phrase names from a description given of her by a member of the novel's white community. In their worldview, the name speaks of a "banshee" from hell who attacks white men from behind, a "devil woman" (143). This name succumbs to a language of resistance invented by slaves who "loud talk" the master by giving the name a new meaning. When the protagonist asks the house slave Jemina why she is so kind to her, the name's double-voiced discourse becomes clear.

" 'Why?' Jemina chuckled softly. 'Why honey, you's the "debil woman." ' " Hurriedly, she told how the [black] people in the neighborhood had coined the name from the slave trader Wilson's description of the uprising. It expressed their derision of slave dealers, whose only god was money, and their delight that a 'devil' had been the agency of one's undoing" (54). Here, the "trickster" gets the best of "Ol' Massah" through name play. In the language of the slaves, *devil woman* meets hostility, renaming occurs, and the epithet fragments. *Devil woman* becomes *debil woman*. Through an utterance of onomastic "loud talking," the epithet refers to Dessa but announces the slaves' animosity toward slave dealers who use the original name to negate Dessa's humanity and (debil)itate her. The words *debil woman* mock and criticize the master— inscribing pride where degradation once ruled and empowering a phrase name that was once (debil)itated by negative intent. Thus, not only is the protagonist's subject position as the "devil woman" redefined, but the new name designating this role undermines and mocks the dominant lifeworld, denying the master's control over a marginalized discourse. Although the authoritative voice of the master dominates the lifeworld of the word in "The Darky," slaves are not without metalinguistic influence. They play a primary role in the inversion of the master's voice. As a reminder of this name play, I use the name *devil woman* instead of *darky, fiend,* or *treacherous nigger bitch* when referring to this subject position.

Unfortunately, this onomastic victory does not change the protagonist's circumstances. In the lifeworld of "The Darky," the consciousness of Dessa remains distanced from the world around her. Her name remains within the dream-lifeworld narration, as does her conscious ability to oppose her physical immobility. She exists in a state of liminality, perched between two lifeworlds, that of her dreams and memories and nat of "The Darky." With her head bowed and her eyes closed, she speaks in a trancelike state without acknowledging Nehemiah or his world. The living words of her dream-lifeworld, the totality of their meaning and intent, do not enter this environment. They remain outside of it and are influenced only by the world behind the woman's closed eyelids, the world of her dreams, a world of potential iconic emergence—the world of *dessa*.

While in this trancelike state, *dessa* relives events of her life. Her stoic voice is audible but disconnected from interlocutory exchange. Only the *devil woman* interacts with the interviewer through dialogue; and she does so with all of the venom and wildness expected of her. Nehemiah notes this split subject: " 'I kill white mens,' her voice overrode mine, as though she had not heard me speak. 'I kill white mens cause the same reason Masa kill Kaine. Cause I can.' It had been an entrancing recital . . . the attack on the master, the darky's attachment to the young buck, that contraception root—all narrated with about as much expression as one gave to a 'Howdy' with any passing stranger. And then that bold statement that seemed to echo in the silence. *This* was the 'fiend,' the 'devil woman' who had attacked white men and roused other niggers to rebellion" (20–21, Williams's italics).

Real dialogue between these two characters does not occur until Nehemiah mentions the name *Kaine*, calling it from the dream-lifeworld into the world of "The Darky." Only then does the woman participate consciously in dialogue with Nehemiah—and then, only occasionally—through the voice of the "devil woman." The voice of *dessa* has not yet entered this lifeworld. Nehemiah stylizes *Kaine* by installing his worldview into the name's contextual aims. The name mutates graphically. " 'Kay-ene—is that it?' People would give darkies these outlandish names, he muttered to himself, and throw the rules of spelling to the winds" (40). As Nehemiah redefines Kaine, the name immediately collects historical content associated with the term *darky*. Kaine's individuality collapses into a generalized category defined by Adam Nehemiah's worldview.

This does not happen to the name *Dessa*. Only the dream-lifeworld sequences of the novel's first chapter contain the main character's name. Outside of internal monologues and dream sequences, neither Dessa

nor anyone else speaks her "true" name at all. Even when Dessa recalls Kaine's dying words, her name stands outside of the text we read.
" 'Nigga,' Kaine say, nigga and my name. He say em ova and ova and I
hold his hand cause I know that can't be all he wanna say. Nigga and my
name; my name and nigga" (20). By refusing to speak her name, Dessa
denies its association with the defining elements of a negative epithet.

The absence of the name *Dessa* from the lifeworld of "The Darky" in
this chapter indicates its suppression within that environment. It also
highlights the self-protecting separation and resistance enacted by the
name-entity *dessa* against the contaminating position effects of "The
Darky." Although Nehemiah attempts to capture *dessa* and redefine it,
his attempts fail. The poetic name violently resists assimilation within
the world of "The Darky." Its elusive discursive action hides, cloaks, and
protects its role as the name through which the protagonist defines herself
and finds confirmation of her experiences.

This evasive action mirrors West African cultural naming practices
used to cloak one's true self from harm or threats from enemies. Gay
Wilentz comments that "the power of a name is so strong in Africa and
the diaspora that often people kept a secret name so that an enemy could
not use it for evil intent; moreover, a name could also be employed as a
counterhegemonic response to one's oppressor, as slaves (who retained
African names or signified in a secret language) were wont to do." [4] The
potential for self-definition represented by the elusive name *dessa* undermines the power of the master's categories to contain the being and
humanity of a self-willed subject position. Therefore, the protagonist
protects it and guards it against hegemonic contempt as if it were a "secret" name.

This battle of resistance culminates in a confrontation between name
and namer when Nehemiah speaks to Dessa and discovers that he cannot
"for the life of him remember her name" (45). His loss of memory stands
in stark contrast to Dessa's existence within memory and her ability to
maintain her autonomy through it. Nehemiah's memory loss highlights
the discursive power and control the poetic name *Dessa* maintains over
the discourses of memory and re-memory. Again, imagination and intuition control events in the surface text. In this novel, memory of a name
is power, and because Nehemiah's experience of this power is one of loss,

the collision between name and namer results in Nehemiah's momentary disempowerment. This struggle leaves Nehemiah without the linguistic control he needs to reinscribe *Dessa* with the contextual aims dictated by his belief system.

The loss does not deter him from pursuing the role of namer. He persists, and in complete disregard for Dessa and her name, he calls her *girl*. " 'Girl,' he said, for at that moment he could not for the life of him remember her name, 'girl, what I put in this book cannot hurt you now. You've already been tried and judged' " (45). Assuming the control of a master namer, Nehemiah assigns Dessa a name designation signifying disrespect, subordination, and inferiority. His success in establishing control over the naming process within the surface text appears to mute the discursive effects of *dessa* and render them ineffective through fragmentation. This is not the case. *Girl* appears in a situation of supranaming through which the deep talk of the name supplement completely subverts its more obvious surface functions.

In the metatext, *girl* functions as an object effect that involves itself in the elusive actions of the poetic name *Dessa*. As a name supplement, *girl* only briefly fills a void or gap left by *dessa's* resistance to the foreign and hostile lifeworld of "The Darky." It does not replace the name within the text. Although a multitude of negative implications accompanies it, its onomastic desire as an object effect subverts those implications. Prior to this name's appearance in the text, both Nehemiah and the narrator refer to the protagonist as the *darky*, a word that objectifies the woman completely—a name stripped of any recognizable human-defining elements. The name *girl*, although not ideal, identifies gender and (on the deepest level of meaning) acknowledges the protagonist's humanity within the lifeworld of "The Darky." Instead of reducing the position of Dessa to that of a child, the epithet *girl* begins the process of humanizing the character in the world beyond her dream experiences.

The name prepares the way for the entrance of the word *Dessa* into the lifeworld of "The Darky" during the novel's second chapter. When telling the story of her attempt to convince Kaine that they should keep their child and run from slavery, our protagonist quotes him. She remembers how painfully sweet her name sounded as he spoke: " 'Dessa,' and I know he don't want hurt me when he call my name, but it so sweet till it do hurt" (46). She repeats the name seven times within a few lines and mentions it again a few paragraphs later. " 'Dessa' just soft like that. 'Dessa' . . . 'Run Dessa.' (Lawd. No one had ever said her name so sweet. Even when he was angry, Dessa. Dessa. She would always know the way he call her name.) 'Dessa, run where?' " (46–47). The repeating of the name is double voiced and contains an internal hidden dialogue through which Kaine tells *dessa* not to escape into a dreamworld, a world that no longer exists. The narrator comments that "his voice seemed to ring inside her head," inside the space of her dream-lifeworld. Kaine's voice works within the woman's words and calls *dessa* into the present, the lifeworld of "The Darky." "Dessa, run where?" Due to this internally hidden dialogue, *dessa* enters the surface text and lifts the woman's conscious mind from its liminal state. She looks at Nehemiah as if seeing him for the first time "and she recoiled, thinking in that first instance of seeing that his eyes were covered by some film, milky and blank. His eyes were 'blue' " (48–49).

Not only is Nehemiah unable to speak Dessa's secret name—he cannot write it. The name-entity *dessa* eludes his ability to categorize it, and he scribbles *Odessa* in his note pad. Again, *dessa* resists the collision it meets in the lifeworld of "The Darky," this time causing a fragmentation through renaming. The result is the creation of a new name, one that Nehemiah claims and uses.

This new name, *Odessa*, represents the hierarchy of the master/slave relationship as well as the stripping away of black humanity and historicity. Mary Kemp Davis comments that "in renaming Dessa, Adam Nehemiah replicates the acts of European enslavers who, in an act of aggression and subjugation, stripped the African of their names and rename[d] them." Although this is one way of viewing the renaming enacted by Nehemiah, the life of the word, its living totality as a name-entity, demands that we consider others. The *O* of the name, for instance, suggests various readings. Adam McKible reads it as "the 'O' of Otherness and objectification, as well as the zero of non-being or worthlessness; it represents what Fredric Jameson might describe as a linguistic 'strategy of containment,' a method of historiographical narration that writes over Dessa and cancels out the actual conditions of her existence." [5] Another way of reading the name is through its deep talk. *Odessa* contains multiple streams of onomastic desire. It is an objectified word with intratextual significance (an "undercover" informant) and a double-voiced word with multiple signifying desires.

Through these desires the name anticipates Nehemiah's forced recognition in the novel's final chapter that he captures only a shadow of *dessa* in his notepad. If the two words forming the name are separated and voiced with a tone of revelation, they read, "Oh! dessa." Used with a different emphasis, a question for instance, they read, "Oh, dessa?" As an "undercover" informant, *Odessa* speaks the revelation and memory of its former self by calling out to *dessa* constantly. Unlike the previous instance of calling, this is not a beckoning, but a celebration. Each time *Odessa* appears in the text it celebrates *dessa*, a secret name and subject position that identifies a self-defined being. "Oh! dessa!"

As separate entities within the metatext, the three subject positions—*devil woman*, *dessa*, and *odessa*—express specific aspects of the protagonist's character. From this point on, the *devil woman* controls her aggressions, *odessa* controls her speech, and *dessa* controls her thoughts and dreams. This body/voice/mind split precludes integration. The hostile and alien discourses of the *devil woman* and *odessa* contain a deep talk contaminated by contempt and dehumanization. McKimble's reading of the *O* as zero points out the subject position of a being existing without true human characteristics, a weak and powerless thing. One might even say that the multiplication of the protagonist's various names by this *O*, or zero, yields nothing. The discursive effects of the void within the name undermine any possibility for productive integration at this point in the novel. The three subject positions must remain separate, or the protagonist is lost—she truly becomes the inhuman zero that Nehemiah and the slave trader Wilson assume she is.

Since integration is not yet an option, the protagonist sits in the cellar or in the yard bemused and isolated. The *devil woman* does not enter the cellar; only the voices and meditations of *dessa*, the ghosts of her dreamlifeworld, and Jemina are allowed within that space.[6] Outside the cellar, the *devil woman* sits with Nehemiah, *odessa* talks to him, and our protagonist, facing a choice of three subject positions, silently observes them all. As the *devil woman*, she is defined by the epithets of the slave trader Wilson. In his worldview she is a "darky," a "fiend," a "treacherous nigger bitch," an animal (22). As *odessa*, she is merely a "hoarse and raspy" voice, a shadow defined by the worldview of Adam Nehe-miah, a zero, a "slut," and a "sly bitch" (57, 71). As *dessa* she is self-defined, elusive, intelligent, able to resist opposition; she has community, friends, and the potential for love and freedom. Which will she choose? The answer to this question composes the first full line of text in the next section of the novel.

In a statement introduced by ellipses are the words "*I chooses me Dessa*" (75, Williams's italics). Charlie, a slave from Dessa's remem-bered past, speaks these words during a corn-shucking contest in which he chooses her as a member of his team. When we first read the words, we do not know who speaks them. This brief moment of ambiguity works to the benefit of the developing metatext as the eruption of the true-real transposes this discourse so that it speaks of Dessa's choice of subject positions.

Another example of transposed discursive action informs the reader of the metatext that Odessa will never return to the lifeworld of "The Darky" after her escape. As distance separates her from the slaveholders' pursuit, rain washes away "all trace of Odessa . . . she would not be a slave anymore in this world," or rather, this *life*world (71, 87). The first part of this quote is from Nehemiah's rendition of the escape episode on the last page of "The Darky." The rest of the quote appears in "The Wench." Just as readers of the surface text combine fragmented elements of a story in order to get the full tale, readers of the metatext also combine them. Although several pages separate these two sentences, they are each a part of the stories that recount Dessa's escape to freedom. They func-tion as two components of one event. Similarly Charlie's statement, "I chooses me Dessa," serves as a component within an event of choice that undergirds the surface narrative of "The Darky" and resolves the pri-mary question of its metatext.

The Wench

And then the rain came up, driven by a furious wind, lashing the needlelike drops into our faces; washing away all trace of Odessa. . . . They had come for her at night. Nathan, Cully, and Harker, whom she hadn't known. Jemina, praising the Lawd in scared whispers, had opened the cellar door and

unlocked her chains. Free, and scrambling up the steep steps, Dess had focused all of her attention on the stranger's whispered instructions, refusing to think beyond the next step. She was free and she walked on, mindful of his hand on her arm, uncaring of anything else save his cautions and the putting of one foot in front of the other. Silently she thanked the Lawd, Legba, all the gods she knew, for Harker and Cully and Nathan, for Jemina herself. She would not be a slave anymore in this world.—(71, 86–87)

This scene contains the second mention of the name *Dess* within the novel. It signals to the reader that a fourth subject position executes the protagonist's escape form the dark cellar. *Dess* fuels the protagonist's desire for freedom and provides her with the necessary mobility, focus, and passion she needs for success. The commodification of Dessa's body in "The Darky" strips her of the capacity to feel and respond to her own desires. Slavery holds *dess* prisoner, and Nehemiah calls her a "slut" (71). "The Darky's" hostile environment obstructs the low-intensity deep talk of the name and prevents it from entering that lifeworld or even being acknowledged correctly.

Only moments of desire, sensuality, love, and intimacy motivate the appearance of this subject position within the surface text. As the protagonist struggles to escape, *dess* keeps her focused on two things: securing her freedom and a man's touch. Just as in the prologue, *dess* is associated with the protagonist's interaction with a male figure (presumably Harker). She is unaware of anything besides his hand on her arm, his instructions, and her own lust for freedom. After the description of her escape, the name *Dess* disappears from the surface text until the final section of the novel. Its voice remains within the dream-lifeworld, shaping memories and influencing action covertly.

This type of covert activity opens this section of the novel. Since the subject position *dess* executes the escape, it controls the narrator's voice in the opening dream sequence. (In fact, the only time we hear its voice in "The Wench" or "The Darky" is when it merges with that of the narrator through internal monologues or dreams.) The description of a corn-husking contest reflects sexualized images of the black female body. This objectification of females through sexual innuendo and humor dominates the first few pages of the section. Through the voice of *dess*, the narrator describes the character Zenobia as "long booty" because she has "ass-for-days." Alex, who "was obviously courting," chooses her as a member of his team. When Charlie selects Dessa, someone comments that "Charlie going [to] try for 'Youth' now he done lost 'Booty' " (74–75). The narrator describes another character, Martha as " 'Booty' and 'Beauty' " (77). The courting ritual simulated here is similar to the ritualistic games of insult known as *signifying, specifying*, and *playing the dozens*. Its use through naming in this scene presents the female body as a site of play, an object at the center of community bonding, and the source of laughter. This type of wordplay promotes intimacy between those present, and no one takes the game seriously. Although it produces a discourse of objectification, this objectification is distinct from the protagonist's experiences as a reproductive machine in the lifeworld of "The Darky."

The primary name-entity of the metatext rejects both forms of objectification through a choice of roles: "I chooses me Dessa." The fact that another character within the dream, not the protagonist nor the voice of *dess*, speaks these words in the surface text confirms this rejection. The name-entity who chooses plays no part in the sexualized game and, therefore, does not speak within the surface events of this memory. We meet this entity only after the objectifying games of the dream sequence ends.

The procreative and nurturing energy manifested by this so far nameless entity functions through a maternal subjectivity. Operating beneath the surface text, it mitigates and eventually eliminates Dessa's role as wench (breeder) and its objectifying deep talk entirely. This name-entity emerges later in the surface text as a distinct, fifth subject position called *Dessa Rose*. Although unfamiliar to the protagonist at first, *dessa rose* stands firmly in opposition to anything that hinders its matrilineal focus and autonomy, even if it is *just* a ritualistic game of community bonding.

Through the use of internal monologue, the protagonist's dream-lifeworld initially controls a great deal of this section's narration, but this worldview loses its ability to mandate the text when the white woman,

Rufel, assumes control of the narrator's voice. As a result, the defining elements of Rufel's worldview inform the life of the word in "The Wench," a lifeworld that maintains the hierarchical master/slave relationships of the previous section with only a few modifications. In this lifeworld, Rufel renames the protagonist "the wench," "the girl," and "the colored girl" (91, 90).

In addition to denoting Dessa in the surface text, "The Wench" identifies a lifeworld where runaways owe their status as ~~free~~ people to a white woman. I employ Derrida's method of identifying a word under erasure—~~free~~ (i.e., free/not free)—to illustrate the tenuous nature of the fugitives' choice, freedom, mobility, and self-determination. Although Rufel allows the fugitives something akin to freedom while at Sutton's Glen (she does not chain anyone to an elm tree or lock anyone in a dark cellar), outside of that space they are looked upon as slaves and subordinates.

Even within Sutton's Glen they are, on occasion, treated as slaves. When Rufel instructs the protagonist to expose the scars of a beating she suffered while enslaved, Rufel acts out the role of master. Dessa compares Rufel's behavior to that of a slave master: "You know they would sometimes make the slave strip when they put them up for auction, stand them up naked, man or woman, for all to see. . . . This the first thing flashed in my mind when Nathan told me she wanted to see them scars, that Miz Lady had to *see* the goods before she would buy the story" (189, Williams's italics). Rufel's inability to interact consistently with the blacks on her plantation as equals renders this lifeworld one of pseudo-freedom and false securities.

Rufel's power as a slave master, represented by her figure standing above Dessa's bed, forces Dessa to withdraw the first time she sees her. Just as in "The Darky," the subject position *dessa* as a speaking entity does not immediately enter the new lifeworld; only her name does. Doris Davenport suggests that "postpartum delirium and illness" cause Dessa's silence.[7] Mary Kemp Davis offers a different psychological reason: amnesia. Although both Davis's and Davenport's clinical explanations for Dessa's silence and withdrawal are correct, there exists one other reason. This is the lifeworld of "The Wench," a world that the subject position *dessa* senses as hostile simply because a white woman controls it: "White woman was everything I feared and hated" (169). This fear and hate restrict *dessa*; therefore, the subject position hesitates before exposing itself through speech. Although both the narrator and the blacks on Sutton's Glen address this entity by name, they cannot coax it into the lifeworld of their existence. Instead, *dessa* remains silent and distanced.

Dessa's delirium provides a narrative space wherein the eruption of the true-real (the emergence of names as icons of meaning) begins. In her delusional state, Dessa sees images she cannot explain, hears voices she does not recognize, and finds comfort in the name *Harker*, a person she has somehow forgotten—a name she knows but does not know. Although Dessa repeats the name because it gives her comfort, it does not release her from her delusions. It only complicates them and prevents the true-real from emerging. This failure indicates the gendered and maternally focused nature of the true-real in this text. Since it cannot emerge through a male name, Dessa's amnesia (and distancing) continues until Rufel's repetition of the name *Mammy* triggers a moment of control.

This name's deep talk speaks of familial bloodlines and communal bonding that remind the protagonist of her personal history. When Rufel uses the name, she violates these cultural meanings. For her, *Mammy* is a pet name denoting a black woman she remembers mothering her, a woman who loved her *like* a mother but who was not her mother. As Rufel repeats the familiar name, *dessa* awakens, so to speak. The scene unfolds like a dramatic dénouement. Rufel talks while our protagonist lies in the feather bed listening silently. The repeated violation of the name's cultural imprint infuriates *dessa*, who uses that anger to force her voice into the lifeworld of "The Wench" and subvert its linguistic foundations. " 'Wasn't no "mammy" to it.' *The words burst from Dessa. . . .* 'Mammy ain't made you nothing! . . . You don't even know mammy' " (118, emphasis added). Even though the protagonist knows the difference between the woman Rufel mentions and her own mother, her subject position as *dessa* finds strength in the chaotic nature of the poetic name's referential proliferation. Dessa uses the name to irritate and frustrate a woman whom she despises.

Mammy, as used by the protagonist, is a caricature of Rufel's word that parodies and challenges the original word's intent. Because Rufel hears only one side of the name's multidirectional, double-voiced deep talk, the volleying of the name between her and Dessa creates confusion and hysteria that eventually result in Rufel's personal crisis and jeopardize her role as a namer:

> "You don't even know 'mammy's' name. Mammy have a name, have children."
>
> "She didn't." The white woman, finger stabbing toward her own heart, finally rose. "She just had me! I was like her child."
>
> "What was her name then?" Dessa taunted. "Child don't even know its own mammy's name. What was mammy's name? What—"
>
> "Mammy," the white woman yelled. "That was her name."
>
> "Her name was Rose," Dessa shouted back, struggling to sit up. "That's a flower so red it look black. When mammy was a girl they named her that count of her skin—smooth black." (119)

Dessa's insistence that a smooth blackness defines *Rose*, her mother's true name, excludes Rufel's familial association with the woman immediately. Rufel's inability to counter *dessa's* assault with the name of her mammy inflames this exclusion. Like Nehemiah earlier, her memory fails her—*dessa* still controls the world of memory. The effects of this name play and memory control are transformational, with each woman responding differently. Dessa discovers that her familial history and memories are the most meaningful forms of self-confirmation she knows.

The eruption of the true-real in this scene gives the protagonist an iconic analogy of familial continuity, the poetic name *mammy*, around which she organizes her memories and validates her newly recovered voice. Within the lifeworld of "The Wench," the name, as defined by Dessa, is an aberrant concept, a foreclosed meaning, whose deep talk brings with it a marginal discourse of familial relations. It gives the protagonist a matrilineal subjectivity and voice that she lacked previously. Because Dessa recognizes the benefits of this discourse, she gains the strength to reclaim her maternal past. She assumes her mother's voice, calling the names of each of her siblings as Rose once did, "lest her poor, lost children die to living memory as they had in her world" (119).

The names Dessa calls speak of living memories that fill the gap between name and history forced upon her in "The Darky." By calling the names of her siblings, she can envision their shared struggles as struggles won through her survival. Even after Rufel leaves the room, *dessa* continues listing names, forging life and voice where death and silence once reigned. Only then does the protagonist speak her own "true" name for the first time. A repressed subject position emerges and proclaims her secret name proudly, "Dessa, *Dessa Rose*, the baby girl" (120, emphasis added).

This name-entity defines itself neither through a man's love nor by association within a community of slaves, but through a subjectivity originating from her mother. As a subject position, *dessa rose* is what her mother left her—an ancestral foundation for self-definition informed by a historical past. The name's deep talk speaks of this past, its beauty, and its pride. Because Rufel leaves the room prior to the emergence of this name, the voice of this subject position speaks within a monologue. This type of self-presentation, as I discuss earlier in this chapter, is a distancing device that keeps the subject position and its name secret. Unlike the name-entity *dessa*, *dessa rose* does not remain in the lifeworld of "The Wench"; nor does she speak her name again in this section of the novel.

Although Rufel questions Dessa about her name later in "The Wench," the protagonist answers using the voices of the name-entity *odessa*: " 'Dessa, Dessa Rose, ma'am,' she said in a raspy voice" (139). Here the subject position *odessa* merges with an identity introduced previously as the *darky* and *devil woman*. Several textual clues direct this reading. The narrator describes the protagonist's voice as "raspy," repeating the description of *odessa's* first spoken words in the previous section. The protagonist's mannerisms, however, repeat those used earlier by the *darky* (who controls the body). The narrator even uses that name when describing her: "The darky kept her eyes downcast." In addition, Rufel questions the protagonist just as Nehemiah did earlier and experiences the same type of memory loss. She forgets the name *Dessa Rose*, calls the protagonist *Odessa*, and continues using *Dessa* or *Odessa*, among other names, even after *dessa rose* shares her secret name near the end of the novel. Since the master's worldview and lack of memory determine the agency of onomastic deep talk in this lifeworld, the situation dictates that *odessa* (the voice of subservience) respond to Rufel's questions, not the self-empowered *dessa rose* or the deceptively stoical *devil woman*. At the end of "The Wench," the *devil woman* or *darky*, subsumed here by *odessa*, doffs the mask of submission to redefine the voice of *odessa*. I demonstrate how and why later in this reading.

Rufel experiences the discourse production of the names *Mammy* and *Rose* quite differently from the protagonist. Note the play on the verb *rose* and the name *Rose* in these excerpts from the passage in which Dessa makes her challenge: "The white woman, finger stabbing toward her own heart, *finally rose*. 'She just had me! I was like her child.'" And later, "'*Her name was Rose*,' Dessa shouted back, struggling to sit up. 'That's a flower so red it look black. . . . smooth black'" (119, emphasis added). Through the phrase *finally rose* and the sentence "*Her name was Rose*" the metatext signals the emerging of a new voice—the maternal voice that the protagonist recognizes and later assumes. Within the metatext, this discursive play also manipulates the identity of Rufel, ironically connecting her to Dessa's mother. Rufel points to herself, her own heart, as if the words "finally rose" mean that she finally *becomes* Rose or, at least, finally acknowledges her heart's desired association with Rose. Rufel, weakened by her inability to validate herself within the sphere of matrilineal subjectivity set before her, fails to justify her right to this association.

The strongest obstacles facing her are familial awareness and cultural relativism. Here I imply an inclusion within both black familial relations and communal languages that are distinct from (and often exclusive of) whites. Rufel lacks an understanding of *Mammy* as a name that masks a historical being whose familial relations are black. This entire scene signifies upon a historical unnaming (and misnaming) of black women traceable to the Middle Passage. Furthermore, Dessa's use of the name *Rose* asserts that, in this case, only race can be a valid indicator of one's familial associations. The scene disavows associations assumed by white women and men who, during and after slavery, knew nothing of the black women they unnamed, yet they insisted upon calling them

Mammy. Many of these whites had little or no concern for the histories, familial relations, or even the names of the women whom they stripped of personal identity. The deep talk produced by *dessa's* vicious name play announces a truth that advocates cultural relativity—or more precisely, "smooth" blackness and a respect for true names—as a necessary prerequisite for calling a black woman *Mammy*.

Through this scene's name play, Rufel unwittingly discovers that the familial history she recalls is alien and superfluous—destructive to her socially constructed self-perception. The eruption of the true-real within the name *Mammy* forges an identity gap that decenters Rufel's historical memory of receiving a black woman's maternal nurturing and proves Dessa's claim that "Mammy ain't made you nothing!" In fact, Rufel's misreading of her own history, her alienation from historical truth, is what makes her "nothing." Instead of producing a discourse of familiarity, the names *Mammy* and *Rose* produce deep talk that first provokes Rufel's erroneous personal identification with Mammy and later exposes the elements of fabrication and denial supporting it.

"Had Mammy minded when the family no longer called her name? Was that why she changed mine? . . . Was what [Rufel] had always thought loving and cute only revenge, a small reprisal for all they'd taken from her?" (129). Dorcas, the slave, renames the child known as Ruth Elizabeth by discarding her birth name and replacing it with one of her own design. Like the relationship between them, Rufel is a fabricated name (created, in part, from the word *rueful*, meaning "sorrow"). Most of the previous situations of name fragmentation in the text result from renaming rituals initiated by obvious hostile intent; but in this case, intimacy and love mask the deep talk of a less obvious hostility. In Rufel's worldview, her symbolic rebirth at the bosom of Dorcas justifies her right to unname the slave and call her *Mammy*: "She had been taken to that cushiony bosom, been named there 'Fel, Rufel" (124). As the irony of this situation reveals itself, revelations unfold that eventually redefine Dorcas as a maid and a nigger. These same revelations cause Rufel to question the real motivations behind her childhood renaming.

Although Rufel wants to maintain her fantasy relationship with Dorcas, her socially constructed self-perception preempts any desire to be the child of Mammy, the slave. She cannot see herself as a "pickaninny" or as someone intimately connected to the plight of those who descended from a black female slave: thus her sudden recollection that Dorcas was not a mammy at all, but a personal maid who had once traveled in France. Rufel elevates the character's social position so that her association with Dorcas is superior to that of the black children she calls "street urchins." To further inflate Dorcas's social position, Rufel recalls that her family named the black woman *Mammy* because it was more prestigious "to have an old servant named Mammy than to have a 'French' maid who couldn't talk French" (129). In this lifeworld, hierarchical social relations outweigh gendered and familial ones, especially false perceptions of the familial. Although Rufel eventually accepts Dorcas's identity as a slave and redefines their relationship as one involving a maidservant and a friend, she does not relinquish her use of the name *Mammy*. She simply redefines it in a futile attempt to maintain her role as namer.

The first subversion of Rufel's role as namer occurs through the manipulation of deep talk within the name *wench*. This epithet, previously introduced in "The Darky" where its deep talk speaks of the protagonist's role as a breeder "ready to be brought to light," is quite inappropriate when speaking of Dessa in this lifeworld (32). This is due, in part, to the name utterances that construct the section's metatext. Deborah E. McDowell credits the use of this inappropriate epithet to Dessa's continued misnaming.[8] I agree, but for slightly different reasons. Instead of denoting Dessa's subject position as Rufel intends, the epithet *wench* functions refractively (it points back to its source), highlighting Rufel's fear of Dessa's youth and the possible sexual attention she might attract. In the metatext, the character identified by the subtitle is not Dessa as we might assume, but Rufel.

The most telling incident supporting this reading of the name occurs at the end of the section. Dessa catches Rufel in bed with Nathan and calls her *Miz Ruint*, a diminutive the fugitives use maliciously when speaking of Rufel amongst themselves. It speaks of the woman's mental state. "I knew you was a fool," Dessa says after calling Rufel out of her name. Since Rufel stands outside the interlocutory community of the fugitives, she does not understand the deep-level meanings of the name Dessa uses. In this instance, the signifying discourses of two name-entities merge to exclude Rufel from the community of namers that her role as master marginalizes. The narration gives us our interpretive direction here: " 'Miz Ruint!' *Odessa* repeated harshly, deliberately" (159, emphasis added). The narrator credits the speech to the name-entity *odessa*, but in the metatext we read the words and sentiments of the *devil woman* who was subsumed earlier by *odessa*. The rebellious spirit of the *devil woman* considers Nathan a part of her world, a comrade against the worldview of the master, a "brother" who aided her escape from the dark world of Adam Nehemiah. It sees Rufel only as an enemy. The protagonist uses this rebellious spirit and worldview to doff the mask of submission. Odessa, whose name represents hierarchical social relationships, speaks but does so with the venom of the *devil woman*.

Rufel interprets the name *odessa* uses, *Miz Ruint*, through an understanding of these hierarchical and adversarial social relationships. In the final line of the chapter, she contemplates the name: "Ruined, that was what the wench had said. Ruined. That was what she meant" (159). Reading these words literally, the *wench* in the lines above refers to whoever used the term *ruined*, and that person is not Dessa—she says, "Miz Ruint." Rufel is the only person using the verb *ruined*. She, not Dessa, has been socialized to think that sex with a black man somehow ruins a woman. Rufel's insistence upon defining herself through socialized constructions of racial relationships causes her to misread *odessa*'s onomastic loud talking and claim inadvertently the subject position of one who has sex without discernment—a promiscuous wench.

Rufel's role as namer is further subverted because she does not control the foreshadowing and homophonic discursive effects created by her own name. Dorcas renames the white child " 'Fel, Rufel," and *fell* is exactly what Rufel thinks she does when discovered in a sexual relationship with a black man. If we combine the most obvious elements of deep talk within each homophonic pet name—'Fel, Rufel (rueful), and Ruint—we read an intratextual foreshadowing of this section's final events as Rufel sees them: she "fell" to being "ruint," and she "rues" her fall.[9] She also "fails" to maintain control of this lifeworld's onomastic discourses. Again, the fall defined through the character's misreading of the name *Miz Ruint* is the most fatal. Rufel's misinterpretation of the name as a negative description of herself costs her control of the conceptual field of language permanently. She relinquishes it to the worldview of the fugitives whose use of the name *Miz Ruint* remains untarnished by Rufel's misreading. This "takeover" begins in the lifeworld of the novel's third and final section, "The Negress."

The Negress

I'd 'gone too far,' she [Ada] say, calling that white woman out her name. Miz Rufel been 'good to us.' Oh, yes, the white woman was 'Miz Rufel' to her then—when *she'd* been the main one started me calling the woman Miz Ruint in the first place. Anyway, far as I was concerned, that white woman was the one'd 'gone too far,' laying up with a black man. And Nathan. I was so mad at him, I could've *spit.*—
(164; Williams's italics)

The controversy surrounding the name *Miz Ruint* introduces *dessa*'s complete linguistic control in "The Negress." The tone of her words in the excerpt above cuts, slices, agitates, and collides with the names and attitudes that defined her existence up to this point. Both her actions and words suggest that a presentation of self seen only in fragments during the previous sections controls this lifeworld. The values, voice, and languages of the protagonist replace those of both the master and the other fugitives within the surface text. Dessa controls the narration, point of view, and story. She determines when and how her name is used and insists that others respect her role as namer, even if they do not always follow it. The worldviews and onomastic deep talk cloaked previously within monologues and dream-lifeworlds reveal their secrets to the reader openly. Now, appropriately armed for battle, Dessa aims her first attack at Rufel's name.

Almost immediately after the protagonist's opening statements, Rufel's name fragments, producing new meanings as well as new names. "Miz Lady—which is what we mostly called her amongst ourselves; to her face, it was always Mis'ess or Miz Rufel. But everyone, Nathan included, called her Miz Ruint, too—amongst ourselfs; this was the name

Annabelle give her. Both names meant about the same to me, though Ruint did fit her. Way she was living. . . . how *poor* she was" (164; Williams's italics). Still not associating the name *Ruint* with Rufel's reading of social and moral downfall, Dessa stylizes the name in this section through its capitalist associations. Rufel has no money and, therefore, no power. Her two-room house and empty bank account as well as her strange behavior define the contextual aims of the names she bears.

Although this section opens with Dessa's manipulation of Rufel's name, the most important statements of resistance constructed by onomastic deep talk in this section have nothing to do with Rufel's various names. In the metatext, *dessa* struggles with a name assigned to a woman the reader might not consider important at all. As a matter of fact, this woman, a seamstress and caretaker of others, has died many years before the day the story begins; but it is through her name, *Dorcas*, that we read and understand the hidden messages of the novel's radical name play. Prior to the role-playing scam enacted by characters in this section, Dorcas is nothing more than a memory, surfacing occasionally without ever appearing "in the flesh"—or so it seems. Tracing this name reveals otherwise. The name is biblical and appears in Acts of the Apostles 9:36–41:

> Now in Joppa there was a disciple whose name was Tabitha, which in Greek is Dorcas. She was devoted to good works and acts of charity. / At that time she became ill and died. When they had washed her, they laid her in a room upstairs. / Since Ladda was near Joppa, the disciples, who heard that Peter was there, sent two men to him with the request, "Please come to us without delay." / So Peter got up and went with them; and when he arrived, they took him to the room upstairs. All the widows stood beside him, weeping and showing tunics and other clothing that Dorcas had made while she was with them. / Peter put all of them outside, and then he knelt down and prayed. He turned to the body and said, "Tabitha, get up." Then she opened her eyes, and seeing Peter she sat up. / He gave her his hand and helped her up. Then calling the saints and widows, he showed her to be alive.

The biblical Dorcas is a seamstress and caretaker of others who dies and is raised from the dead by the apostle Peter. He reinstates her presence in the lives of those who thought she was gone forever. As a result of the role-playing enacted in the final chapters of this novel, Dessa becomes the caretaker for whom Rufel has longed. Although a complex and reciprocal relationship develops between Dessa and Rufel, the role-playing scam metaphorically resurrects Dorcas in the figure of Dessa, if only briefly.

The resurrection of Dorcas begins in "The Wench." Rufel contemplates the possibility that Dessa's mother Rose and her Dorcas are the same person. By focusing on two names and their relationship with color, she considers the possibility: "What had the colored girl called her Mammy? *Rose*. Dorcas. *Rose—smooth black*. . . . Dorcas. Rose?" (130, Williams's italics). Rufel's use of names merges the two characters, and beneath the surface text, the names *Dorcas* and *Rose* also merge. If we remove the end punctuation separating these names, the quoted material reads: Rose Dorcas Rose—smooth black Dorcas Rose. Through the discourse production of these names, Rufel calls out to the subject position *dorcas*, and (like *dessa*) *dorcas* rose.[10] The discursive force that Rufel's words animate functions as a name-entity that seeks a physical body. Its search ends when Dessa agrees to play the role of mammy in "The Negress."

Our second clue in decoding the discursive relationship between *Dorcas* and *Dessa* is the author's choice of subheading, "The Negress." The surface text defines *negress* as a French word meaning "black woman." This reference to the word as a French term recalls Rufel's description of Dorcas as a " 'French' maid who couldn't talk French." The epigraph, written in French, reinforces this connection, setting the stage for Dorcas's embodied resurrection: "Ma négresse, voulez-vous danser, voulez-vous danser avec moi, ici?" (20). When Harker asks Dessa to dance (in French) and she does not understand him, the association between the two names and characters strengthens. Dessa's role-playing completes the resurrection. Like Dorcas, she is a black woman who does not speak French and who serves in the role of maid and mammy.

This brief resurrection endangers Dessa's freedom (Nehemiah almost recaptures her), her life (to return means to hang), her generations (her true name will not pass on). *Dorcas* contains a sociotypical desire that relays a message of warning vital to African Americans during the era in which this text was written and published. Blacks, female and male, of the 1980s lived in a world that seemed to want to resurrect a past many had fought hard to overcome, a past thought of as a memory—shadows, gone forever. The sociotypical deep talk of the name *Dorcas* warns black Americans to beware of playing roles that can strip one of power and identity, roles that seem to forget "the struggle," roles that lead to the repetition of a dangerous past—life-threatening roles that impose and demand a facade of submission yet play into a politics of self-denial and social regression.

By choosing to name a memory *Dorcas*, Williams develops Dessa's ability to control and determine the world of her existence through resistance. Although this character "plays at" being mammy and maid, the resurrection of Dorcas never achieves permanence. This is *dessa's* world; she controls both the arena of memory and language. Dessa tames the influencing power of the name-entity by not allowing its memory nor the hierarchical social values of its deep talk to exist in her personal relationship with Rufel outside of the role-playing scam. By novel's end, Rufel understands this and joins Dessa in rejecting the implications of Dorcas's return. Instead of a resurrection installed with previously established hierarchical social value, the characters Dessa and Rufel achieve an egalitarian friendship that precludes adherence to socialized identities.

Just as Dessa briefly assumes the role of the " 'French' maid who couldn't talk French," other characters adopt uncharacteristic roles as well (129). Cully plays the role of Rufel's white brother from Charleston; Nathan plays the role of a driver; Rufel plays the role of a "quiet and respectable," "high-class lady"; and the others play the role of property for sale (199). As the characters role-play, the utterances of signifying names interact more than ever to inform and restrict socialized power relations.

The names *Mistress* and *Odessa, Dessa* and *Miz Lady* (*Mis'ess* or *Miz Rufel*) represent not only the individuals signified by the names but the power relations between master and slave, free black and free white, respectively. The dialogical exchanges among these words occur so frequently within the text that a battle between hierarchical and egalitarian control appears within the discourse of the metatext. This battle ends after Nehemiah misrecognizes or, rather, misnames, Rufel. He calls her *Miz Janet*, the name of a society woman and member of the "planter aristocracy" mentioned earlier in "The Darky" (28). Rufel's misnaming is an instance of unnaming that "calls out to" a bond of slaveholding relations (master/mistress), which does not achieve the effect Nehemiah hopes. Rufel continues to claim that Dessa is not the slave he is hunting.

Next Nehemiah calls Rufel "out of her name"; he calls her *slut*: " 'You-all in this together' . . . 'womanhood' . . . 'All alike. Sluts' " (232). Through these misogynist statements Nehemiah characterizes Rufel and Dessa in a manner that negates all hierarchical relations between them. Their moral character is attacked on a level of debasement where there is no master (except for white males) and no slave. In this space of gendered sameness, they accept the names preferred by each other and repeat them together: " 'My name is Ruth,' she say, 'Ruth. I ain't your mistress.' . . . 'Well, if it come to that,' I told her, 'my name Dessa, Dessa Rose. Ain't no *O* to it.' . . . 'Ruth,' 'Dessa,' we said together" (232–33). Note that Ruth does not speak Dessa's secret name; she says *Dessa*, not *Dessa Rose*. *Dessa Rose* remains evasive, indicating that not even this version of Rufel (Ruth) can accept fully the demand for equality and respect that speaks through it.

Prior to this moment of reconciliation (and renunciation), the use of names in the role-playing and out-of-role-playing portrayals of master and slave and "partners in crime" parallel the hierarchical status of the characters. Dessa carefully uses the right name, *Mistress*, when in character as a maid and mammy, but she blurs the boundaries between the white woman's names when she is out of character. This blurring signifies the tenuous nature of her status as a free individual, given her physical location in a world of slaves and enslavers. Rufel, on the other hand, does not recognize the differences as associated with role-playing; she uses the names *Dessa* and *Odessa* in both situations. For Rufel, the distinction between the names does not depend on *where* she uses each name but *how* she uses them.

When assaulted by the intoxicated Mr. Oscar, Rufel uses both names together: " 'Dessa,' she called. 'Odessa, help me get this man out the bed' " (200). The sense of the name *Dessa* is one of familiarity. Rufel uses it in response to the nickname *Mis'ess* used earlier by the protagonist in the same scene. The name *Odessa*, on the other hand, opens a command and speaks of a master/slave relationship. These characters maintain the hierarchical relationship of master/slave in this manner throughout the remainder of the text. For Rufel, *Dessa* identifies the black woman's subject position as a friend, while *Odessa* represents the slave and ~~free~~ fugitive.

A refined utterance develops within the textual spaces of the name *Dessa* later in the novel. In the jail scene, Rufel uses both names again. She enters the jail and addresses the sheriff, asking, "Is somebody trying to steal Dessa?" A few lines later she calls to the woman behind bars: "Odessa! . . . You come out of there right this minute!" (226). The name *Dessa* in the first quote is a name with an "undercover" sideward glance toward freedom. It anticipates Nehemiah's claim that the protagonist is a runaway. The sentence also contains a loophole, *steal*, that provides the name with a new contextual aim and a new utterance, suggesting that in order for anyone to claim *dessa* as property they must first steal her freedom. The hierarchical social relationships indicated by the names remain untouched by the new deep talk of *Dessa*. Just as in the previous example, *Odessa* indicates a master/slave relationship, and *Dessa* indicates a more egalitarian one.

The protagonist never accepts the subject position *odessa* as she does the other subject positions represented by her various names. As mentioned earlier, the historical content of inhumanity, vacuity, and hierarchical submission associated with *Odessa* must never become defining elements of the poetic words *Dess*, *Dessa*, or *Dessa Rose*. " 'Ain't no *O* to it' " (323). Mae Gwendolyn Henderson comments that "Dessa's repudiation of the *O* (Otherness?) signifies her always already presence—what Ralph Ellison describes as the unquestioned humanity of the slave." [11] Throughout the novel, *Dessa* and *Dessa Rose* maintain onomastic desires that struggle to achieve equality, resistance, pride, subversiveness, and multiple "human" subjectivities. The protagonist accepts these names as subject positions of empowerment and self-definition long before the opening lines of "The Negress." The discursive veracity and fecundity they represent make possible her "rise" within the lifeworld of "The Wench." Her acceptance of them gives her the confidence and vitality she needs to embrace that part of herself called *dess*.

This name and subject position makes brief appearances in each lifeworld, excluding "The Darky." Its appearance within "The Negress" maintains its original contextual aims, especially its sexually focused tasks. Just as before, *dess* enters the surface text during situations of male/female intimacy and bonding. Harker beckons this subject position and coaxes it into the lifeworld of "The Negress." " 'Dess,' he say and it was like he'd never called my name before, just 'Dess,' soft like that" (187). The protagonist experiences a sensual awareness of the name similar to her experiences earlier when Kaine coaxes *dessa* into the lifeworld of "The Darky."

After the subject position *dess* enters the surface text of "The Negress," the protagonist becomes more physically focused. She compares Kaine's body with both Nathan's and Harker's: "Kaine was slight built; hugging him was like hugging a part of myself. Harker wasn't big like Nathan—Nathan's muscles bulged like a stuffed cotton sack" (190). When the name appears again a few pages later, the protagonist's narration of her experiences and actions once again becomes sexually oriented. "Dess," Harker says, "Voice quiet as the night. . . . His head was right by my leg and he turned and lifted my dress, kissed my thigh. Where his lips touched was like fire on fire and I trembled" (191). The provocative nature of the passions, desires, and freedoms spoken from within the name *Dess* bring the protagonist face-to-face with her own sexuality for the first time since the prologue.

Throughout the novel the estrangement between the subject position *dess* and the protagonist cloaks sexuality. Like a secret name, this cloaking device prevents anyone other than the protagonist from defining her sexuality. Keeping it secret impedes the possible stereotypical sexual identities that her designation and roles as breeder in "The Darky," wench in "The Wench," and mammy in "The Negress" might impose upon her. In "The Negress" she subverts the idea of asexuality usually associated with mammy figures (and Dorcas) by removing the cloak and sharing *dess* with a man.

The narrative use of estrangement between the protagonist and the poetic name *dess* also subverts possible misreadings of her behavior. Without an interpretive consideration of this secret name, a reader might easily conclude that the protagonist's violent reaction to Nathan and Rufel's sexual intimacy results from her own interest in this man. The character Harker draws this conclusion and asks, "You liking Nathan for your man now?" (187). Dessa is incapable of such desires during her outburst because she and *dess* are not yet integrated in "The Wench." Harker, not Nathan, acts as a catalyst for the reintegration of the protagonist with this subject position. Only after that reintegration does she possess the ability to desire more than familial affections with a man. She tells us this following her first kiss with Harker. "Kaine had been my dream and I didn't spect to do no more dreaming about a man—least not no time soon. Yet, there I was, casting eyes at someone else [Harker]" (191). Dessa reacts to Harker's reading of her anger by laughing and reducing the implications of his question to something similar to a ritualistic insult (as practiced in the game of verbal agility called *the dozens*). "I laughed. . . . 'That's all it come down to, huh? . . . Somebody fumbling under somebody else's cloths'" (187)? The reason for her anger is not that simple.

Dessa's affection for Nathan stems from her love for him as a brother figure. "I had a powerful feeling for him, but as a brother; he was like a brother to me" (187). Even after her integration with *dess*, the protagonist expresses no physical attraction to Nathan. To her, his body looked "like a stuffed cotton sack" (190). Later in the narrative, when Nathan attempts to heal their broken friendship, he uses the name *Dess*: "Dessa—Dess, why can't I like you and her, too?" The protagonist rejects the use of her once secret name within the context of their friendship. More specifically, her awareness of *dess* as the sexual part of herself causes her to read Nathan's statement as a suggestion that she play the role of the other woman. "It seemed to me that one rubbed out the other," she tells the reader (205). Her ability to make this distinction and choose how and when *dess* influences her choices indicates her complete integration with and control over this subject position.

By novel's end, Dessa and Ruth stand together in full acceptance of their true selves and with mutual respect for each other. Both women accept the humanity and equality of the other, both acknowledge and respect the other's name, and both understand the hazards of nurturing their friendship within a society that devalues such bonds of friendship. Because of southern slavery and social pressures demanding segregation of free blacks and whites during this period, the two women are not allowed to remain together without compromising their relationship. The only socially acceptable role for whites desiring harmonious interactions with free blacks in Arcopolis is that of protector, not friend. "We couldn't hug each other, not on the streets, not in Arcopolis, not even after dark; we both had sense enough to know that" (233).

Arcopolis. This name contains a sideward glance that forces the reader to look a second time at the name *Odessa*—this time reading the discourses produced by the distinctions these two names share. Both words have Greek origins, and both stand at the end of the text as unresolved anomalies with political and social significance for the characters. *Odessa*, a name derived from an ancient Greek colony called *Odessos*, is the capital of a seaport city located on the northwest coast of the Black Sea. Its mixed population consists of Ukrainians, Jews, and nonwhite (or ethnic) Russians. The continual appearance of *Odessa* within this novel seems unresolved until we read it against the name *Arcopolis*. Only then can we "hear" the meanings associated with peaceful interracial coexistence nestled deeply within the utterances of *Odessa*.

The lexical meaning of the word *acropolis* informs the deep talk of its derivative, *Arcopolis*, and guides my interpretation of that name. In ancient Greece, the acropolis was a fortress perched upon a city's highest point, well out of the reach of the city's enemies. The acropolis of ancient Greek cities (such as Athens) was the last defensive stronghold. The word's mutated appearance in this text, *Arc*opolis (note the spelling change from *acr* to *arc*), contains a graphic imprint that signifies the last object of attack. The discourse production of the two names, *Arcopolis* and *Odessa*, designates the world beyond Sutton's Glen as the next place of attack against the dehumanizing effects of slavery, prejudice, and racial hostilities. Peaceful integration and coexistence are impossible until those within the last defensive stronghold of oppression surrender. Dessa Rose explains it this way in the epilogue: "Negro can't live in peace under protection of law, got to have some white person to stand protection for us. And who can you friend with, love with like that? Oh, Ruth would've tried it; no question in my mind. Maybe married Nathan—if he'd asked her . . . but Ruth went East and we all come West" (236).

The epilogue of *Dessa Rose* ends with the protagonist contemplating the story of her history, repeating it, naming it. None of her various names appear; only her memories and her voice do. "I never will forget Nemi trying to read me," she says. "Well, this the childrens have heard from our own lips" (236). Nehemiah's attempts to "read" *Dessa Rose* fail because he reads the metatext of a name *he* creates and owns (inscribes and ascribes, to borrow from Henderson), not the name she creates and lives through. Dessa's story proves that the only definitions of self important enough to value are the ones defined from within oneself, the place and origin of all "secret" names.

6

Reading Ernest Gaines's
A Gathering of Old Men

A GATHERING OF *Old Men* plays out a mission which *Dessa Rose* merely suggests through the deep talk of two names, *Arcopolis* and *Odessa*. While the characters in Williams's novel leave the acropolis of prejudice and racial hostility virtually unchallenged, the men of *A Gathering* organize a sortie against this last bastion of oppression. Like the characters in Williams's novel, they doff the shield of white protection; but, unlike Dessa and her friends, the black men in Gaines's novel arm themselves for further action. Of interest to this study is the peculiar weapon they choose in the final battle of a war waged first with empty guns. Surrounded by a courtroom of "enemy forces," they fight the acropolis of St. Raphael Parish with their names.

This novel is a montage of names, complete with lists and roll calls. Formal names, nicknames, pet names, diminutives, epithets, and phrase names come together to tell the story of old men who, after years of submissiveness, finally confront their oppressors. As noted by Joseph Griffin, Gaines's use of names reveals the growth of a community in transition "from uncertainty and fear to self-assurance and responsibility," a community of men "coming of age." [1] Manliness and black male empowerment stand at the forefront of this growth. The novel's primary name utterances speak of manhood as a motivating idea and confrontational self-respect as a method of action. The metatext develops these ideas, with internalized relational subjectivity taking a comfortable "back seat."

This is a major distinction between Williams's use of names and Gaines's. Through pivotal moments of renaming, *Dessa Rose* develops its protagonist's internalization of familial relations while resisting socialized black female identities. In Gaines's text, familial associations succumb to socialized identities of manhood and outward expressions of it through unnaming. Throughout the following pages, I note moments when such differences reveal themselves. I give particular attention to how poetic names influence the relationships between external and internal identity conflict as well as their impact upon intuitive and expressive change. My main focus, however, concerns the development of onomastic deep talk through the adoption of socialized ideas.

The characters of *A Gathering* face a dilemma they consider one of incomparable dimensions—a white man has been murdered by a black man. Although tensions between the white and black communities of St. Raphael Parish have always been high, never before has a black man been "bold" enough to kill a white man, especially not one of the nightriding, "Negro"-lynching Boutans. Everyone understands the repercussions of such an act to mean mayhem and perhaps death for not only the murderer but the other blacks in the parish as well. Even in the face of such potential danger, the old black men of St. Raphael respond to a call designed to protect the assumed killer. According to the instructions given by the white woman, Candy, who devises the plan, she and the old men stand together, each proclaiming that he or she killed Beau Boutan. Candy hopes to shield "her people" from harm by making it appear that the men, holding twelve-gauge shotguns with an empty number-five shell inside, are there to protect her. The old men see her call as an opportunity to protect one of their own and a chance to take a stand against those who have dominated and abused them all of their lives.

The controlling question or plot focus of the novel is, who killed Beau Boutan? Although everyone, including the reader, assumes that Mathu (Candy's black friend and substitute father figure) is the murderer, only Mathu knows who is really responsible for the death of the white man; only he knows the name that resolves the novel's puzzle. Through several incidents of role-playing, those claiming responsibility present various scenarios and motives for murder. As the list of the guilty grows, the novel's controlling question moves closer to its resolution. Even though Mathu remains virtually silent throughout the novel—never revealing what he knows of the incident—three answers emerge: one names a man, another names an idea, and a third names a method of action.

A Gathering of Old Men is a mystery that appears to defy a crucial law of mystery writing: do not resolve the mystery too early. In classic detective fiction and in the best whodunits, tensions build upon a gathering of facts and the withholding of a name. In Gaines's novel, this does not appear to happen. The novel exposes four suspects and four names within the first eighteen pages. The mystery seems solved by the beginning of the third chapter; we *know* that Mathu killed Beau Boutan. At this point, we assume that the remainder of the novel presents the success or failure of a cover-up. Later we discover that we have been deceived.

As readers, we buy into a delusional experience (role-playing) that allows the name of the man who killed Beau Boutan to avoid our grasp. Of course, this is what happens when we read only the surface level of action. Reading through the name *Mathu* reveals the story of a mystery unfolding. The name works beneath the surface text to subvert the assumed resolution that Mathu killed Beau Boutan. In the metatext, the name-entity *mathu* gathers facts about itself through constant interactions with other names and voices. The name continually acts and creates dramatic tension as it seeks to uncover the mystery of the novel's controlling question. Unlike the interactions of characters and names in William's novel, *mathu* is a subject position seeking its subject and true name, not a subject persona seeking its name and true position (social role). After a search that covers most of the text, the subject position *mathu* discovers its own "true" name.

Mathu, the Man Who Killed Beau Boutan

The name *Mathu* begins its journey speaking of an unknown. Its break with established naming patterns gives us our first clue to reading its deep talk. Chapter headings develop the most noticeable interpretive patterns involving names in Gaines's novel. They suggest the importance of discourses produced through informal and formal name play. A name introduces each of the novel's twenty chapters. Fifteen of these chapter headings follow the structural pattern of formal (or legal) name, "aka," informal name (diminutive or nickname). The remaining five chapters are headed by informal names and introduce a second (or third) monologue by a former speaker. For example, the first chapter is headed *"George Eliot, Jr. aka* Snookum" (Gaines's italics). The seventeenth chapter is headed "Snookum." Interestingly, Mathu's name does not serve as a title for any of the twenty chapters. This absence, or lack, sets him apart from the other central male characters and accentuates his virtual silence throughout the text. Because his name breaks with the pattern of naming established by the text, Mathu draws our attention. We ask *what is his "aka"* and discover that the name he bears is its own "other name," an "aka" whose movements and deep talk appear only within the metatext.

Mathu is the only major character whose surname we never learn. He also has no nickname.[2] Although Charlie addresses him as *Parrain* (a title meaning godfather) during the final pages of the novel, his full formal name remains a mystery. In this sense, *Mathu* denotes a subject persona whose formal name is unknown. The metatext takes full advantage of this mystery. There the truncated discourse that speaks of something "unknown" informs the name's function as the subject position of the man who killed Beau Boutan.

Because this subject position refers to an unknown, it can be assumed by anyone who claims responsibility for murder, with very few exceptions. Among its strongest textual constraints are gender and race. When Candy claims the role of murderer, the contextual aim of the name identifying that role excludes her as a viable candidate; she is a white female. The purpose of *mathu*'s search is to find a *man*, more specifically, a *black man*. Although Candy "plays at" being a murderer in the surface text, neither her name nor her voice enters the deep talk of the word *Mathu*. In the metatext, her name mocks her and *mathu* excludes her.

When the old men play the role of murderer, this does not happen. Clatoo's name, for instance, briefly fills the gap between subject position and true name when he says: "No use talking to Mathu. He didn't do nothing. I did it" (87). The name as subject position still refers to the man who killed Beau Boutan, and because Clatoo identifies himself as that man, he is *mathu*—at least in the metatext. This brief name and subject persona substitution brings with it information that stylizes *mathu*'s theme without affecting its object-oriented tasks. The name-entity *mathu* interacts with the role-playing character, gathers information concerning probable motives "the man" has for committing murder, and continues its search until it finds the right man. Clatoo claims he killed Beau because he was tired of "keeping [his] militance down" (87). This information becomes a part of *mathu*'s theme of militancy and rebellion against "the law," white laws embedded with white prejudice.

This discursive action repeats itself as each old man role-plays. Their names merge briefly with the subject position *mathu*; they provide it with a motive and, in return, they inherit the subject position's name and its defining elements. This is quite different from the subject positions *dessa*, *odessa*, *dess*, and *dessa rose* in Williams's novel. These names are not transitory or assumable; they denote at all times the protagonist, or an alter ego that is sometimes imposed. The use of these names by other characters offers the protagonist an awareness of situations where confrontation might occur while also offering her a way to assert herself through verbal play. They organize the various subjectivities from which Dessa chooses. The "aka" *mathu*, on the other hand, denotes several different characters at various times throughout the novel.

The subject position *mathu* moves through the text as an assumable energy that provides the old men with a vehicle for self-transformation. Each old man loses his formal name through a process of unnaming that encompasses the entire narrative. This unnaming transforms not only the information *mathu* gathers about itself but also the names of each old man. In *The Myth of the Negro Past*, Melville J. Herskovits comments that an African (male or female) may change his or her name as a rite "marking a new stage in his development" or on the occasion of "some striking occurrence in his life." [3] In *A Gathering*, name changes follow this West African naming custom. As the old men mature from fear and submission to confidence and aggression, their names change. Nicknames, the names through which the old men find voice and camaraderie, briefly become synonymous with *mathu, the man who killed Beau Boutan*, and replace formal names within the text. The surface text signals the progressive nature of this change by first merging nicknames and diminutives with the surnames. Grant Bello becomes Cherry Bello, Joseph Seaberry becomes Rufe Seaberry, Matthew Lincoln Brown becomes Mat Brown, Clabber becomes Clabber Hornsby, Bing becomes Bing Lejeune, and so forth. As the novel progresses, all remnants of family and formal names disappear from the text completely, leaving behind only redefined nicknames.

Billy Washington is one exception. This character does not loose his surname. Its deep talk functions differently from that of the other old men's formal names. He is the oldest member of the black community, and his family name speaks of honor and respect within the quarters— not of denied desires, as the others do. The name's interaction with the subject position *mathu* merely adds the idea of militancy and rejection of white prejudice to its deep talk. Another exception to the unnaming fragmentation of formal or family names occurs in cases where only full formal names identify characters. The character Jacob Aguillard is one such example. Only his family name disappears from the text. Because this character stood outside of the black community prior to the day the novel documents, he has no nickname. His redefined given name remains and functions like a nickname within the metatext.

Charlie's unnaming is the most profound of all. Murder is the materialization of this character's internal conflict, a striking out against abuse and an action that initiates a split between responsibility (man) and fear (boy). Before the opening line of the text, Charlie murders Beau and gives the murder weapon to Mathu, the only "real" man he has ever known. Through this act, he relinquishes his manhood and with it his intuitive understanding of himself as defined through the name he later adopts, *Mr. Biggs*. Not only does Charlie unname himself through this act, but he assigns the subject position of a murderer to a name other than his own. He renames *Mathu*. The ability of the subject position *mathu* to merge with other names and transform them begins with this initial fragmentation. Since these events take place outside the text proper, we read the deep talk of the revised name only after Mathu speaks.

In the novel's seventh chapter, the inactive and usually silent Mathu speaks of his guilt for the first time. "When the man get here, I'll turn myself in" (52). Unlike the other old men who subsequently assume the role of murderer, Mathu's confession is not a direct admission of guilt. His pensive behavior and laconic tone merely suggest or imply guilt. The voice of the subject position *mathu* motivates this confession by indirect admission. The protagonist's pensive state of mind during the scene is a focusing inward that signals a space within the surface text through which the voice of *mathu* enters. A fragmentation of the original name occurs as a result of two distinct voices—that of the subject persona (or character) and that of the name-entity *mathu*—merging and speaking within one contextual space.

In the confession, "the man" becomes a double-voiced phrase name through which Mathu, the subject persona, refers to Sheriff Mapes. Within the same unit of speech, the distinct voice of the subject position or name-entity *mathu* refers to "*the man*" who killed Beau Boutan. This dualistic interaction of voices within the confession produces two distinct utterances. On the surface, Mathu reveals that he will formally confess his guilt and play the role of a murderer when the sheriff arrives. In the metatext, the name-entity speaks and communicates a message concerning the intent of a self-seeking subject position. When *the man* who killed Beau Boutan arrives, the subject position *mathu* will turn itself in.

There is also an unwritten play on the descriptive terms *boy* and *man* within *mathu*'s announced intent that defines a dichotomy between two modes of being. The name's ability to supraname, unname, and rename other characters—its role as a discursive force—results from its interaction with individuals who develop from boyhood into manhood or who demonstrate that such growth has taken place. "When the man get here, I'll turn myself in," the voice of the *mathu* tells the reader, and this is exactly what happens. When the "real" murderer, Charlie, arrives at Mathu's house to explain how and why he killed Beau Boutan, he first announces that he is a man. His emphatic, spoken confession of personal growth separates him from the role-playing old men who do not identify themselves in this manner:

> "I'm a man, Sheriff," he said. "I'm a man." . . .
>
> "I want the world to know I'm a man. I'm a man, Miss Candy. I'm a man, Mr. Lou. I want you to write in your paper I'm a man."
>
> "I'll write it, Charlie," I said, looking up at him. He was three or four inches taller than I, and outweighed me, I'm sure, by at least a hundred pounds.

> "I'm a man," he said. "I want the world to know it. I ain't
> Big Charlie, nigger boy, no more, I'm a man. Y'all hear me?
> A man come back. Not no nigger boy. A nigger boy run and
> run and run. But a man come back. I'm a man." . . .
> "I'm a man, Sheriff," he said. "That's why I come back.
> I'm a man. Parrain. I'm a man, Parrain."
> Mathu, standing in the corner by the fireplace, nodded his
> white head.
> "You want to tell us about it, Charlie?" Mapes asked him.
> "I'll tell you about it, Sheriff," Charlie said. He started,
> then stopped, because something else had suddenly popped
> in his mind. "Sheriff, I'm a man," he said to Mapes. "And
> just like I call you Sheriff, I think I ought to have a handle,
> too—like Mister. Mr. Biggs." (186–87)

This passage offers several opportunities for comparison between *Dessa Rose* and *A Gathering*. The descriptive terms *man* and *boy* in the excerpt define two alter egos of the character Charlie. The names *Big Charlie* ("*nigger boy,*") and *Mr. Biggs* (the man who returned) represent subject positions controlling the actions of the character's conflicting alter egos. Each of these poetic names results from a moment of renaming that splits two internalized and hostile forces. Renaming in *Dessa Rose* also results in a subject position split. There, fragmentation produces not two but four separate subject positions (*dessa, dess, dessa rose,* and *odessa*). Like *big charlie* and *mr. biggs*, these subject positions speak through the narrative's metatext. Unlike *big charlie* and *mr. biggs*, none of the name-entities that result from Dessa's renaming stand in hostile conflict with the others.

The most diverse of the name-entities produced by renaming in *Dessa Rose* stands in the surface narrative as a memorial to a desired state of being. The name *Odessa* undermines its own use by alien speakers (or namers) by calling out to *dessa,* celebrating its successful resistance of a hostile influence (oh! dessa). The protagonist uses the subject position as a mask and a protective shield, never buying into the ruse herself. "I chooses me Dessa. . . . Ain't no *O* to it" (75, 244). Dessa never identifies herself as Odessa, keeping the two completely separate.

Charlie, on the other hand, loses the ability to distinguish between who he is and who he pretends to be. "I ain't Big Charlie, nigger boy, no more." His phrasing of this statement alludes to his past acceptance of a role he finds hostile to his intuitive self-image. Within the character, the two identities form a contradictory union. Instead of using a mask to fight the voice of an external force, Charlie internalizes the mask and suffers the psychological conflicts these diverse voices create within him.

His failure to resist external naming mutates his intuitive subject position as *mr. biggs*, erasing the name—but not its voice—from most of the novel. The position effects of *mathu* consume this subject position and unname *it*, not *big charlie*. This unnaming forecloses *Mr. Biggs* prior to the opening lines of the novel, leaving only *Charlie* to designate the subject persona. The name remains foreclosed until chapter 15 when the character admits to murder. Only then does *Big Charlie* enter the referential chain describing *mathu* and merge briefly with that subject position. Since *mathu* seeks a *man*, not the boy *Big Charlie* represents, it rejects the discourses that speak of unmanliness. This rejection fragments *Big Charlie* through renaming. Defining elements that designate a boy split off and are not a part of the new name's deep talk. In a moment of self-recognition and intuitive reflection, the name *Mr Biggs* emerges in the surface text. " 'Sheriff, I'm a man,' he said to Mapes. 'And just like I call you Sheriff, I think I ought to have a handle, too—like Mister. Mr. Biggs.' "

A second point of comparison between *A Gathering* and *Dessa Rose* demonstrated by Charlie's speech exists in the function of word repetition. Charlie's repetition of *man* validates a history of white naming privilege over black self-naming, whereas Dessa's repetition of *mammy*, during her verbal attack on Rufel, agitates and inverts this history and privilege. Unlike Dessa's outburst, which originates from self-confirmation, Charlie's originates from a need for confirmation outside of himself. His speech plays out the struggle of a black man who tries to convince a white world of his manhood, his humanity, and his human value. Dessa does not have this struggle, and any suggestion of it remains within the name she rejects, *Odessa*. Although the novel acknowledges a need for conquering the world beyond self and immediate community, this victory never becomes a requisite to Dessa's self-definition. For Charlie it is foundational.

Although Charlie and Dessa are accused of murdering their oppressors, there is a major difference between how they assert their definitions of self. This is a third difference between the two novels. Dessa speaks herself into being without physical confrontation or the approval of others, whereas Charlie attempts to gain external acceptance of his new identity and later acts out his understanding of that identity through the violence of a miniature race war.

Charlie's announcement of his manhood appears in the chapter spoken by Lou Dimes, a white reporter. Similar to the revisiting of events leading to Dessa's captivity in "The Darky," we read the recording of events, of (his)tory, through a white male voice. Whereas Adam Nehemiah never captures the essence of Dessa's story—never getting it quite right—Lou Dimes appears to capture every word and inflection of Charlie's tale. In doing so, he represents an opportunity for the confirmation of black manhood within the white community, an opportunity Dimes rejects.

Although he mentions the sheriff's sincerity in addressing Charlie as Mr. Biggs (more than once), he never admits his own. Instead, Mr. Lou, as Charlie labels him, draws a picture of intimidation and submission to intimidation. His rendition of events confirms the threat Charlie's physical presence represents. " 'I'll write it, Charlie,' I said, looking up at him. He was three or four inches taller than I, and outweighed me, I'm sure, by at least a hundred pounds." Dimes agrees to publish a written statement concerning Charlie's manhood because of his threatening physical size, not because he acknowledges Charlie's maturity and responsibilities as a man. Lou Dimes does not see Mr. Biggs; he still sees *Big* Charlie. Not until the shooting begins does Lou Dimes acknowledge Charlie's manhood through a serious use of the name *Mr. Biggs*.

Williams avoids white confirmation of black self-identity through the use of Dessa's dream-lifeworld and name play. Dessa works against white namers, disavowing them with conviction while turning their rationale for naming and unnaming the other against them. Whereas Dessa easily finds an internal and secret place of self-definition within her dream-lifeworld, Charlie has no similar place of self-assurance. His claims of manhood read almost as if he is uncomfortable with the idea unless he gains external approval. Before confessing, he sends for "the law," and the other "white folks" follow. Not only does Charlie need approval, but he needs it from the whites who gather around him.

Each of the individuals he addresses by name has, at some point in the novel, represented various white ideologies and prejudices Charlie feels he must change in order to confirm his manhood. Mapes, who earlier in the text slaps several of the old men and knocks them down, represents law enforcement officials who have no respect for black human dignity and who brutalize blacks in the name of justice. Candy represents those whites, male and female, who live in the past and think of African Americans as inferior, "black and helpless," incapable of protecting themselves or speaking for themselves without direction (67). Mr. Lou, or Lou Dimes, represents the media, and other institutions of financial profit under white control, who view black male empowerment as a threat and who create images of black males that keep that power "at bay" through subtle caricature and subversion.

The last of those named by Charlie, Mathu, symbolizes the disease of intraracial prejudice and the disquieting image of the outsider inside that results. In *Black Feminist Thought*, Patricia Hill Collins, speaking of black women who work in white institutions and homes, describes an *outsider-within* as an individual with "a distinct view of the contradictions between the dominant group's actions and ideologies. . . . [A]n outsider-within stance functions to create a new angle of vision on the process of suppresion." [4] My description of Mathu as an *outsider inside* revises Collins's discussion and identifies Mathu as a character who resides within a particular ethnic and racial community but rejects some aspect of that association because his worldview is aligned with the oppressor—a dominant other. Because of his attitude toward various members of his own racial group and ethnic community, Mathu is an outsider existing inside that group and community. This outsider inside has a unique angle of vision on the process of self-denial and self-denigration practiced by the black men of St. Raphael parish. Prior to the day the novel depicts, Mathu harbors resentment for the other black men in the quarters and stands apart from them. He dismisses them just as whites dismiss them: "I felt . . . you never would 'mount to anything" (181). Their unmanly submission to fear and to whites blocks Mathu's ability to bond with them or respect them. Ironically, he bonds with Sheriff Mapes, fishing and talking with him in mutual respect—like "real men." When Charlie calls his name, "Mathu, standing in the corner by the fireplace, nodded his *white head*" (emphasis added). Mathu thinks "white"; therefore Charlie struggles to convince him, as well as the other representations of the outsider in the room, that he, Charlie Biggs, is a man.

As Charlie tells the story of his abuse at the hand of St. Raphael's white citizens, he paces the floor, moving "toward the door, or the window." Appearing agitated and nervous, he reveals that the boy who had once controlled his life and his responses to life allowed himself to be beaten and degraded—"and long as I was Big Charlie, nigger boy, I took it" (189). He explains that the man hidden inside that boy could no longer allow such behavior to continue. His voice mounts and his pacing ceases. The character enters a state of mind the text describes as a "trance." Within this dream experience, the "impossible" occurs and the true-real emerges.

Several times throughout the text characters admit the impossible nature of the events revealed in the novel. During the dénouement we are told again. "Mathu was looking at [Charlie] as though he was not absolutely sure he was seeing him there" (188). And again a few pages later: "he wasn't sure that it was Charlie doing this talking. The rest of the people seemed to feel the same way" (191). But the man standing before them *is* the person known previously as Charlie. The narrator's dramatic and somewhat phallic descriptions (tree limbs and cannon*balls*) of the speaking character emphasize Charlie's physical presence, *his* physical relationship to space and none other. It confirms the impossible—Charlie finally took a stand—and with the impossible confirmed, the true-real emerges in the form of a motivating idea: "Like some overcome preacher behind the pulpit, he cried out: 'But they comes a day! They comes a day when a man must be a man. They comes a day!' The two big tree limbs with big fists like cannonballs shook toward the ceiling, and we watched in awe, in fear, in case he decided to whirl around, or fall. He did neither. He brought his arms down slowly, breathing heavily, while he stared over our heads toward the wall. 'They comes a day,' he said to himself, not to us. 'They comes a day'" (189).

Although Lou Dimes's narration confirms that the body of Charlie stands before the group of onlookers, their suspicions that something or someone other than Charlie acts and speaks in this scene are correct. The name-entity *mathu* usurps and subsumes the monologue of the subject persona Charlie, controlling both his voice and his actions. Charlie submits to the generative powers of *mathu* in the same way that an "overcome preacher behind the pulpit" submits his body and voice to God. This image of an emerging supreme energy silences everyone—even the sheriff, who speaks only after "a respectful moment of silence" (189). The eruption of the true-real in this scene allows *mathu, the man who killed Beau Boutan*, to speak boldly concerning his reason for killing: "They comes a day when a man must be a man. They comes a day!"

Ernest Gaines commented once that "we don't know who killed Beau. I still don't know who killed Beau, and I wrote the damned thing three or four years ago. Mathu could have very easily killed Beau."[5] I agree. The name-entity *mathu* did kill Beau Boutan. The poetic name answers the novel's controlling question by providing deep talk that reveals the name of a murderer and more. The position effects of *mathu* create a motivating idea that each man who tells his story adopts. The decision to finally take a stand against injustice is common in Charlie's story and in each of the old men's stories. This decision is motivated by an idea that says "I wasn't go'n 'low that no more" and "they comes a day when a man got to stand" (190, 191). Each man's story refines this idea until *mathu*'s motive for murder includes revenging an entire history of injustices the black community of St. Raphael parish has experienced at the hand of white society. This discourse fragments into at least three independent voices; one names a method of action (murder), another names *the man* who killed Beau Boutan (Mr. Biggs), and a third names the idea that killed him (manhood as confrontational self-respect). Each of these discourses speaks through the deep talk of a single multidirectional signifying name: *Mathu*.

The (God)father

Sometime round sundown—no, just 'fore sundown, I heard a voice calling my name. I laid there listening, listening, listening, but I didn't hear it no more. But I knowed that

voice was calling me back here. . . . He passed his hand over his sweaty face and head; then he looked at Mathu. "All right, Parrain?"—(192–93)

Charlie realizes the meaning of responsibility and its relationship to real manhood only after he hears a disembodied voice calling his name. He identifies the owner of the voice when he looks at Mathu and calls him *Parrain*, a poetic name whose deep talk identifies a namer. In French *Parrain* means "godfather" and "namer." These lexical meanings speak of Mathu as the only person who could have, but did not, reveal the identity of the murderer. In this sense, *Parrain* calls out to the deep talk and discursive action of *mathu*. Note the structural positioning of the names in the quote: "he looked at Mathu. 'All right, Parrain?' " *Parrain* functions reflectively (as in a mirror) to transpose or, rather, expose the deep-level discourse of the name *Mathu* in the preceding sentence. It points back at *mathu* and identifies that entity as one that "names" a killer.

When we unpack *Parrain* further, we find that it is a title with several levels of meaning. First, *Parrain* refers to a familial relationship, "godfather"; second, and more importantly, it identifies Mathu as the "godfather figure" for all of the old men in Marshall Quarters who carry guns. They admire him and look up to him, even if he does not always return their admiration. Because they consider Mathu "a man" who always stands up to the community's adversary (white society), he earns the community's respect. "Mathu was the only one we knowed had ever stood up" (31). On the day of Beau Boutan's murder, they welcome into their communion both Mathu and the opportunity to be like him. Third, the name identifies Mathu as a supreme namer, a (god)father. I place the word *god* in parenthesis to highlight the deep talk of Godliness contained within the title. Mat credits God for giving him the opportunity to stand against his adversaries. "He works in mysterious ways. . . . Give a old nigger like me one more chance, and I'm taking it, I'm going to Marshall [Quarters]" (38). Mat and the other old men follow Mathu, proclaiming him their unofficial leader. Metaphorically, he is the (god)father who provided "a way." This poetic word's association with God also influences the name-entity *mathu* so that when it speaks through Charlie's voice a supreme energy surrounds him and gives him the appearance of an "overcome preacher."

The supranaming transformations of *Mathu* are particularly interesting when juxtaposed to the events involving external namers in the novel *Dessa Rose*. Whereas *A Gathering* inflates the power and significance of Mathu (both on the surface and within the metatext), Williams's novel reduces Dessa's primary external namers, Nehemiah and Rufel, in status and significance through renaming. Nehemiah's name fragments to *Nemi*. "I never will forget Nemi trying to read me," Dessa says, emphasizing the impotency of the character as namer and interpreter of her identity (236). Rufel's name also fragments and announces her incompetence as namer. She is "'*Fel*" or, rather, she "fails." Mathu, in contrast, becomes *Parrain*, (god)father, the ultimate namer.

Mathu plays out this role when, at the end of the day, he addresses each old man by name and tells them to go home. "He looked at Johnny Paul a good two seconds; then he looked at somebody else. He would call that person's name, look at him awhile, then turn to somebody else" (182). Mathu takes control of the situation and issues orders to his company of armed men (and unarmed women) like a (god)father, a penultimate namer and law giver. Through his roll call, he commends the men by acknowledging their militancy: "Rooster with a gun, Dirty Red with a gun—Chimley, Billy" (181). Mathu's use of nicknames sanctions them as independent utterances of self-respect and manliness. They are instruments of black male empowerment.

Later, he acknowledges his own transformation. "'I been changed,' he said. 'Not by that white man's God. I don't believe in that white man's God. I been changed by y'all. Rooster, Clabber, Dirty Red, Coot—you changed this hardhearted old man" (183). Mathu redefines the source of linguistic value by denouncing the "white man's" God, the symbol of language and linguistic order (such as "In the beginning was the Word, and the Word was with God, and the Word was God"). His statement also denounces white men's ability to act as messengers of a "law giver," a rejection that becomes vital to the inversions that occur in the trial scene. Mathu *is* Parrain in Marshall Quarters, the (god)father, and like a god ordaining his priests, he decrees that the old men holding guns have their own powers, the power to change the heart of a "god."

The Battle of Names

Charlie's proclamation of his manhood and Mathu's confirmation of the old men's militancy culminate in a miniature race war. By novel's end, Charlie is dead, and with him dies the subject position of the man who killed Beau Boutan. Although the name *Mathu* lives on within the metatext and surface narrative texts, only one method of action speaks through it—that of standing against injustice through onomastic resistance. The war fought with guns offers little in the way of transformative influence when compared to the accomplishments the novel's battle of names achieves. Beyond the outward aggressive appearance of old men who hold empty guns and eventually load those guns are the battles of civil disobedience and linguistic resistance enacted through their manipulation of formal and informal names.

In both *Dessa Rose* and *A Gathering*, black namers enter into a battle with whites for control over the naming process. Both texts reject the deep talk that character names collect when used by whites, while allowing black characters to subvert white names when speaking among themselves. Just as the fugitives of Sutton's Glen call Rufel *Miz Ruint* when beyond her hearing, Gaines's characters call the white woman Mertle Bouchard *Miss Owl* among themselves. In her presence, they address her as *Miss Merle*. This masking through poetic name play is a shield of protection for the characters' true selves. It also serves as a defining mechanism, distinguishing the insider from the outsider in both texts.

Another difference in these texts is their use of informal names. Most informal names in Williams's novel appear as given names such as *Dorcas*, *Nathan*, *Kaine*, *Dante*, *Janet*, and *Dessa*, among others; as diminutives like *Rufel*, *Ned*, *Ada*, and *Flora*; or as epithets. Names we usually consider nicknames are presented by Williams as the given names of slaves—perhaps in an attempt to duplicate the naming practices of masters who considered their slaves chattel and, therefore, gave them nontraditional names like *Harker*. Williams reminds us of this by blurring the line of distinction between nicknames and given names. This type of creativity and blurring may also be a form of resistance through naming initiated by the slaves themselves and duplicated in the text. In any case, the only clearly defined nicknames of equal value to those in *A Gathering* are names like *Red, Button, Mony, Dess, 'Fel, Miz Ruint, Miz Lady, Master man,* and *debil woman.* Each of these expresses charatonymic desires much like the nicknames and pet names in Gaines's novel.

Informal names in Gaines's novel are representative words whose meanings as established among blacks mutate when used with hostile intent. Nicknames that speak of physical characteristics such as *Chimley, Dirty Red, Clatoo, Clabber,* and *Cherry,* for instance, turn into weapons aimed against the name bearer, verbal weapons that disavow claims of pride and communal bonding. Each of these names describes skin color; Chimley has the darkest complexion of all—something that makes him sensitive to who uses his nickname and how. "He didn't mind his friends calling him Chimley, 'cause he knowed we didn't mean nothing. But he sure didn't like them white folks calling him Chimley. He was always telling them that his daddy had named him Robert Louis Stevenson Banks, not Chimley. But all they did was laugh at him, and they went on calling him Chimley anyhow" (40). When "white folks" use the nickname with the intent of mocking or belittling Chimley, he hears the name as he would a centered epithet; it is a personal insult. Black characters speak the nickname without derogatory intent. It offers them a sense of familiarity, camaraderie, and communion. Similarly, in *Dessa Rose* the name *debil woman* builds a sense of camaraderie and support within the slave quarters.

Formal names, on the other hand, speak of black characters' desires and familial associations. Chimley's insistence on being addressed by his formal name only when the speaker is white emphasizes his alienation from that community, his place as an outsider. Derived, in part, from the name of the Scottish author who wrote *Dr. Jekyll and Mr. Hyde,* the name *Robert Louis Stevenson Banks* embodies whiteness, duality, and Otherness. It speaks of a desire for acceptance and equality within the white world while also speaking of the evil behind the character's forced estrangement and exclusion from that world. The name's association with Jekyll and Hyde also speaks of the character's duality, his ability to react in diverse ways to various users of his name. Formal names such as this, and all others in the text, provide information concerning the bearer's ancestral, social, and attitudinal identity. They connect an individual to a familial past and represent her or his desire for gaining respect, inclusion, and equality beyond the black community.

Maternal given names subordinate this type of ancestral and attitudinal identity in *Dessa Rose*. In fact, we never learn Dessa's family name nor that of any other black character. The only formal names presented in the text are those of white slave traders like Wilson, law enforcers like Sheriff Hughes, the white upper class like the Mims, and white plantation masters like Smith and Sutton. *Dessa Rose* celebrates black, maternal ancestry, continuity, and pride—not black paternal relations nor a desire to gain the respect of a white patriarchal society. The protagonist rejects the idea of naming her son after his father, for instance—at least initially; and she changes his name from *Desmond Kaine* ("'Des' for Odessa, 'mond' to represent the men, Nathan, Cully, and Harker") to *Mony* because she "felt him to be as good as gold" (148). Perhaps Williams avoids formal names in her novel because they announce a paternal ancestral identity (maybe even a white ancestral identity, as Malcolm X would charge), which the novel intends to mute. In Gaines's text, paternal identity silences the maternal, but this is the only part of traditional formal naming that the text celebrates.

We usually think of formal names as those we use in official documentation or in recording legal matters—births, deaths, marriages, property ownership, and so on. They are the names that somehow mark an individual as a human being in society. Gaines denies this function to African-American formal names. Instead of gaining the white community's respect, Chimley's insistence on being addressed by his formal name results in laughter and negation. The use of formal names by blacks in this text exposes a white sociolinguistic structure that rejects black humanity and black formal names. This pattern does not change, not even after the old men claim guilt in Beau's murder. The white deputy, Griffin, documents Yank's confession while spelling out the letters of his nickname: "Yank. Y-a-n——". Yank stops him and insists that Griffin write his name in the official record of events as Sylvester J. Battley. "Be sure and spell Sylvester and Battley right, if you can. When my folks read about me up North, I want them to be proud" (99). Deputy Griffin ignores the request, and once again, a member of the novel's white social structure rejects the idea of black humanity, historicity, and pride through the denial of a formal name.

During the trial, the old men resist this history of denigration and denial by refusing to use names whose deep talk speaks of that history: "The trial went on for three days, and it was orderly most of the time. But every now and then one of the old black fellows, arm in sling, would go just a little overboard describing what happened. Besides, he would use all nicknames for his compatriots—Clabber, Dirty Red, Coot, Chimley, Rooster. This would bring the court to laughing, especially the news people, who took the whole thing as something astonishing but not serious" (212). By not using their formal names, the old men invert the object of denial; and like their West African and diaspora ancestors, they cloak their names' deep-level discourses within a second, secret language, a language the white spectators of the trial cannot hear. Through this secret language and its use in a formal situation, the old men make the rules of acceptability and the legal value of formal names as defined within the white lifeworld subordinate to the value of nicknames within the margins. Note that the names listed (*Clabber, Dirty Red, Coot, Chimley, Rooster*) are the same ones Mathu, the (god)father, ordained as instruments of empowered manhood and change. This secret use of nicknames inverts Chimley's earlier insistence on being addressed by his formal name. The results in the surface text are similar (laughter and rejection and, therefore, unnaming). The use of nicknames in formal situations is unacceptable within the dominant social order, and the whites, of course, reject them—leaving the old men virtually nameless within that sphere. But in the redefined sociolinguistic order of those who live within the margins, nothing exists but nicknames—redefined, powerful, and proud nicknames.

Instead of honoring the Euro-American idea of what constitutes a formal name, the old men repeat the traditions of their ancestors, making nicknames formal and, therein, exerting the power and influence of their communal language as a form of resistance. P. Robert Paustian comments that slaves' self-naming practices assigned as much value to nicknames as they did biblical or European-derived names. He also comments that these appellatives that "later became formal names were based on occupations or physical characteristics, just as European as well as African names had once been." [6] For the old men, then, their nick-names are just as powerful as the formal names of whites, which were also, at one time, considered "mere" nicknames. The old men's nick-names and their subversion of formal names are the only weapons they use by novel's end. Although they continue to stand against injustice, they do so within the realm of civil disobedience and resistance through self-naming.

One of the most interesting messages of this novel's battle of names is the one communicated through the blurring of lines separating formal names, nicknames, and the names of animals during Yank's confession. This merging of voices disintegrates lines of class differences that distinguish those who own and those who are owned in a mesh of names. In chapter 9, Yank lists the names of the men whose horses and mules he has tamed. In the same sentences, he lists the names of the animals themselves: "Snook, Chip, Diamond, Job. I broke Tiger, Tony, Sally, Dot, Lucky, Cora, John Strutter, Lottie, Hattie, Bird, Red, Bessie, Mut, Lena, Mr. Bascom. For Dr. Morgan, I broke Slipper, Skeeter, Roland. I broke 'em all" (99). In this reading, I assume that *Dr.* Morgan is the name of an animal owner and that the other names Yank mentions refer to mules and horses. If this is true, then the names *John Strutter* and Mr. Bascom mark points of narrative dissonance. These names break with the pattern of naming. *John Strutter* combines two names while Mr. Bascom is prefaced by a title. Because both names deviate from the established norm, the nature of the name bearers, whether men or beasts, completely disappears.

Even race disappears in Yank's list of names. Only characters familiar with the bearer of the names he calls know their intended meaning and referent. Gaines does not give the reader that privilege. Even more essential to this example is my assumption that John Strutter and Mr. Bascom might denote people. Because Yank's intent is not clear, we cannot be sure if the second sentence of his list denotes only animals or owners and animals. In either case, our confusion makes the hypothesized author's point. Joseph Griffin argues that the juxtaposition of this chain of names with an early list of individuals who gather at Marshall's Quarters highlights the similarities between animal names and black characters' names—their interchangeable nature, discourses of inhumanity, and (I might add) their use as signs of commodification and disfranchisement.[7] I also read in the deep talk of these names the spirit of displacement and dissolution. The hypothesized author's point is to blur the lines of racial division and equate the giver of inhumane treatment with those who receive such treatment—to "mix it all up" until the onomastic assaults against black humanity and the economic disfranchisement of "mules and men" disappear.

In a 1987 interview, Ernest Gaines responded to the question "What causes you the most continuing unrest?" with a one-word answer, "Reagan," a name he goes on to define as "people who build bombs and might use them one day."[8] In *A Gathering of Old Men*, a world in which old men carry guns they might (and do) use one day, Gaines presents his concern for "Reagan" through the deep talk of the name *Mathu*. *Mathu* is a metaphorical bomb that explodes within St. Raphael Parish, an idea that motivates aggressive action against years of racial injustice.

This idea manifests itself in the form of murder, a race war, and rebellion through civil disobedience—a battle of names that breaks laws and transforms "boys" into men. Names, not guns, are their most powerful and successful weapons. The old men of St. Raphael Parish challenge the unofficial laws of American socialization and legal address by using nicknames instead of formal names in a court of law, and they break judicial laws when they refuse to reveal the name of the man who they believe murdered Beau Boutan. Perhaps the message of the true-real developed through this battle of names is simply that *men* suffering injustice must take a stand against that injustice by taking control of the words and actions that name them, by being "real men," not by arming themselves with deadly weapons they might use one day.

The novel demonstrates the hope of "real men" through the deep talk of the names *Salt* and *Pepper*. These characters are football players at Louisiana State University. "Wherever you went, people spoke of Salt and Pepper of LSU. Both were good powerful runners, and excellent blockers. Gil blocked for Cal on sweeps around end, and Cal returned the favor when Gil went up the middle" (112). Gaines introduces these two young men as individuals who successfully work together not only for their mutual benefit but for the benefit of their community. Although one character is black and the other white, their names, Calvin "Pepper" Harrison and Gilbert "Salt" Boutan, reflect a mutual acceptance of parallel roles.[9]

Through the characterization of these two football players, the novel suggests that in the development of a joint society it is only when diverse cultures accept the humanity and productive value of one another that success and peaceful coexistence can be achieved. Violent relationships between whites and blacks that culminate in race wars of any kind (onomastic or physical) are destructive. But relationships like the one represented by Salt and Pepper are mutually beneficial. The ultimate message of the deep talk of these names is that black and white Americans must stop fighting one another; they must join forces and block for one another in order to combat the injustices of our present age. Like salt and pepper, we should work together to season America until it "tastes" right.

7

Within the Bend of Race

T HE DISCOURSE production of poetic names in African-American literature contains streams of gendered difference that intersect with race, blend with it, and, sometimes, completely lose force under the weight of it. Race dismantles difference, rendering all it claims (un)sexed and equally debased through the utterances of pejorative unnaming. Hortense Spillers and Evelyn Higginbotham have argued previously that gender is racially inflected, that race not only levels difference but circumscribes and genders social relations.[1] This chapter traces a few streams of gendered difference as they meet the bend of racially constructed social relations—not only to emphasize individual authors' use of names but to accentuate cross currents of gendered specificity as they merge with the difference race makes.

Maya Angelou's use of name fragmentation in *I Know Why the Caged Bird Sings* (1970) demonstrates the subversive complexities and resistive nature of black names' deep talk when confronted with racist opposition. This is the point of her autobiography's sixteenth chapter. I say this not to argue the irrelevance of gender to black literary naming (that is certainly not true) but to highlight its inflection by race when determining culturally coded languages of resistance. Through Marguerite's renaming, Angelou stresses the violent effects of being renamed through the contaminating sieve of racism.

All characters involved in Marguerite's renaming are women (they call her Margaret and Mary). Their gender, however, does not appear to have any effect on the mode of name fragmentation nor the discursive force of naming events. Although Angelou never mentions gender as responsible for Marguerite's name fragmentation, the historical interpolation of gender through racist name calling suggests that it is an implicit part of the event: "Every person I knew had a hellish horror of being 'called out of his name.' It was a dangerous practice to call a Negro anything that could be loosely construed as insulting because of the centuries of their having been called niggers, jigs, dinges, blackbirds, crows, boots and spooks" (91). In each of these pejorative names, gender (and any suggestion of the genitalia) is usurped by racist desexualization.

Regardless of the form name calling takes, whether unnaming or renaming, being called out of one's name, especially by a racist, is an insult. Angelou's expression of why Marguerite reacts in anger to her renaming defies any reading of this chapter of her autobiography as gendered difference exclusively. Like many black writers, Angelou uses the conflicts of renaming as a method of enunciating resistance to a history of racially motivated onomastic shifts and as a means of communicating deep-level confrontations of linguistic control.

Mrs. Cullinan's use of the name *Margaret* appears to be the result of a mispronunciation, at least initially, whereas the name *Mary* functions as a violent verbal assault against the child's race and her self-image. Both names are derivatives of the original, *Marguerite*, and both continue to evolve and mutate throughout the chapter until they express a multitude of onomastic desires and interpolated voices. Ultimately, the names and the individuals who use them enter into a battle for domination and control over the naming process.

Although Angelou's original name does not surface within chapter 16, it works beneath the surface challenging each new name assigned to her. During the first name fragmentation, the name-entity *marguerite* functions as an absent presence whose discursive force evokes a facetious discussion of pity. When the white employer, Mrs. Cullinan, mispronounces the name, calling the child *Margaret*, Angelou explains in narration: "Poor thing. . . . couldn't even pronounce my name correctly." This sarcastic announcement of pity changes into unabridged anger when another white woman suggests that the name is too long. "I'd never bother myself. I'd call her Mary if I was you" (90). In agreement with her friend, Mrs. Cullinan adopts the shortened name and uses it.

The young Marguerite refuses to be stripped of her name by a racist disregard for her autonomy and decides to quit the job. She devises a plan for retribution that also provides a reason for quitting that her mother will accept—she breaks a few cherished possessions of the offender. After this act of revenge, Mrs. Cullinan once again addresses her as Margaret: "Everything was happening so fast I can't remember whether her action preceded her words, but I know that Mrs. Cullinan said, 'Her name's Margaret, goddamn it, her name's Margaret!' And she threw a wedge of the broken plate at me. It could have been the hysteria which put her aim off, but the flying crockery caught Miss Glory right over her ear and she started screaming. I left the front door wide open so all the neighbors could hear" (93). It seems that the child wins her battle for dignity and the right to name herself, but the name-entity *marguerite* still haunts the margins of the text.

That this absent presence has the ability to reshape discourse compromises what a reader might otherwise consider a victory. Because Margaret is not the child's true name and because of the tone used by Mrs. Cullinan, it is clear that *Margaret* is almost as much of an insult as *Mary*. Mrs. Cullinan does not surrender to defeat; she strikes back with a tone of sarcasm that gives new meaning to the name she thinks the child accepts. The deep talk of the diminutive acknowledges Marguerite's revenge but also strikes a blow against her true name. The discursive effects of the name *Margaret* acknowledge the child's autonomy by mocking it through caricature. In other words, the deep-level communications of the name confirm a victory and verify a defeat. This struggle for onomastic control does not end here.

The catalyst for further engagement, *marguerite*, a name-entity whose border-crossing existence lies between the marginal lifeworld of shared cultural languages and the alien lifeworld of Mrs. Cullinan's onomastic intent, undermines the aim and meaning of all its diminutives. It does not allow the deep talk of *Margaret* to succeed in defining or mocking the child's true self. Instead of evoking pity for an unwanted namer, as it did at the opening of the chapter, *marguerite* manipulates the reader's interpretation of the name *Margaret* so that its use ultimately provokes humor, a laugh on the alien namer, which subverts Mrs. Cullinan's intent.

Angelou is aware of both the partial failure in the name play she pursues and *Margaret*'s new deep talk. She speaks of both in the subdued humor of the chapter's last line: "Mrs. Cullinan was right about one thing. My name wasn't Mary" (93). Her name wasn't *Margaret* either. *Margaret* speaks from an alien sociolinguistic space and is regarded as an onomastic comedy when juxtaposed with the discursive impulses and cultural languages of the original name's deep talk.

Kimberly Benston, arguing that onomastic revisions, such as those in Angelou's autobiography, are a tropologic feature of African-American literature, calls this feature *genealogical revisionism*. Unfortunately, Benston's essay gives women's writing only a cursory glance. This omission raises a few questions concerning his telos of naming and "(un)naming." [2] Does he mean that male authors alone engage in genealogical revisionism, or do women authors also engage in this type of naming and unnaming? Are there differences in the discourses that unnaming produces in male and female texts even when the framing stories are similar?

Richard Wright's autobiography, *Black Boy*, and Toni Morrison's novel *Song of Solomon* each contain scenes of misnaming that are very similar. Each revisits James Pennington's observations concerning the improper recording of black names in public records, thereby amplifying Pennington's discourse while creating their own. Morrison fictionalizes the situation by presenting characters (Sing and Jake) who accept the loss of a name and revise their assigned new name, *Dead*, through a personalized act of renaming. Years later the renaming of *Dead* leads to silence and historical forfeiture. Wright, on the other hand, describes misnaming as a grave loss that dispossesses and silences his grandfather's public identity immediately:

> From Granny I learned—over a course of years—that [Grandpa] had been wounded in the Civil War and had never received his disability pension, a fact which he hugged close to his heart with bitterness. I never heard him speak of white people; I think he hated them too much to talk of them. In the process of being discharged from the Union Army, he had gone to a white officer to seek help in filling out his papers. In filling out the papers, the white officer misspelled

Grandpa's name, making him Richard Vinson instead of Richard Wilson. It was possible that Grandpa's southern accent and his illiteracy made him mispronounce his own name. It was rumored that the white officer had been a Swede and had had a poor knowledge of English. Another rumor had it that the white officer had been a Southerner and had deliberately falsified Grandpa's papers. Anyway, Grandpa did not discover that he had been discharged in the name of Richard Vinson until years later; and when he applied to the War Department for a pension, no trace could be found of his ever having served in the Union Army under the name of Richard Wilson. (153)

Benston describes the story of Wilson's unnaming as a recitation through which black linguistic poverty forecloses public identity and disempowers the narratives of self. He comments that "having lost his name even as 'trace' to the archives of a bloody past, [Wright's grandfather] can achieve no authentic public identity . . . his private narrative voice is rendered ineffective." [3] Although I agree that the misnaming prevents an "authentic public identity," I must disagree with Benston's conclusion that the name is lost even as a trace of the past. A trace of the name does exist, a renaming trace (*Vinson*) that marks the site of personal disfranchisement. Richard Wilson's renaming as *Richard Vinson* forces a loss of reward, acknowledgment, and confirmation that might otherwise offer him inclusion in the roll call of patriotic American warriors. Because Wright's grandfather does not allow the revised name to foreclose his personal identity as *Richard Wilson*, this is a case of oppositional renaming.

As in Pennington's narrative, the improper recording of a name shuts down Richard Wilson's ability to confirm his experiences as a man in the public sphere. Renaming compounds its effects by rendering his memory invalid within the public arena of white authorial discourses. "He would name persons long dead, citing their ages and descriptions, reconstructing battles in which he had fought, naming towns, rivers, creeks, roads, cities, villages, citing the names and numbers of regiments and companies with which he had fought. . . . he tried desperately to persuade the authorities of his true identity right up to the day of his death, and failed" (154). Nothing Richard Wilson remembers, not even the dates and times of his activities, has meaning in the world beyond self, family, and friends without a name supporting it. Yet, he continues to remember and seeks reparation until his death.

Whether a careless mistake or an intentional assault, the improper recording of Wright's grandfather's name excludes him from an American legacy of economic reward, commemoration, and recognition for human sacrifice and service in the public sphere. Instead, the defining elements and deep talk of *Vinson* speak of loss through communicative fracture and political invisibility. In the world extending beyond self and community, *Vinson* renders the public "body" of the man it renames as impotent and soundless as a stillborn, but it does not kill his "flesh" (i.e., spirit).

For Toni Morrison's family of Deads, the body is not stillborn; it commits suicide. Instead of attempting to reclaim an identity that misnaming dismantles, Sing revises the defining elements of the name *Dead* by inverting its connotations of death and baptizing it as a symbol of new life. This renaming projects memories of the past beyond the historical circumstances of unnaming and cloaks them beneath the guise of a homophonic imprint. Gay Wilentz comments in *Binding Cultures* that Sing's act of "naming is a method of regaining control of one's life. . . . [it] demonstrates the pattern of passing on the unique cultural traits of Africa within the context of the African-American community." [4] In this context, the name *Macon Dead* functions as the mask for a second name, a "secret" name reflecting the West African tradition of cloaking and protecting one's true self from danger and harm through a hidden name. Embodied by the name is an oral history silenced by a story of unnaming:

> When freedom came. All the colored people in the state had to register with the Freedmen's Bureau . . . Papa was in his teens and went to sign up, but the man behind the desk was drunk. He asked Papa where he was born. Papa said Macon. Then he asked him who his father was. Papa said, "he's dead." Asked him who owned him, Papa said, "I'm free." Well, the Yankee wrote it all down, but in the wrong spaces. Had him born in Dunfrie, wherever the hell that is, and in the space for his name the fool wrote, "Dead" comma

"Macon." But Papa couldn't read so he never found out what he was registered as till Mama told him.

He didn't have to keep the name, did he? He could have used his real name, couldn't he? [Milkman asks].

Mama liked it. Liked the name. Said it was new and would wipe out the past. Wipe it all out. (53–53)

Unlike Wright's recitation of the events and ambiguous causes of his grandfather's misnaming, Morrison's fictional story offers an example of a white man who undoubtedly has no regard or respect for accuracy when inscribing a public record of black nomenclature. Sing's renaming splits the drunken "Yankee's" error, *Dead*, into two names: one functions as a homophonic imprint and the other as a word with a sideward glance. These two names develop along parallel lines that never merge.

The intent of Sing's renaming wipes the past from the view of others, but not from the "secret" name with a sideward glance, the name "undercover." Each time it appears in the text it looks back at what its homophonic imprint "wipes out"—the original name—containing it, cloaking it, and protecting it from further mutation or abuse. The name hides not only the past but also the real names of everyone its homophonic imprint claims: Macon *Dead*, Pilate *Dead*, Reba *Dead*, Hagar *Dead*, Ruth Foster *Dead*, Magdalene called Lena *Dead*, First Corinthians *Dead*, and Sing *Dead*. Everyone connected in any way to the past becomes a part of the name with an undercover sideward glance; this includes each family member since the deep talk of the name they recognize, the homophonic imprint, renders them all "dead."

Macon remembers his family name as one of unnaming because he cannot read beyond the curtain of a homophonic imprint. Instead, he reads the play of death before it. Although he can read the word and understand its lexical meaning, he cannot read the name's deep-level communications nor the hidden effects of its sideward glance. In this sense he is like his father, illiterate.

Both Morrison and Wright mention illiteracy as a cause of unnaming. Unlike Wright's grandfather, Jake does not discover his misnaming in a helpless state of linguistic disadvantage without remedy. He has a choice;

he chooses to accept Sing's act of renaming, not the homophonic imprint of a white man's unnaming. Unfortunately, Sing dies without explaining the name's meaning, without passing on stories that give it life and split the curtain that hides the name with a sideward glance. The legacy of the homophonic imprint locks her children in a cycle of linguistic poverty and perpetual death.

Benston comments that Richard Wright distances himself from the history of "linguistic poverty" and silences his grandfather's experiences by giving a literary voice to that silence. In other words, instead of accentuating the power of oral history, Wright privileges writing. Morrison privileges writing also, but as an aid to memory (Pilate's earring contains the written record of her name). Morrison's novel condemns those who devalue oral tradition and its linguistic richness, those who foreclose history by denying it, and those who allow the deterioration of names that speak of the past (*Shalimar* to *Solomon* to *Sugarman*, for instance). Her text celebrates the deep talk of her characters' names, "names they got from yearnings, gestures, flaws, events, mistakes, weaknesses." It venerates African-American oral history and rejects the silencing of voices that tell stories. More importantly, *Song of Solomon* honors the voices that speak through the deep talk of names, names that give life to history, names that remember both "the struggle" and its reward, names from the past, "names that bore witness" (333).

Song of Solomon rebukes those who deny the subversive nature and historical deep talk of names by depicting characters who pay a high price for doing just that. Macon Dead, for instance, loses an understanding of his identity as substantial, as real. "Surely, he thought, he and his sister had some ancestor . . . who had a name that was real. A name given to him at birth with love and seriousness. A name that was not a joke, nor a disguise, nor a brand name. . . . His own parents, in some mood of perverseness or resignation, had agreed to abide by a naming done to them by somebody who couldn't have cared less" (17–18). By erasing Jake and Sing's act of renaming from Macon and Milkman's reading of the name, Morrison questions the value of subversive renaming for those who cannot read or, more specifically, those who cannot hear the deep talk of the names they bear.

In many black texts, male or female authored, the mother, or her female surrogate, symbolically serves as a physical, "flesh and bone" incarnation of the onomastic sign. Her name conjures a deep talk of historical value of which her voice speaks. In this way she is the caretaker of familial identity and history. Through her name and voice, her heirs inherit an understanding of themselves and the oral histories that speak through *their* names. Sing violates this charge when she "rereads" *Dead* as a censuring of history. Her propitious desire to rename defaces her symbolic role and projects her beyond the memory of her heirs. Pilate "never knew her mother's name," and when Milkman asks his father to tell him the family's original name, Macon Dead responds, "I don't remember my mother too well" (18, 297). Sing's act of renaming "wipes out" the onomastic sign she embodies, and her physical death kills any chance her children have of hearing, knowing, remembering, and understanding the deep talk of that sign.

Through Sing's death, Morrison brings depth to our understanding of the mother's name as oral history. "After she died Macon wouldn't let anybody say it aloud. That was funny. He wouldn't speak it after she died, and after he died that was all he ever said—her name" (298). Sing's name and the history it tells die with her. To restore what was lost through a repeated story of unnaming, Jake's ghost attempts to resurrect Sing's name by telling it to Pilate: "Sing. Sing" (148). There are four problems with this attempt at resurrection: Jake is a man; his voice cannot serve as a surrogate to the maternal voice. Pilate does not know this name and, therefore, cannot sense the word's onomastic intent. She has not heard the stories that give life to memory and thus has no way of understanding the name's deep talk. Finally, she never passes the name on. Pilate misinterprets Jake's message and sings.

Pilate's song assists Milkman by changing his search for gold into a search for his true name. While visiting Danville, Pennsylvania, and a town called Shalimar, Virginia, he encounters two women who provide the maternal voices he needs to complete his journey. Circe serves as Sing's first surrogate to Milkman and tells him his grandmother's name is *Sing*. The process of restoring the family history continues in Virginia with Milkman's second surrogate mother, Susan Byrd, who confirms Sing's true name, *Singing Bird*—the maternal name "wiped out." Through this discovery, Milkman finally understands his need for ancestral identity and history.

Although this information assists Milkman in realizing his desire for self-discovery, it does not provide him with all he needs. Milkman hears the deep talk of his own name only after hearing its oral history spoken aloud by Susan Byrd. He sits in her living room and listens "to gossip, stories, legends, and speculations" until he understands that "under the recorded names were other names." He then reads *Macon Dead* as a cloak that "hid from view the real names of people, places, and things. Names that had meaning . . . Solomon's Leap, Ryna's Gulch, Shalimar, Virginia . . . Macon Dead, Sing Byrd, Crowell Byrd, Pilate, Reba, Hagar" (327–33). The sideward glance of the name-entity *macon dead* shifts its status from an agent of undercover discourses that cloak and protect to an active mnemonic name that gives pride and value to those it names.

A similar subversion through renaming occurs in Alice Walker's short story "Everyday Use," but with results that are more immediate and obvious. Although Dee unnames herself by replacing her given name with *Wangero Lee-wanika Kemanjo*, Walker does not allow the effects of this unnaming to stand unchallenged. The name passed down for generations and given to her by her mother remains in the text. The narrator calls the character either *Dee* or *Dee (Wangero)* for most of the story. By merging two names, Walker allows the discursive strategies of renaming to overpower the influences of the character's self-unnaming, producing a metatext that both embodies and inverts *Wangero*. *Dee* holds a position of sovereignty within the text. The loophole that provides the second name, *Dee (Wangero)*, with a way to avoid unnaming maternal history (suggested by *Wangero*) is the parentheses that embody the name *Dee* opposes. *(Wangero)*'s revised graphic makeup speaks of the name's status as a secondary, ineffectual, and parenthetical event. The continuity between a maternal line of naming and familial history remains intact. Added to this history is the character's self-definition and the history it tells.

This same type of renaming and historical reappropriation occurs in Gloria Naylor's *Women of Brewster Place* when Mrs. Brown confronts her daughter, Kiswana, concerning her name change. Like Macon Dead and Dee (Wangero), Kiswana cannot hear the deep talk of the name she inherits; therefore, she finds no historical value or meaning in it. Her mother reads the name quite differently—she knows, hears, and understands its deep talk. In a moment of anger and frustration, Mrs. Brown gives Kiswana the oral history, the deep levels of meaning, she needs to redefine her name:

> My grandmother, she began slowly in a whisper, was a full-blooded Iroquois, and my grandfather a free black from a long line of journeymen who had lived in Connecticut since the establishment of the colonies. And my father was a Bajan who came to this country as a cabin boy on a merchant mariner. . . . I am alive because of the blood of a proud people who never scraped or begged or apologized for what they were. . . . It broke my heart when you changed your name. I gave you my grandmother's name, a woman who bore nine children and educated them all, who held off six white men with a shotgun when they tried to drag one of her sons to jail for "not knowing his place." Yet you needed to reach into an African dictionary to find a name to make you proud. (86)

Mrs. Brown ends her speech by speaking the name *Melanie*. She never uses her daughter's new name. Instead the two words, *Kiswana* and *Melanie*, coexist in this chapter, allowing supranaming to dominate the interpersonal and ancestrally defined encounter. Kiswana hears her familial oral history through her mother's voice and learns the value of the name *Melanie*, but only after this history redefines her chosen name's deep talk is the process of renaming complete.

This occurs later in the scene as the narrator describes an event that merges the images of mother and daughter through tears that symbolically blend the diverse onomastic tasks of the character's two names: "Kiswana followed her reflection in the two single tears that moved down her mother's cheeks until it blended with them into the woman's copper skin" (87). In the metatext, Kiswana's doubled reflection, her duality and the deep talk of her two names, merge into the symbolic "flesh" of an incarnate onomastic sign—her mother. The name *Kiswana* emerges from this encounter redefined, renamed, and full of new historical content.

The maternal signifier and the maternal namer often remain silent in male-authored texts. When the invisible man, hurt and disoriented, hears the question "WHAT IS YOUR MOTHER'S NAME?" he answers, "Mother, who was my mother? Mother, the one who screams when you suffer—but who? This was stupid, you always knew your mother's name. Who was it that screamed? Mother? But the scream came from the machine. A machine my mother? . . . Clearly, I was out of my head" (240). Surrounded by doctors and nurses, the invisible man contemplates several names, none of them his mother's, until he "had become submerged within them and lost" (241). This lifeworld suffocates and silences the maternal signifier.

For the invisible man, not knowing his mother's name is not being— not existing at all. Ellison emphasizes this displacement by reflecting upon the value of maternal names to African-American identity. As Mary Rambo and "Jenny Johnson's boy," Ralston, drag the invisible man (still disoriented) to the safety of Mary's home, she gains a sense of Ralston's identity through the mention of his mother's name. She gains a way of knowing that moves beyond recognition to claiming: "*My name's Mary Rambo, everybody knows me round this part of Harlem, you heard of me, ain't you?* And the fellow saying, *Sure, I'm Jenny Jackson's boy, you know I know you, Miss Mary.* and her saying, *Jenny Johnson's boy, you know I should say you do know me and I know you, you Ralston, and your mama got two more children, boy named Flint and gal named Laura-jean, I should say I know you—me and your mama and your papa useta—*" (252, Ellison's italics). This reflection of the social real is also a reflexive meditation on community and maternal naming that allows the narrative to distance the invisible man from the source of his true name and alienate him.[5]

This tradition of linking familial associations maternally extends from West Africa. In some African societies, children follow unilineal descent through the mother. In many cases, this method of identifying familial associations and kinship ties is so thorough that if a child's parents die the mother's brother, not her husband's, assumes responsibility for the infant. During slavery a maternal line of descent determined one's legal status as free or bound. In the light of these traditions, the invisible man's inability to name or remember his mother renders him void of a public and familial identity. He has no way of locating himself that others can *see*; therefore, they (we) have no way of connecting to him beyond the color of his skin and the personal experiences he shares.

Ellison uses the absence of a maternal name as a way of distancing his protagonist from the reader and characters in the text, just as Robert Louis Stevenson Banks in Gaines's novel uses the name "his daddy had named him" to distance himself from white insult and disrespect (40). Maternal names in female-authored texts are a presence that strengthens the public, familial, and personal identities of the individual named if— and this is crucial—the character recognizes, acknowledges, and accepts the oral history contained within the name's deep talk. Morrison, Walker, Naylor, and many others celebrate the value of reclaiming the past through recuperative acts that link the defining elements of a name with maternal ancestral memory. Their use of mnemonic names redefine and refashion history in ways that forbid foreclosure and distancing. Not only do their texts call forth racial relationships between the reader and their characters, but the play of names and naming speaks to a remembrance of historical relationships as well.

Paternal ancestral names, on the other hand, often function as instruments of historical grieving that are mutated in some way, infrequently used, or not present at all. This is where the current of gendered difference begins to thin, giving away beneath the weight of race and the shared memories of historical unnaming. Alex Haley's *Roots* demonstrates most effectively the successful struggle of one family against the threat of this loss. In other texts, nicknames, such as those in Gaines's *A Gathering of Old Men*, function as "real names" that silence or weakened the paternal signifier through a deterioration of its ancestral themes. Female-authored texts like Williams's *Dessa Rose* silence paternal ancestral themes through the complete absence of a surname, not even replacing it with an *X*. Others, like Morrison's *Song of Solomon*, distort the social implications of these names by aligning them with a legacy of female namers, historical fracture, or ominous fragmentations. We never discover the surname of Shalimar, for instance, who is the representative of male ancestry for Morrison's family of Deads. At novel's end, his ominous unnaming remains unresolved. It is *the lost African name.*

Another area of difference between black male-authored and female-authored writing is in the relationship of name fragmentation to the development of public identity and personal subjectivity. Morrison, Williams, Walker, and Angelou, among others, use name fragmentation as a method of voicing their characters' identity and subjectivity through and beyond the already present, whereas characters in male-authored texts—like *Black Boy, Invisible Man*, and *A Gathering of Old Men*—form identities through external struggle, striking out against the *effects* of the already present. A desire for identity confirmation outside the self permits unnaming or a sense of public namelessness to serve as dominating forces within many of their texts. For Wright's grandfather the loss of external name confirmation is tantamount to the death of his public identity, but for Singing Bird it is an opportunity for new life, an opportunity to claim individual subjectivity and to rename. In defiance of her maternal role as the custodian of familial history, she welcomes the "wiping out" of the past, an act for which her son and grandson pay with their personal, not public, sense of self.

Tensions between alien (usually white) naming influence and self-reappropriation are present in all the texts studied. Maya Angelou's Marguerite, Toni Morrison's family of Deads, and Richard Wright's Richard Wilson (Vinson) each struggle for self-reappropriation when confronted by misnaming influences beyond their control. Gendered difference surfaces in how the discourse production of poetic names defines these influences and identities, how those names reveal the construction of power and undermine imposed parameters of linguistic control, and how names determine the measure of success the speaking subject achieves while resisting racialized identities. In the metatext of each novel mentioned above, onomastic deep talk provides the named with varied vehicles for success. Onomastic narrative effects allow *vinson* to doff the "body" of death and function as "living" proof of a black man's economic and political disfranchisement. The liberated "flesh" of *marguerite* generates facetious pity and a laugh on the alien namer, and *dead* acts undercover to cloak and protect original or, rather, true names from hostile alien assault.

Since several of the readings presented in this book follow a pattern of male unnaming and female renaming, this discussion of gendered difference would be remiss if it did not delve more deeply into this issue.

What is the influence of gender upon the authorial use of name fragmentation rituals? Does an author's gender govern her or his artistic manipulation of onomastic deep talk, or do literary name fragmentations reflect the unpredictability of the social real? The following section addresses these questions and proposes that in literature and the social real, name fragmentations reveal a chaotic displacement and recuperation of gendered difference that can only be defined as supranaming.

Don't Call Him Boy, Girlfriend

I began my investigation of literary name fragmentation with a hypothesis: black male writers unname their characters whereas female writers rename. I based this hypothesis initially on the fragmentation of *boy* to *man* and *girl* to *girlfriend* I observed in a variety of texts as vastly different as those of Terry McMillan and Ralph Ellison. The pattern was also present in my memory of shared cultural languages within the social real. It appeared in the form of gendered sociolinguistic instruction from my mother when I suddenly adopted my older male cousin's habit of saying *man* at the beginning of almost every sentence: "girls don't say *man*." It was also present in her descriptions of her friends: "She was a girl-friend of mine at Fayetteville State." In the world beyond my parents' home, the differences held fast: "Who you callin' boy? You see a boy here, slap him" and "He sure is fine, girlfriend."

The use of *boy* and *girl* within a broader social arena provided further proof that my gendered hypothesis was correct. Typically, individuals use these terms to communicate a nonculturally specific message of camaraderie, youth, or gender. As pet names they may denote a sweetheart or friend, and as nicknames they describe socialized behaviors and racialized expectations. This is where the bend of race begins to mutate the deep talk of *boy* and *girl*, communicating racially constructed meanings. By this I mean that the deep-level utterances communicated depend more upon who speaks the name and under what circumstances than anything else.

Girl, when used by Anglo-American men and women among themselves, for instance, indicates a socialized identity of female goodnaturedness, gaiety, inexperience, youthfulness, submissiveness, or pleasure. When whites, male or female, use the term to denote blacks, the deep talk changes and speaks primarily of childlike dependence, manageable irresponsibility, and white superiority; it becomes an utterance of mockery, disrespect, and denunciation—this because of a history of racist unnaming. Generally, neither *girl* nor *girlfriend* is shared across racial lines in the United States, at least not without a meaning experience of displacement and disjunction that often offends. In an episode of the now defunct television sitcom *The Crew*, titled "The T&A of PSA," a white female attempts to join a discussion between four black women (her roommate and three others) by addressing them as "girlfriends." In return for her efforts, she receives an invitation to leave.[6] No matter what the intent of the speaker, echoes of the past disfigure the utility of these terms in interracial exchanges—especially those between adults.

Historically, racists used *boy* and *girl* so frequently when speaking of blacks that, in many cases, they substituted these terms for the names of the individuals addressed. No matter how mature in age the individual was, white slave masters, and later racist white employers, referred to black men and women as *boys* and *girls* (and various other patronizing derivatives such as *son* and *gal*). For African Americans the terms became hated epithets, pejorative descriptive names.

Anna Julia Cooper, in *A Voice from the South*, attributes the pejorative use of *girl* to individual white Americans' "poor training" and ignorance: "When a great burly six feet of masculinity with sloping shoulders and unkempt beard swaggers in, and, throwing a roll of tobacco into one corner of his jaw, growls out at me over the paper I am reading, 'Here gurl,' (I am past thirty) 'you better git out 'n dis kyar 'f yer don't, I'll put yer out,'—my mental annotation is *Here's an American citizen who has been badly trained. He is sadly lacking in both 'sweetness' and in 'light'*" (95, Cooper's italics). Cooper's dignified response to the white man growling at her in a public train is to consider the source of "calling" and dismiss the speaker while ignoring the racist name. This was the response of many African Americans during the nineteenth century, at least while in the presence of racist whites.

Long before the nineteenth century, African Americans understood that accepting the pejorative use of *boy* and *girl* without rejecting the deep talk meant a submission of their humanity and name to the authority of those who consider blacks inferior, docile, and, even worse, less than human. To counteract, or revise, the pejorative name assigned to them, black men insisted upon an acknowledgment of their manhood, referring to themselves as *men* and demanding that others use the descriptive term—if any description at all. In contrast, black women revised the pejorative name assigned to them by redefining its intent, calling each other *girl*, *gal*, *girl-friend*, and, more recently, *girlfriend*, so that the intent expressed shared intimacy or shared communal recognition.

These culturally coded subversions of white naming practices are more than a reaction to racist unnaming; they are a form of resistance. The deep talk of the term *man* violently strikes out against *boy*, disempowering it by unnaming it and denying its history of control. In contrast, black women's use of *girl* and *girlfriend* redefines and renames white racist discourses in a manner that does not obliterate the history connected to it. Instead, these names' double-voiced desires call out to the struggles of a common history and revise that history through the deep talk of a homophonic cultural imprint. Whether the tonal inflection used when speaking the name is one of sympathy, shock, outrage, or love, the history of a shared historical past resonates within it.

Many texts follow this pattern of female renaming and male unnaming: Sherley Ann Williams's renaming of Dessa, Ralph Ellison's unnaming of the invisible man and Tod Clifton, Maya Angelou's renaming of Marguerite, and Malcolm X's unnaming as El-Hajj Malik El-Shabazz, among others. Short stories like Alice Walker's "Everyday Use" follow the pattern also. These texts represent the "easy fit" that justified my original hypothesis and almost convinced me of its accuracy. After seeing the pattern of male unnaming and female renaming repeated so often, I assumed that my hypothesis was "fail-proof." I soon discovered that reading name fragmentation as gendered difference is not that simple. The hypothesized model circumscribes boundaries that are too confining to describe the resistance, rhapsody, and playfulness of names and naming within either context—African-American literature or the social real.

As the boundaries of comparison expand beyond the "easy fit," a spirit of disruption, reenunciation, inversion, and restructuring of gendered fragmentation paradigms presents itself. The straight-jacket effects of male unnaming/female renaming often defy the spirit of supranaming honored by authors like Nella Larsen, James Baldwin, Toni Morrison, Richard Wright, Zora Neale Hurston, and Gloria Naylor. As previous readings demonstrate, renaming occurs just as easily inside James Baldwin's fictional church and on the army discharge papers of Richard Wright's grandfather as it does inside the kitchen of Angelou's Mrs. Cullinan and in the tears of Naylor's Mrs. Brown. Each of these authors, and others like them, violate my original hypothesis either through the discourse production of supranaming or by fragmenting names in ways that are just the opposite of what I anticipated. These types of violations are especially true when reading the fragmentation and extended discourse production of *boy*, *girl*, and *man* in African-American literature and pop culture.

Consider, for instance, the use of *boy* and *gal* in a dialogue between the slaves Gabriel and Juba from Arna Bontemps's *Black Thunder* (1936). In this novel, Gabriel Prosser plans a rebellion against slavery that he eventually aborts. As he and his lover, Juba, recline on the floor of a dark hut, they contemplate Gabriel's name and how it will read on a note written like the one Toussaint L'Ouverture used in his call to insurrection:

> "My name is Gabriel — Gen'l Gabriel, I reckon — you's heard
> tell about me by now." Ha-ha! How that sound gal?
> "Right pretty, boy" [Juba says]. . . .
> "That was right pretty how Toussaint writ that note all
> right."
> "What else he say?"
> "*Come and unite with us, brothers, and combat with us
> for the same cause.*" He slapped his flank. "Sing it, church!
> Ain't that pretty?"
> "Pretty 'nough boy." (1161–17, Bontemps's italics)

This scene, written by a black man, is about language, power, influence, and *renaming*. As Gabriel and Juba contemplate a written call for others to join their insurrection, their use of nicknames acts out a miniature revolt of its own. Unlike Gabriel's carefully laid plans, this rebellion is successful. The characters' use of a cultural imprint enacts a revolt against the master's control of language and the words that name.

Renaming subverts and disavows the negative deep talk of *boy* and *girl*, replacing it with meanings derived from a distinctly black cultural language, a language existing beyond the master's sociolinguistic domination and control. This use of onomastic deep talk suggests the intimate nature of Gabriel and Juba's relationship and duplicates the covert nature of the slaves' plans for rebellion. In other words, Gabriel and Juba's subversion of *girl* and *boy* reflects and embodies the conspiratory nature of rebellion itself—and it does so through the hidden discourse production of renaming.

More recently a group of young black men, recording on the Motown label, presented America with a moment of supranaming by calling themselves *Boyz II Men*. Within the deep talk of *Boyz* a constant collision of meaning occurs, a collision that *Men* resolves. The word *boyz* revises the cultural imprint *boy* as used by Bontemps (and others) by exposing its covert nature and exploiting the animosity it conceals. The recent popularity of this term signals a desire in black male self-naming patterns that offers no suggestion that the individuals so named celebrate being childlike. The internal conflict of the nicknames' deep talk seeks further linguistic engagement with a past that continues to haunt the present (something clearly demonstrated by the 1995 focus on the word *nigger* in the media and in Judge Ito's courtroom). *Boyz* and its cultural sibling *B-boys* internalize, duplicate, and then aggressively oppose the intent of the derogatory epithet used historically by white racists. These revised names speak of manliness, but only as aggressive posturing, intimidation, and unresolved violence, as demonstrated in James Earl Hardy's 1994 novel *B-Boy Blues*:

> Here are "men" who throw their masculinity around for the entire world to not only see but swallow. . . . Of course, it is a rather grotesquely exaggerated take on manhood. But, when you are on your way to growing into a man (at least in years) and nobody has told you how to be one and almost all the "men" you see around you walk, talk, dress, and act like this, how else do you prove that you are a man but by joining them? Yes, you too have to be one bad mothafucka, the one they'll fear the most. It's a man thang, nothin' but a man

thang, and only the roughest survive. Banjeeness has become a boyz2men rite-of-life for many preteen/teenage/post-teen males in the so-called inner city. . . . B-boys do come in all ages (uh-huh, forty-year-olds nursin' a "40"), persuasions (the girlz are down, too), mutations (white boys like the down-with-the-homies-phony and Great-White-Aryan-Muscle-Boy-Hope Marky Mark), and orientations [some are homosexual]. (27)

Hardy introduces to African-American literature its first gay hip-hop love story and with it a new cultural accent in the renaming fragmentation of *boy*. Mitchell, the novel's protagonist and narrator, summarizes his definition of *boyz* and its supplement *B-boys* in one word—"banjeeness." For him, the cultural imprints of *boyz* and *B-boys* are synonymous. They interpolate the cultural languages of the inner city (including the renaming fragmentations of *boy* in the form of *block boy*, *homeboy*, or *"banjee/banji/banjie boy"*) and draw a picture of the African-American male defined by class on one level and by highly stereotypical and exaggerated imitations of black masculinity on another. Furthermore, "banjeeness" has no gender or racial boundaries. "The girlz are down, too" and so, Mitchell believes, are white imitations of blackness. According to *B-boy Blues*, anyone who accepts and acts out the stereotypical image of a black "ruffneck" can claim "banjeeness" (25–27).

Mitchell (who, by the way, is not characterized as a "ruffneck") uses *B-Boy* much as white racists use *boy*—as an assault against those whom he spends three pages describing. *B-boy* renames *boy* but does so with a heavy hand of negativity and denunciation that in many ways reclaims the master's word and supplements its deep talk with out-of-control aggressiveness, hate, and hostility. That this text celebrates homosexuality and chastises the public display of machismo does not affect its supranaming fragmentation and metatextual development of *boyz*, *B-Boy*, and *man*. In this novel, being a "real man" stands beyond aggressive posturing and intimidation; but most importantly, it stands beyond sexual orientation.

In the midst of its vigorous name play and crafty celebration of homosexuality, *B-Boy Blues* ends on a note reminiscent of many other

African-American, male-authored texts—with a confirmation of its protagonist's manhood. After making love "fiercely" to his B-boy partner
Raheim, Mitchell asks: " 'Who's tha man? / [Raheim] chuckled. 'You,
Little Bit.' / 'And . . . who is *yo'* man?' / [Raheim] smiled. 'You, Little
Bit' " (283, Hardy's ellipses and italics). Through the reenunciation of
man that the intimacy of *Little Bit* calls forth, the metatext redefines the
deep talk of *B-boys*. Mitchell defines manhood through an identity that
is proudly homosexual. This is the most profound difference between the
idea of "real" manliness as asserted by Hardy's protagonist and the protagonist of the other black male-authored texts presented in this book.

A second series of name fragmentations, standing outside the "easy
fit," provides evidence of the aggressively resistant activities female
supranaming practices offer. While black men asserted (and redefined)
their various definitions of manhood in literature and the social real,
black women responded to their public unnaming by insisting upon a
social and political recognition of their womanhood. Sojourner Truth's
much debated and much quoted charge "Ain't I a Woman?" unnames
girl, striking out at its demeaning history of disrespect in a manner similar to that used by black men during the same era. *Woman* also takes
a swipe at the paper-doll term *lady*, unnaming what was, at the time, a
word enunciating both a classist and racist exclusivity.

In the 1980s, the word *womanish* (defined by Alice Walker in *In
Search of Our Mother's Gardens* as the opposite of *girlish*) found its way
from the intimate spaces of private mother-to-daughter discourse to a
place of broad popular favor in the form of a new name, *womanist*. Walker defines the term, in part, as "a black feminist or feminist of color." [7]
With the acceptance of this politically charged name, black women engage in a definitive act of unnaming that rejects white, middle-class exclusions often conjured through the deep talk of the word *feminist*. At the
same time, the name subverts all notions of exclusion by including *feminist* within its deep talk.

Whereas *boyz* and *B-Boy* merge with *man* to speak a supranaming
discourse of manhood within public, communal, and private spaces,
woman and *womanist* break with the dominate pattern of female renaming to move parallel to it. These names command a political and social
role that operates as a counterpart to the discourses of private communal

bonding usually associated with *girl*. Like *man*, the terms *woman* and *womanist* have the potential to unname but are used by African Americans as a supranaming supplement; they do not foreclose the use of *girl* or *girlfriend* in broadly defined social discourses. Also *woman* and *womanist*, like *man*, are preferred in exchanges with white Americans. They claim a public role both within and outside of communal spaces while the playfulness of *girl* enjoys the comforts and securities of home.

Girlz, on the other hand, renames *girl* while internalizing and engaging the same historical conflicts as *boyz*. It speaks a "don't take no mess" discourse of confrontation and communal bonding within public and private spheres. I use the phrase *communal bonding* instead of *female bonding* here to suggest the cross-gender functions of this term. Both *girlz* and *girl* are appropriated by some men, especially gay men, when addressing women and each other. The cultural imprint reflects fellowship among peers and respect for personal identity similar to the use of *baby* among heterosexual males during the second and third quarters of this century. Conversely, the interracial use of *girlz* and *boyz* is acceptable most frequently when they appear in pop culture as the title of groups like *Boyz II Men* or films like John Singleton's 1991 *Boyz N the Hood*. Even then, the mnemonic utterances of an inauspicious past haunt the internal spaces of its deep talk.

The chaotic displacement and recuperation of gendered difference in name fragmentation practices appear, at first, to form distinct patterns of male unnaming and female renaming, but as the crosscurrents of gendered difference fade so do the patterns. African-American writers, regardless of gender, use renaming and unnaming for contemplating the subversive power and influence of cultural language coding. Some shape moments of character identity formation through simultaneous unnaming and renaming whereas others use both to express their character's existence in and knowledge of the sustaining powers offered by the "flesh."

It is through the liberated "flesh" of supranaming deep talk that the currents of gendered difference quiet completely. Through it black authors develop deep-level narratives that defy imposed constructions of race. Names challenge racist claims on language and dismiss oppressive name calling while covertly enacting their own forms of exclusion and black communal bonding. By tracing the events of surface and metatextual supranaming, an active reader discovers that deep within the bend of race there is a "mooring place" where the most durable resistance to racial constructions abides.[8] There, in that place, we find that for the characters of all black-authored texts, names are possessions more consequential, more substantial, than their oppressors or their oppression.

Conclusion:
Reading for the Deep Talk

S HAKESPEARE'S JULIET was perhaps the first literary character to ask, "What's in a name?" Since then, critics have quoted her in the title of books, essays, and articles that evaluate the meanings of names within literary utterances. By seeking the meanings of utterances within literary names, *Deep Talk* inverts their search and answers Juliet's question a bit more literally. Throughout the preceding pages the question "What's *in* a name?" has been the impetus of interpretation, commentary, and analysis.

In my attempt to address Juliet's question, I have argued that a plethora of utterances developing concrete themes and deep-level meanings exists within names. By presenting readings of names within various texts, this study has demonstrated how the functions, discursive force, and interlocutory nature of African-American literary names produce and organize multiple levels of interpretive discourse that motivate and violate the surface narrative, recuperate and revise the historical past, organize existence, and assist in developing narratives of self and various ideological constructs.

The method of interpretation I call *Reading through Names and Naming* is a vehicle for conceptualization that exposes the activities and discursive missions of poetic names without imposing restrictions that violate the meaning proliferation of their deep talk. Theories of names and other language theories like them variably acknowledge and dismiss meaning as an important element in understanding how names in literature function.[1] In some cases researchers acknowledge abstract or dictionary meanings as valuable interpretive tools. More often, they avoid issues of meaning proliferation by pointing out interesting parallels between a name and a character's behavior, evaluating the appropriateness of character name selections, highlighting neologisms, exploring numerical values, noting paronomasic use (punning), tracing ethnology, or mentioning briefly a character's, community's, or author's preoccupation with and concern for names. These narrowly focused investigations often usurp deep-level meaning, replacing it with interpretations that reveal nothing more than a name's potential for meaning.

Take, for instance, Ruth Rosenburg's essay " 'And The Children May Know Their Names': Toni Morrison's *Song of Solomon*." Rosenburg dismisses the interpretive value of the novel's biblical names completely, claiming that *Song of Solomon* "can only be explicated in its own terms." She says nothing about the terms created by the deep talk of the names speaking beneath the novel's surface. For Rosenburg, names reflect the themes and meanings of the primary story. They do not develop concrete themes, meanings, and stories of their own. Rosenburg regards Morrison's use of jostling meanings, paradoxes, and name-centered mutinies as "frustrating" (her word, not mine) and ultimately meaningless. I read them as I would a road sign. They indicate a name's meaning proliferation as well as its importance and value within the interpretive discourse of a metatext. The only interpretive value biblical names have in Morrison's novel, according to Rosenburg, is a sociological one. After establishing this as her thesis, she proceeds to catalogue the "three-generational saga" of black naming practices as represented in the novel.

Although Rosenburg's sociolinguistic interpretations yield unique insights into the novel's surface construction and the roles names play in that construction, her cataloging of names produces little in terms of their deep-level communications. A researcher who reads biblical names in Morrison's novel as transposed signifying utterances with discrete onomastic desires discovers not only the sociological importance of these names but the deep-level connotative and denotative positions they signify and develop as well. Such a reader discovers the story of resistance, death, and resurrection written and played out by the name *Pilate* in the novel's metatext. Reading the streams of meaning extending from a name such as *Pilate* is an act of discovery that engages the reader in the creation of narrative discourse. If we ignore the deep-level performances of onomastic meaning proliferation, we frustrate ourselves and the ability of name-focused themes to develop coherent metatexts.

The novels of Toni Morrison are filled with onomastic deep talk that transforms and illuminates surface narratives on multiple levels. Her use of names and naming deserves extended consideration in future studies. My intent in this book has been to move beyond the shadowy figure of potential meaning, such as that described above, toward an understanding of the deep-level communications of poetic names and the effects of their incantatory textual presence in the works of several black authors. Any analysis of literary onomastics should embody a search for the discourse-producing magic of naming. Without such a search, the examiner approaches the gates of onomastic deep talk without walking through them.

Names must be evaluated as enunciative acts that develop, interpolate, transpose, and speak concrete themes and a variety of contextual aims. These vehicles of deep-level communication give names their invasive force while repetition increases their discursive impact and liberates their "flesh." Each time a name appears in a text, its themes and contextual aims become more distinct, more tangible and interpretable. The proliferation of concrete themes within a name empowers the invasive performance of its deep talk so that it creates name-entities and metatexts of its own. A poetic name so empowered is a boundless, liminal, and flexible rhetorical device.

The seven guiding principles and three categories of onomastic desire discussed in this study assist the reader in discovering the discourse production of poetic names. Earlier, I described unpacking a name's onomastic desires as analogous to the investigative quests of an archeologist. To build upon this analogy, I now add that the seven guiding principles are maps and interpretive tools much like those in the archeologist's backpack and lab. They assist readers in discovering avenues of meaning and moments of onomastic engagement that might otherwise be ignored. The principles offer an experience of meaning and an understanding of the poetic archives of naming. More than this, they verify that beneath the primary structures and plausibility of all narratives lie the treasures of onomastic deep talk.

In African-American literature these treasures have a special place of honor. For black writers an awareness of their unique position as masters of Mae Henderson's "simultaneity of discourse," as subjects of DuBois's double consciousness, and as subversive opponents of race, class, and gender oppression erupts in their writing as a dialogic interaction between and *within* words. The utterances of diverse social and cultural accents resonate beneath almost every situation, every image, and every word, including names. This text, for instance, privileges an African legacy in almost every element of its interpretive methodology while also acknowledging its indebtedness to Western theoretical paradigms.

Present within each reading *Deep Talk* offers are West African and diasporic traditions of changing names in celebration of monumental or life-shaping events, using secret names as acts of self-protection and resistance, and believing in names as creative life forces. Even the gerund phrase and title of the reading process I describe, *Reading through Names and Naming*, grows out of an African legacy of naming practices. I use it to demonstrate the dualistic nature of names as storehouses of meaning and action. As "body" and "flesh" of an interpretive act, the name speaks on two levels of meaning simultaneously. It functions as the description of an interpretive process and as a name whose discursive makeup and deep talk honor West African and diasporic traditions of phrase naming.

In addition, names and naming in the texts I have surveyed (which by no means constitute the whole of African-American literature) repeat acts of subversive resistance similar to those used by captured Africans to resist the adverse effects of their slave masters' dubious naming practices. In like manner, I use *deep talk* to resist and reject the adverse political implications of subsuming white critical practices within my own. The name's deep-level communications "loud talk" issues of exclusion and separatism based upon race and gender. Mine is an appropriative gesture that transforms some of the fundamental concepts within a few white theoretical paradigms (aspects of Fish, Bakhtin, Lacan, and Kristeva primarily). I have attempted to revise these paradigms in ways similar to that acknowledged by Henry Louis Gates, who claims that theorizing the black text is, by definition, transformative; Karla Holloway, who employs the language of "Western theoretical" discourses in *Moorings and Metaphors* to emphasize the "generative potential" of her text; and Mae Henderson, whose own "simultaneity of discourse" appropriates and transforms theories from Teresa de Lauretis to Hans-Georg Gadamer and Mikhail Bakhtin.[2] Each reading presented in this study examines the generative potential and magic of transformative black discourse. My selection of the term *deep talk* as the title of my text privileges this Afrocentric focus.

Deep Talk embodies a West African and diasporic tradition of seeking the re-creative spirit of utterances that speak beneath the obvious. Between its covers, the magic of naming moves and, to the active reader, whispers: do as West Africans do. Just listen for the deep talk.

Notes

Introduction

1. Maya Angelou interviewed by Oprah Winfrey, *Oprah Winfrey Show*, CBS, March 1993.

2. Bakhtin, "Word in Dostoevsky," 150.

3. Morson and Emerson, *Mikhail Bakhtin*, 139.

4. Ellison, "Hidden Name and Complex Fate," in *Shadow and Act*, 144–66.

5. Spillers, "Mamma's Baby, Papa's Maybe," 68.

6. Benston, "I Yam What I Am," 152.

7. Gates, *Signifying Monkey*, 46. Gates borrows the title of his book from African-American folk poems (known as "toasts") about the signifying monkey, a descendant of the African trickster Esu-Elegbara (71, 11).

8. Gates, *Signifying Monkey*, 55, xxvii, 82. According to Gates, "pastiche is literary history naming itself, pronouncing its surface content to be the displaced content of intertextual relations themselves, the announcement of ostensibly concealed revision. Pastiche is an act of literary 'Naming'; parody is an act of 'Calling out of one's name' " (124).

9. Shanley, letter to author, 13 Jan., 1997.

10. Shanley, conversation with author, 14 Oct. 1995.

11. K. Holloway, *Moorings and Metaphors*, 1.

12. Lipsitz, *Life in the Struggle*, 228.

13. Carby, *Reconstructing Womanhood*, 16–17; Ann duCille, *Coupling Convention*, 9.

14. Levinson, "Intention and Interpretation," 224.

15. Morson and Emerson, *Mikhail Bakhtin*, 136. An eponym is a personal

name that becomes so closely associated with an idea, event, object, or time that it denotes that idea, event, object, or time—e.g., using the phrase name "Hoover Times" to denote the depression era.

16. Kristeva, "True-Real," 216–17. Also see Toril Moi's introduction to Kristeva's essay. Moi explains: "Kristeva coins the term 'le vréel' in order to account for the modernist revolution in Western thought and art, which she sees as the effort to formulate a truth that would *be* the *real* in the Lacanian sense of the term, or in other words: a 'true-real' or *vréel* (from *le vrai* [the true] and l*e réel* [the real])" (214).

17. According to Frege, literary names have no true means of denoting meaning or reference because their objects do not exist in the real world; they have no truth-value. Instead of denoting, they only "seem" to denote ("On Sense and Reference," 56–78). Since this study focuses on fictive referents located within a fictive universe "vividly" imagined (a term Linda Hutcheon uses) by its readers, issues of real world truth-value are of no importance and are not considered here (Hutcheon, "Metafictional Implications for Novelistic Reference," 5). Alan Gardiner challenges Russell's theory of names in his *Theory of Proper Names* as being "unsound" and "lamentably confused" (59). Julia Kristeva considers Russell's comparison of proper names to demonstratives a "logical embarrassment" ("True-Real," 234).

18. Habermas, "Technical Progress and the Social Life-World," 50–51; Hutcheon, "Metafictional Implications for Novelistic Reference," 5–8; Gates, *Signifying Monkey*, 53.

19. As Hortense Spillers and Evelyn Brooks Higginbotham have demonstrated elsewhere, class and gender are racially inflected (Spillers, "Mama's Baby, Papa's Maybe," 65–81; Higginbotham, "African-American Women's History," 91–113).

20. According to Voloshinov, "Only theme means something definite" (*Marxism and the Philosophy of Language*, 101). Understanding arises only after acknowledging and evaluating theme—not the novel's or story's theme, but the name's theme—which is the only true proprietor of a name utterance's deep-level meanings. With this in mind, I use the terms *concrete theme* and *contextual aim* interchangeably. Both terms refer to the objects, ideas, actions, or perceptions articulated by the full expression of a name's tasks and creative functions within particular narrative situations.

21. Renaming includes shifts from the original to the mesonymic (e.g., Liza taken from the middle of E*liza*beth) or ouronymic (Beth taken from the end of Eliza*beth*) as well as the addition of affixes (*O*dessa from Dessa and Hart*ley* from Hart) or the merging of names that produces what linguists call a *portman-*

teau word (*Rufel* from *Ru*th *Eli*zabeth). Other varieties of renaming include ana-grams, acronyms, abbreviations, and initialism. For more information on these terms and other introductory linguistic and onomastic concepts see Langacker, *Language and Its Structure*, and Nuessel, *Study of Names*.

22. Henderson, "Speaking in Tongues," 22; K. Holloway, *Moorings and Metaphors*, 43, 20; Gates, *Signifying Monkey*, 50–51.

23. Bakhtin, "Discourse in Dostoevsky," 181–269.

24. There are two types of epithets: *centered epithets* designate and de-scribe particular individuals and thereby name them; *passing epithets* collapse individuality into systems of generalized group classification.

25. I make a distinction between ethnicity and race. Ethnicity is a con-struct defined by ancestry, real or assumed, through which individuals share a common history, language, and sociocultural experience. Race is a construct that relegates and stereotypes identity for social and political purposes based upon cultural orientation or physical characteristics such as skin color. For a more detailed discussion of race and ethnicity see Feagin and Feagin, *Racial and Eth-nic Relations*.

1. On the N(yam)a Level

1. Harrison, *Drama of Nommo*, xxi; also see Griaule, *Le Renard Pâle*, 36–40.

2. Bedaux, Comments, 158. For additional discussion concerning the va-lidity of Marcel Griaule's ethnographic studies see van Beek, "Dogon Restu-died," 139–58 as well as the comments written by Suzanne Preston Blier, Jacky Bouju, Peter Ian Crawford, Mary Douglas, Paul Lane, and Claude Meillassoux that follow van Beek's remarks.

3. Jahn, *Muntu*, 125; Griaule, *Conversations with Ogotemmêli*, 139; Gri-aule, *Dieu d'eau*, 166.

4. Metzer and Murphy, *New Oxford Annotated Bible with the Apocrypha*, "The Letter of Jeremiah," 6:2–3 in the Apocrypha, 169–70. I thank Barbara Williams Lewis of the University of Texas at Austin for information leading to my search of the Apocrypha. Also see Jer. 29:10–14. Another point of interest to this reading is God's command to the freed Hebrews concerning slavery. Sev-eral times the Old Testament commands that the Hebrew people release their slaves after six years of service: "In the seventh year thou shalt let him go free from thee" (Deut. 15:12). See also Exod. 21:2 and Jer. 34:14. All biblical cita-tions are to the New Revised Standard Version.

5. Baker, *Long Black Song*, 120.

6. Cooke, "Naming, Being, and Black Experience," 170–71.

7. For more information on African naming practices see Paustian, "Evolution of Personal Naming Practices," 177–91, and Jackson, "Black Americans," 61–62. Several books and articles present the customs of specific societies: Baird, Commentary, 75–86; Adzei's "Meaning of Names in Ghana," 95–97; Mafukidze's "Origin and Significance of African Personal Names," 4–6; S. Johnson's *History of the Yorubas*, 79–89; and Beers, "African Names and Naming Practices," 206–7. For a study concerning the spread of African names and naming customs in America see Puckett, "Names of American Negro Slaves," 471–94, as well as his book *Black Names in America*. Also see Dillard, *Black English*, especially the subsection of chapter 3 titled "West African Naming Practices outside Gullah Territory"; Herskovits, *Myth of the Negro Past*, J. E. Holloway, *Africanisms in American Culture*, and Dillard, *Black Names*, especially chapter 1, "Personal Names," 17–35.

8. Gutman, *Black Family*, 230–56.

9. Gutman, *Black Family*, 231.

10. Gates, *Loose Canons*, 132–33.

11. Gates, *Loose Canons*, 133. The deep-level discourse implicit in Gates's remembered story establishes itself through a culturally informed name utterance, an epithet. *George*, as used by Mr. Wilson, is not a proper name, but a unit of speech used throughout northern and southern parts of the United States to denote a position or role of subordination and inequality. It is a name loaded by a cultural history that dismisses any preexisting human expectations, values, and equalities assumed by or associated with the individual it unnames. As a cultural imprint that undermines assumptions of equality, *George* circumscribes a way of being in the world that disciplines and wounds liberated "flesh."

12. Low, *Encyclopedia of Black America*, 657.

13. J. E. Holloway, *Africanisms in American Culture*, xx.

14. J. E. Holloway, *Africanisms in American Culture*, xix.

15. Morrison, *Playing in the Dark*, 47.

16. Malcolm X, *Autobiography*, 199.

17. B. T. Washington, *Up from Slavery*, 41; Spillers, "Permanent Obliquity," 130.

18. Spillers, "Mama's Baby, Papa's Maybe," 468.

19. Boskin, *Sambo*, 19–21. Boskin offers an excellent source for tracing the patterns of unnaming associated with the treatment enslaved Africans received from the English and Spanish.

20. Quoted in Dow, *Slave Ships and Slaving*, 295.

21. Pennington, *Fugitive Blacksmith*, 201–2.

22. Pennington, *Fugitive Blacksmith*, 247.

23. Gates, *Figures in Black*, 5–6, in which he quotes from Thomas Jefferson, *Notes of the State of Virginia* (London: Stockdale, 1787), book 2, 196.

24. I thank Jane Curran for bringing this reading of the name *Loveless Babies* to my attention.

25. Gutman, *Black Family*, 193.

26. Gutman, *Black Family*, 193.

27. duCille, "Postcolonialism and Afrocentricity," 28–29.

28. Paustian, "Evolution of Personal Naming Practices," 184.

29. Jackson, "Black Americans," 60.

2. Reading through Names and Naming

1. Pondrom, "Role of Myth," 182.

2. Sir James George Frazer argues that the Greek and Italian people of ancient times considered Janus/Jana and Dianus/Diana duplicates of each other. Only the dialect of the tribe who worshipped them varied, thus, the name differences (*Golden Bough*, 190–93). Throughout my reading of the metatext, I follow Hurston's lead and use the name *janie* (although written in lowercase letters) to represent these deities. Likewise, the lowercase names *janie woods* and *vergible woods* denote the correlating name-entities developed by the metatext. The name *Diana* I use only when speaking of the original ancient myths.

3. Frazer, *Golden Bough*, 9; Lowe, *Jump at the Sun*, 199 n. 5. Lowe comments briefly upon this and other similarities between Hurston's characters and classical gods.

4. Frazer, *Golden Bough*, 9; Hurston, "My Most Humiliating Jim Crow Experience," 164.

5. This name phrase associates Tea Cake with Osiris. For information concerning this god see Budge, "Legend of Osiris." Pondrom cites this source and explains the significance of Osiris to Hurston's novel.

6. Frazer, *Golden Bough*, v, 196–204, 214.

7. Lowe, *Jump at the Sun*, 199; Kravitz, *Who's Who in Greek and Roman Mythology*, 79, 189; Dillard, *Black English*, 124–29.

8. Dixon, *Preconscious Processing*, 4–5.

9. Cultural meanings assumed by the reader through an awareness of associations existing outside the text are cultural imprints.

10. Turner, *Ritual Process*, 95.

11. K. Holloway, *Moorings and Metaphors*, 26.

12. 2 Kings 18:1–4, 2 Chron. 29:3–36 NRSV. Hurston's brother's name

was also Hezekiah, further indicating a familial association and creating discourses that this reading does not broach.

3. Unpacking, Categorizing, and Interpreting Treasures

1. Bakhtin, "Discourse in Dostoevsky," 181–269. The categories described in this chapter deviate from Bakhtin's original model.

2. Bakhtin, "Discourse in Dostoevsky," 198.

3. Bakhtin uses a similar analogy (scaffolding) when discussing the recognizable extratextual associations of referentially oriented discourse. For Bakhtin, the extratextual material is scaffolding for the builder, or author, while in this text it is a ladder for the reader's descent into the metatext (Bakhtin, "Discourse in Dostoevsky," 187).

4. Dowling, "Song of Toni Morrison," 41.

5. Morrison, quoted in LeClair, "Language Must Not Sweat," 28. Ruth Rosenburg notes Jake's aesthetic choice of names but suggests that names such as *Pilate* are "lexically opaque, because they were 'picked blind' " (" 'Children May Know Their Names,' " 195).

6. Stryz, "Inscribing an Origin," 33.

7. My use of discourse stylization parallels Bakhtin's ("Discourse in Dostoevsky," 189).

8. Stryz, "Inscribing an Origin," 33.

9. Carmean and Lewis, "Song of Solomon," 513.

10. Nadel, *Invisible Criticism*, 82.

11. Fish, *Is There a Text*, 159.

12. Biblical references for the stories discussed in this reading include Gen. 16:1–15, 17:15–21, 21:1–20; Dan. 12:1, and Mark 15:17, 22, 34, NRSV.

13. African Americans have always identified with Hagar's story—some, because of her status as a slave, and others, because they believe she was black. Renita J. Weems comments that social and economic differences were the most divisive elements separating Hagar and Sarai, but the ethnic differences between them would manifest themselves today as those of an "African woman and a Hebrew woman, a woman of color and a white woman, a Third World woman and a First World woman" (*Just a Sister Away*, 1). Also see Hayes, *Hagar's Daughters*.

14. Dake, *Annotated Reference Bible*, n. h, 14.

15. Kristeva, "True-Real," 235. Kristeva reads the inscription of Schreber's name and his mother's maiden name within his discourse of invasion. The

names of those who "invade" and virtually emasculate Schreber bear names (or portions of names) extending from Schreber's own "historical truth." Kristeva describes this as an explosion of signified identity that confronts an unnamable semiotic "space of need" through a "multiplication of proper names."

4. Onomastic Resistance and the True-Real

1. Benston, "I Yam What I Am," 151–52. Benston observes that Malcolm's question and answer levels divisive structures of class, rank, training, and pretense "by reminding the professor of a shared origin, returning him to the debasing ground of Middle Passage and slavery."

2. Spivak, *In Other Worlds*, 77–78; Gates, *Signifying Monkey*, 53; also see Habermas, "Technical Progress and the Social Life-World," 50–51.

3. Lacan, *Ecrits/A Selection*, intro., x.

4. Kristeva, "True-Real," 216–17; 228. Because Kristeva's definitions of iconic hallucination (what I call *iconic emergence*) and the true-real appear within an essay defining the pathological itinerary of psychosis, it might appear that I am commenting upon the psychological implications of intuitive or subconscious writing and speech. This is not the case (or at least not my intent).

5. K. Holloway, *Moorings and Metaphors*, 178; McKible, " 'These are the facts' " 232.

6. Cixous, "Laugh of the Medusa," 875–99.

7. Here, I imply both Kristeva's sense of intertextuality as well as signifying practices within the text that comment upon extratextual social ideologies or sociopolitical commentaries extending from the social real (see Kristeva, *Desire in Language*, 15).

8. Goldstein, "Talk with Gloria Naylor," 36. The quote is Naylor's.

5. "Callin' Her Out Her Name"

1. M. K. Davis, "Everybody Knows Her Name," 545–47. Although several historical accounts of slave uprisings mention Dinah's participation in the uprising, none of them acknowledge her by name. David Walker notes the incident in his *Appeal to the Colored Citizens of the World* ([1829], 1965), Herbert Aptheker mentions it in *American Negro Slave Revolts* (1974), and Angela Davis speaks of the woman in a 1971 essay entitled "Reflections on the Black Woman's Role in the Community of Slaves."

2. M. K. Davis, "Everybody Knows Her Name," 545–47.

3. Names and the physical presence of characters are not always synonymous in the analyses of this chapter. To minimize the confusion, my readings follow the standard use of capitalization (Dessa, for instance) to identify characters as physical subjects—as subject personae. Names in italics and lowercase letters (*dessa*) identify subject positions, name-entities, and discursive effects (position effects or the eruption of the true-real, for instance).

4. Wilentz, *Binding Cultures*, 90.

5. M. K. Davis, "Everybody Knows Her Name," 548; McKible, " 'These are the facts,' " 233. Mae Gwendolyn Henderson mentions the *O* of Otherness but comments that Dessa's "rejection of the *O* signifies her rejection of the inscription of her body by the other(s)" ("Speaking in Tongues," 32).

6. Nehemiah attempts to enter the cellar once but finds himself "fearful of being drawn into the shadows" (30). The experience infuriates him, and from that point on he sits with the protagonist beneath an elm tree.

7. Davenport, review of *Dessa Rose*, 338.

8. McDowell, "Negotiating between Tenses," 151. A later version of the essay appears as "Witnessing Slavery after Freedom."

9. I thank my colleague David Leverenz at the University of Florida for pointing out this reading of Rufel's various names.

10. Neither the subject position *dorcas* nor the voice of the subject position *dessa rose* emerges within the lifeworld of "The Wench." The original subject positions of the protagonist, *odessa* and *dessa*, continue to respond in dialogue as two separate selves. And although this lifeworld lays the foundations for Dessa's later transformation into Dorcas, the protagonist does not speak through that voice either.

11. Henderson, "Speaking in Tongues," 32.

6. Reading Ernest Gaines's *A Gathering of Old Men*

1. Griffin, "Calling, Naming, and Coming of Age," 90.

2. Joseph Griffin notes that *Mathu* "is an anglicized pronunciation of the French Christian name *Mathieu*" ("Calling, Naming, and Coming of Age," 93).

3. Herskovits, *Myth of the Negro Past*, 191.

4. Collins, *Black Feminist Thought*, 11–12.

5. Quoted in Gaudet and Wooton, *Porch Talk*, 100.

6. Paustian, "Personal Naming Practices," 183.

7. Griffin, "Calling, Naming, and Coming of Age," 94.

8. Quoted in Gaudet and Wooton, *Porch Talk*, 131.

9. Griffin, "Calling, Naming, and Coming of Age," 96.

7. Within the Bend of Race

1. Spillers, "Mama's Baby, Papa's Maybe"; Higginbotham, "African-American Women's History."

2. Benston, "I Yam What I Am," 152. The parenthetical bracketing of the term *(un)naming* is Benston's.

3. Benston, "I Yam What I Am," 152.

4. Wilentz, *Binding Cultures,* 90.

5. Karla Holloway distinguishes between the mirrorlike quality of reflection and the "meditative posture" of *reflexion,* "which has a depth and resonance not possible with mere refection. . . . The combination of these permits a text that is at once emblematic and interpretive of the culture it describes" (*Moorings and Metaphors,* 196 n. 2).

6. "The T&A of PSA," *The Crew,* Fox Network, 9 November 1995. Other cultures adopt this form of calling also. Latinos, for instance, use *man, girl, girlfriend, homeboy,* and *homegirl* much as African Americans do. The only name among these five that is easily shared between members of diverse racial and ethnic groups is *man.*

7. Walker, *In Search of Our Mother's Gardens,* xi.

8. Karla Holloway defines a *mooring place* as "cultural ways of knowing as well as ways of framing that knowledge in language" (*Moorings and Metaphors,* 1).

Conclusion

1. Arguments concerning names and their ability to produce meaning include the work of Pulgram, Gardiner, Algeo, Nicolaisen, and Zabeeh. Although these theorists do not necessarily focus on literary names, each considers proper names void of meaning. Nicolaisen points out the connotative value of names, reserving meaning as the domain of other types of words. See Ernst Pulgram, *Theory of Names*; Gardiner, *Theory of Proper Names*; Algeo, *On Defining the Proper Name*; Nicolaisen, "Are There Connotative Names?"; and Zabeeh, *What Is in a Name?*

2. Gates, *Black Literature and Literary Theory,* 4; K. Holloway, *Moorings and Metaphors,* 22; Henderson, "Speaking in Tongues," 144–66.

Bibliography

Abrahams, Roger D. *Deep Down in the Jungle: Negro Narrative Folklore from the Streets of Philadelphia*. Chicago: Aldine, 1970.

———. "Playing the Dozens." *Journal of American Folklore* 75 (1962): 209–20.

———. *Talking Black*. Rowley MA: Newbury House, 1976.

Ackerman, Diana. "Proper Names, Propositional Attitudes and Non-descriptive Connotations." *Philosophical Studies* 35 (1979): 55–69.

Adzei, Kwaku. "The Meaning of Names in Ghana." *Negro Digest* 12 (1962): 95–97.

Algeo, John. "Is a Theory of Names Possible?" *Names* 33, no. 3 (1985): 136–44.

———. *On Defining the Proper Name*. Gainesville: Univ. Press of Florida, 1973.

Alvarez-Altman, Grace. "A Methodology to Literary Onomastics: An Analytical Guide for Studying Names in Literature." *Literary Onomastic Studies* 8 (1981): 220–30.

Angelou, Maya. *I Know Why the Caged Bird Sings*. New York: Random House, 1970.

Aptheker, Herbert. *American Negro Slave Revolts*. 1943. Rpt., New York: International, 1974.

Asante, Molefi Kete. *The Book of African Names*. Trenton NJ: African World Press, 1991.

Babuts, Nicolae. *The Dynamics of the Metaphoric Field: A Cognitive View of Literature*. Newark: Univ. of Delaware Press, 1992.

Baird, Keith E. Commentary. In *Names from Africa*, by Ogonna Chuks-Orji, 75–86. Chicago: Johnson, 1972.

Baker, Houston A., Jr. *Long Black Song: Essays in Black American Literature and Culture*. Charlottesville: Univ. Press of Virginia, 1972.

Bakhtin, Mikhail. "Discourse in Dostoevsky." In *Problems of Dostoevsky's Poetics*, trans. Caryl Emerson, 181–269. Minneapolis: Univ. of Minnesota Press, 1984.

———. "Discourse in the Novel." In *The Dialogic Imagination*, trans. Michael Holquist, 259–422. Austin: Univ. of Texas Press, 1981.

———. "The Word in Dostoevsky." *Problems of Dostoevsky's Poetics*, trans. R. W. Rotsel, 150–227. Ann Arbor: Ardis, 1973.

Bal, Mieke. *Narratology: Introduction to the Theory of Narrative*. Toronto: Univ. of Toronto Press, 1985.

Baldwin, James. *Go Tell It on the Mountain*. New York: Dell, 1953.

Bedaux, R. M. A. Comments. *Current Anthropology* 32, no. 2 (April 1991): 158.

Beers, H. Dwight. "African Names and Naming Practices." *Library of Congress Information Bulletin* 36 (25 March 1977): 206–7.

Benston, Kimberly W. "I Yam What I Am: Topos of (Un)naming in Afro-American Literature." In *Black Literature and Literary Theory*, ed. Henry Louis Gates Jr., 151–72. New York: Methuen, 1984.

Blackwell, James E. *The Black Community: Diversity and Unity*, 2d ed. New York: Harper and Row, 1985.

Bloom, Harold. *A Map of Misreading*. New York: Oxford Univ. Press, 1975.

Bontemps, Arna. *Black Thunder*. 1936. Rpt., Boston: Beacon Press, 1992.

Boskin, Joseph. *Sambo: The Rise and Demise of an American Jester*. New York: Oxford Univ. Press, 1986.

Brown, William Wells. *Narrative of William Wells Brown: A Fugitive Slave*. 1847. Rpt., Reading, MA: Addison-Wesley, 1969.

Budge, E. A. Wallis. "The Legend of Osiris." In *The Egyptian Book of the Dead*. 1895. Rpt., New York: Dover, 1967.

Bungert, Hans. "Functions of Character Names in American Fiction." In *The Origins of Originality of American Culture*, ed. Frank Tibor, 165–75. Budapest: Akadémiai Kiadó, 1984.

Burelback, Frederick M. "Names as Distance Controllers in Literature." *Literary Onomastics Studies* 13 (1986): 171–82.

Buttrick, George Arthur. "The Bible and Preaching." In *The Interpreter's One-Volume Commentary on the Bible*, ed. Charles M. Laymon, 1254–63. Nashville: Abingdon Press, 1971.

Cangield, John V. "Names and Causes." *Philosophical Studies* 35 (1979): 71–80.

Carby, Hazel. *Reconstructing Womanhood: The Emergence of the Afro-American Woman Novelist*. New York: Oxford Univ. Press, 1987.

Carmean, Karen, and Leon Lewis. "Song of Solomon." In *Masterpieces of African-American Literature*, ed. Frank N. Magil, 512–16. New York: HarperCollins, 1992.

Cixous, Hélène. "The Character of Character." *New Literary History* 5 (1974): 384–402.

————. "The Laugh of the Medusa." Trans. K. Cohen and P. Cohen. *Signs* 1 (1976): 875–99.

Collins, Patricia Hill. *Black Feminist Thought: Knowledge, Consciousness, and the Politics of Empowerment*. Vol. 2, *Perspectives on Gender*. Boston: HarperCollins, 1990.

Cooke, John. "Understanding the Lower Frequencies: Names and the Novel." In *Approaches to Teaching Ellison's* Invisible Man, ed. Susan Resneck Pharr, 112–18. New York: Modern Language Association, 1989.

Cooke, Michael G. "Naming, Being, and Black Experience." *Yale Review* 67 (winter 1978): 167–86.

Cooper, Anna Julia. *A Voice from the South*. 1892. Rpt., New York: Oxford Univ. Press, 1988.

Culler, Jonathan. *Ferdinand de Saussure*. Ithaca: Cornell Univ. Press, 1986.

Dake, Finis Jennings. *Dake's Annotated Reference Bible*. Lawrenceville GA: Dake Bible Sales, 1961.

Davenport, Doris. Review of *Dessa Rose*, by Sherley Ann Williams. *Black American Literature Forum* 20 (1986): 335–40.

Davis, Angela. "Reflections on the Black Woman's Role in the Community of Slaves." *Black Scholar* 3, no. 4 (1971): 2–15.

Davis, Mary Kemp. "Everybody Knows Her Name: The Recovery of the Past in Sherley Anne Williams's *Dessa Rose*." *Callaloo* 12, no. 3 (1989): 544–58.

Derrida, Jacques. *Glas*. Trans. John P. Leavey and Richard Rand. Lincoln: Univ. of Nebraska Press, 1986.

————. *Of Grammatology*. Trans. Gayatri Chakravory Spivak. Baltimore: Johns Hopkins Univ. Press, 1974.

————. *On the Name*. Trans. David Wood, John P. Leavey, and Ian McLeod; ed. Thomas Dutoit. Stanford: Stanford Univ. Press, 1995.

Dillard, J. L. *Black English: Its History and Usage in the United States*. New York: Random House, 1972.

————. *Black Names*. The Hague: Mouton, 1976.

Dion, Kenneth L. "Names, Identity, and Self." *Names* 31, no. 4 (1983): 245–57.

Dixon, Norman F. *Preconscious Processing*. Chichester UK: Wiley, 1981.

Dodson, Jualynne. "Conceptualizations of Black Families." In *Black Families*, ed. Harriet Pipes, 77–90. Newberry Park CA: Sage, 1988.

Douglass, Fredrick. *Narrative of the Life of Frederick Douglass: An American Slave*. New York: New American Library, 1968.

Dow, George, ed. *Slave Ships and Slaving*. Port Washington NY: Kennikat Press, 1962.

Dowling, Colette. "The Song of Toni Morrison." *New York Times Magazine*, 20 May 1979, 41.

duCille, Ann. *The Coupling Convention: Sex, Text, and Tradition in Black Women's Fiction*. New York: Oxford Univ. Press, 1995.

———. "Postcolonialism and Afrocentricity: Discourse and Dat Course." In *The Black Columbiad: Defining Moments in African-American Literature and Culture*, ed. Werner Sollors and Maria Diedrich, 28–41. Cambridge: Harvard Univ. Press, 1994.

Dunn, Margaret M., and Ann R. Morris. "The Narrator as Nomenclator: Narrative Strategy through Naming." *CEA Critic* 46, no. 1–2 (1983): 24–29.

Ellison, Ralph. *Invisible Man*. New York: Random House, 1952.

———. *Shadow and Act*. 1953. Rpt., New York: Random House, 1972.

Equiano, Olaudah. *The Life of Olaudah Equiano; or, Gustavus Vassa, the African*. 1837. Rpt., New York: Negro Universities Press, 1969.

Evans, Gareth Evans. "The Causal Theory of Names." In *Naming, Necessity, and Natural Kinds*, ed. Stephen P. Schwartz, 192–215. Ithaca: Cornell Univ. Press, 1977.

Feagin, Joe R., and Clairece Booher Feagin, *Racial and Ethnic Relations*, 4th ed. Englewood Cliffs NJ: Prentice Hall, 1993.

Fish, Stanley. *Is There a Text in this Class? The Authority of Interpretative Communities*. Cambridge: Harvard Univ. Press, 1980.

Fishman, Charles. "Naming Names: Three Recent Novels by Women Writers." *Names* 32, no. 1 (March 1984): 33–44.

Frank, Francine, and Frank Anshen. *Language and the Sexes*. Albany: State Univ. of New York Press, 1983.

Frazer, Sir James George. *The Golden Bough: A Study in Magic and Religion*, 3d ed., vols. 1–3. 1911. Rpt., London: Macmillan, 1922.

Frege, Gottlob. "On Sense and Nominatum." In *Readings in Philosophical Analysis*, ed. Herbert Feigl and Wilfred Sellars, 86–102. New York: Appleton Century Crofts, 1949.

———. "On Sense and Reference." In *Translations from the Philosophical Writings of Gottlob Frege*, 56–78. Oxford: Blackwell, 1952.

French, Peter A., Theodore E. Uehling Jr., and Howard K. Wetstein, eds. *Contemporary Perceptions in Philosophy of Language*. Minneapolis: Univ. of Minnesota Press, 1979.

Gaines, Ernest J. *A Gathering of Old Men*. New York: Vintage, 1984.

Gardiner, Sir Alan. *The Theory of Proper Names: A Controversial Essay*, 2d ed. London: Oxford Univ. Press, 1954.

Gates, Henry Louis, Jr. *Figures in Black: Words, Signs, and the Radical Self*. New York: Oxford Univ. Press, 1987.

———. Intro. to *Our Nig; or, Sketches from the Life of a Free Black*, by Harriet E. Wilson, xi–lix. New York: Random House, 1983.

———. *Loose Canons: Notes on the Culture Wars*. New York: Oxford Univ. Press, 1992.

————. *The Signifying Monkey: A Theory of Afro-American Literary Criticism.* New York: Oxford Univ. Press, 1988.

————, ed. *Black Literature and Literary Theory.* New York: Methuen, 1984.

Gaudet, Marcia, and Carl Wooton. *Porch Talk with Ernest Gaines: Conversations on the Writer's Craft.* Baton Rouge: Louisiana State Univ. Press, 1990.

Goldstein, William. "A Talk with Gloria Naylor." *Publishers Weekly,* 9 Sept. 1983, 35–36, 43.

Griaule, Marcel. *Conversations with Ogotemmêli: An Introduction to Dogon Religious Ideas.* London: Oxford Univ. Press, 1965.

————. *Dieu d'eau: Entretiens avec Ogotemmêli.* Paris: Editions du Chêne, 1948.

————. *Le renard pâle.* Paris: Institut d'Ethnologie, 1965.

Griffin, Joseph. "Calling, Naming, and Coming of Age in Ernest Gaines's *A Gathering of Old Men.*" *Names* 40, no. 2 (June 1992): 89–97.

Gutman, Herbert G. *The Black Family in Slavery and Freedom, 1750–1925.* New York: Pantheon Books, 1976.

Habermas, Jürgen. "Technical Progress and the Social Life-World." In *Toward a Rational Society: Student Protest, Science and Politics,* trans. Jeremy J. Shapiro, 50–61. Boston: Beacon Press, 1970.

Haley, Alex. *Roots: The Saga of an American Family.* New York: Doubleday, 1976.

Hardy, James Earl. *B-Boy Blues.* Boston: Alyson, 1994.

Harrison, Paul C. *The Drama of Nommo.* New York: Grove Press, 1972.

Hayes, Diana L. *Hagar's Daughters: Womanist Ways of Being in the World.* New York: Paulist Press, 1995.

Heller, Murray. *Black Names in America: Origins and Usage.* Boston: G. K. Hall, 1975.

Henderson, Mae Gwendolyn. "Speaking in Tongues: Dialogics, Dialectics, and the Black Woman Writer's Literary Tradition." In *Changing Our Own Words: Essays on Criticism, Theory, and Writing By Black Women,* ed. Cheryl A. Wall, 16–37. New Brunswick NJ: Rutgers Univ. Press, 1989.

Herskovits, Melville J. *The Myth of the Negro Past.* Boston: Beacon Press, 1941.

Higginbotham, Evelyn Brooks. "African-American Women's History and the Metalanguage of Race." In *Revising the Word and the World,* ed. VèVè A. Clark, Ruth-Ellen B. Joeres, and Madelon Sprengnether, 91–113. Chicago: Univ. of Chicago Press, 1993.

Hogue, W. Lawrence. *Discourse and the Other: The Production of the African-American Text.* Durham NC: Duke Univ. Press, 1986.

Holloway, Joseph E. *Africanisms in American Culture.* Bloomington: Indiana Univ. Press, 1991.

Holloway, Karla. *Moorings and Metaphors: Figures of Culture and Gender in Black Women's Literature.* New Brunswick NJ: Rutgers Univ. Press, 1992.

hooks, bell. *Talking Back: Thinking Feminist, Thinking Black*. Boston: South End Press, 1989.

Hull, Gloria T., Patricia Bell Scott, and Barbara Smith, eds. *All the Women Are White, All the Blacks Are Men, But Some of Us Are Brave*. New York: Feminist Press, 1982.

Hurston, Zora Neale. "My Most Humiliating Jim Crow Experience." In *I Love Myself When I Am Laughing*, ed. Alice Walker, 163–64. New York: Feminist Press, 1979.

———. *Their Eyes Were Watching God*. 1937. Rpt., Urbana: Univ. of Illinois Press, 1978.

Hutcheon, Linda. "Metafictional Implications for Novelistic Reference." In *On Referring in Literature*, ed. Anna Whiteside and Michael Issacharoff, 1–13. Bloomington: Indiana Univ. Press, 1987.

Inscoe, John C. "Carolina Slave Names: An Index to Acculturation." *Journal of Southern History* 49 (1983): 527–54.

Iser, Wolfgang. *The Implied Reader: Patterns of Communications in Prose Fiction from Bunyan to Beckett*. Baltimore: Johns Hopkins Univ. Press, 1974.

Jackson, Edward M. "Black Americans: The Naming of Themselves; A Historical and Literary Approach." *Connecticut Onomastic Review* 3 (1990): 60–71.

Jahn, Janheinz. *Muntu: An Outline of the New African Culture*. Trans. Marjorie Grene. New York: Grove Press, 1961.

Johnson, James Weldon. *The Autobiography of an Ex-Colored Man*, 1912. Rpt., New York: Viking Penguin, 1990.

Johnson, John L. *The Black Biblical Heritage: Four Thousand Years of Black Biblical History*. Nashville: Winston-Derek, 1991.

Johnson, Samuel. *History of the Yorubas*. London: Routledge, 1921.

Joyce, Ann. "The Black Canon: Reconstructing Black American Literary Criticism." *New Literary History* 18 (1987): 335–44.

Kochman, Thomas, ed. *Rappin' and Stylin' Out: Communication in Urban Black America*. Urbana: Univ. of Illinois Press, 1972.

Kravitz, David. *Who's Who in Greek and Roman Mythology*. New York: Clarkson Potter, 1975.

Kripke, Saul A. "Identity and Necessity." In *Naming, Necessity, and Natural Kinds*, ed. Stephen P. Schwartz, 66–101. Ithaca: Cornell Univ. Press, 1977.

———. *Naming and Necessity*. Cambridge: Harvard Univ. Press, 1980.

Kristeva, Julia. *Desire in Language: A Semiotic Approach to Literature and Art*. Ed. Leon S. Roudiez; trans. Thomas Gora, Alice Jardine, and Leon S. Roudiez. New York: Columbia Univ. Press, 1980.

———. "The True-Real." Trans. Seán Hand. In *The Kristeva Reader*, ed. Toril Moi, 214–37. New York: Columbia Univ. Press, 1986.

Lacan, Jacques. *Ecrits/A Selection*. New York: Norton, 1977.

Langacker, Ronald W. *Language and Its Structure: Some Fundamental Linguistic Concepts*. New York: Harcourt Brace Jovanovich, 1973.

Larson, Charles, ed. Intro. to *An Intimation of Things Distant: The Collected Fiction of Nella Larson*. New York: Doubleday, 1992.

Larsen, Nella. *Passing*. 1929. Rpt., New Brunswick: Rutgers Univ. Press, 1986.

Lawson, James Weldon. "Odysseus's Revenge: The Names on the Title Page of *The Autobiography of an Ex-Coloured Man*." *Southern Literary Journal* 22 (1989): 92–99.

LeClair, Thomas. "The Language Must Not Sweat." *New Republic*, March 1981, 28.

Leitch, Vincent B. *Deconstructive Criticism: An Advanced Introduction*. New York: Columbia Univ. Press, 1983.

Levinson, Jerrold. "Intention and Interpretation: A Last Look." In *Intention and Interpretation*, ed. Gary Iseminger, 221–56. Philadelphia: Temple Univ. Press, 1992.

Lincoln, Abbey. "Who Will Revere the Black Woman?" In *The Black Woman*, ed. Toni Cade, 80–89. New York: New American Library, 1970.

Linsky, Leonard. *Names and Descriptions*. Chicago: Univ. of Chicago Press, 1977.

Lipsitz, George. *A Life in the Struggle: Ivory Perry and the Culture of Opposition*. Philadelphia: Temple Univ. Press, 1988.

Lorde, Audre. *Sister Outsider*. Freedom CA: Crossing Press, 1984.

Low, W. Augustus, ed. *Encyclopedia of Black America*. New York: McGraw-Hill, 1981.

Lowe, John. *Jump at the Sun: Zora Neale Hurston's Cosmic Comedy*. Urbana: Univ. of Illinois Press, 1994.

McAdoo, Harriette Pipes. *Black Families*, 2d ed. Beverly Hills CA: Sage, 1988.

McDowell, Deborah E. "Witnessing Slavery after Freedom—*Dessa Rose*." In *"The Changing Same": Black Women's Literature, Criticism, and Theory*. Bloomington: Indiana Univ. Press, 141–55.

———. "Negotiating between Tenses: Witnessing Slavery after Freedom—*Dessa Rose*." In *Slavery and the Literary Imagination*, ed. Deborah E. McDowell and Arnold Rampersad, 144–63. Baltimore: Johns Hopkins Univ. Press, 1989.

MacKethan, Lucinda H. "Names to Bear Witness: The Theme and Tradition of Naming in Toni Morrison's *Song of Solomon*." *CEA Critic* 49: 199–207.

McKible, Adam. " 'These are the facts of the darky's history': Thinking History and Reading Names in Four African American Texts." *African American Review* 28, no. 2 (1994): 223–35.

Mafukidze, Takawira. "The Origin and Significance of African Personal Names." *Black World*, 9 (1970): 4–6.

Malcolm X. *The Autobiography of Malcolm X*, as told to Alex Haley. 1965. Rpt., New York: Random House, 1973.

Meeter, Glenn. "Names and Naming in Fiction and Life: A Personal Onomastics Odyssey." In *From Oz to the Onion Patch*, ed. Edward Callary, 117–29. Dekalb IL: North Central Name Society, 1986.

Metzer, Bruce M., and Roland E. Murphy, eds. *New Oxford Annotated Bible with the Apocrypha: An Ecumenical Study Bible.* 1973. Rpt., New York: Oxford Univ. Press, 1991.

Mill, John Stuart. "Of Names." In *A System of Logic: Ratiocinative and Inductive.* Vol. 7 of *Collected Works of John Stuart Mill*; book 1, *Of Names and Propositions*, ed. J. M. Robson. Toronto: Univ. of Toronto Press, 1973.

Morgan, Jan, Christopher O'Neil, and Rom Harré. *Nicknames: Their Origins and Social Consequences.* London: Routledge and Kegan Paul, 1979.

Morris, Pam. *Literature and Feminism.* Oxford: Blackwell, 1993.

Morrison, Toni. *Beloved.* New York: Knopf, 1987.

———. *Playing in the Dark: Whiteness and the Literary Imagination.* Cambridge: Harvard Univ. Press, 1992.

———. *Song of Solomon.* New York: Knopf, 1977.

———. *Tar Baby.* New York: Knopf, 1981.

Morson, Gary Saul, and Caryl Emerson, eds. *Mikhail Bakhtin: Creation of a Prosaics.* Stanford: Stanford Univ. Press, 1990.

———. *Rethinking Bakhtin: Extensions and Challenges.* Evanston: Northwestern Univ. Press, 1989.

Murray, Heller. "Black Names in America: History and Meaning." Ph.D. diss., Ohio State University, 1974.

Nadel, Alan. *Invisible Criticism: Ralph Ellison and the American Canon.* Iowa City: Univ. of Iowa Press, 1988.

Naylor, Gloria. *The Women of Brewster Place.* 1982. New York: Penguin Books, 1983.

Neussel, Frank H. *The Study of Names: A Guide to the Principles and Topics.* Westport CT: Greenwood Press, 1992.

Nicolaisen, W. F. H. "Are There Connotative Names?" *Names* 26, no. 1 (1978): 40–47.

Norris, Christopher. "Deconstruction, Naming, and Necessity: Some Logical Options." *International Review of Applied Linguistics in Language Teaching: An International Review* 13, no. 3 (1984): 159–81.

Pamp, Bengt. "Ten Theses on Proper Names." *Names* 33, no. 3 (1985): 111–18.

Paustian, P. Robert. "The Evolution of Personal Naming Practices among American Blacks." *Names* 26, no. 2 (1978): 177–91.

Pennington, James W. C. *The Fugitive Blacksmith; or, Events in the History of James W. C. Pennington, Pastor of a Presbyterian Church, New York, Formerly a Slave in the State of Maryland.* 1849. In *Great Slave Narratives*, ed. Arna Bontemps, 193–267. Boston: Beacon Press, 1969.

Petrey, Sandy. *Speech Acts and Literary Theory.* New York: Routledge, Chapman & Hall, 1990.

Pickerill, Donald. Intro. to "The Song of Solomon." *Spirit Filled Life Bible: The New King James Version.* Nashville: Thomas Nelson, 1991, 946–48.

Pondrom, Cyrena N. "The Role of Myth in Hurston's *Their Eyes Were Watching God.*" *American Literature* 58, no. 2 (1986): 750–58.

Puckett, Niles Newbell. *Black Names in America: Orgins and Usage,* ed. Murray Heller. Boston: G. K. Hall, 1976.

———. "Names of American Negro Slaves." In *Studies in the Science of Society,* ed. George P. Murdoch, 471–94. New Haven: Yale Univ. Press, 1937.

Pulgram, Ernst. *Theory of Names.* Berkeley CA: American Name Society, 1954.

Rabinowitz, Paula. "Naming, Magic, and Documentary: The Subversion of the Narrative in *Song of Solomon, Ceremony,* and *China Men.*" In *Feminist Re-visions: What Has Been and Might Be,* ed. Vivian Patraka and Louise A. Tilly, 26–42. Ann Arbor: Women's Studies Program, Univ. of Michigan, 1983.

Reed, Ishmael. *The Last Days of Louisiana Red.* New York: Macmillan-Atheneum, 1989.

———. *Mumbo Jumbo.* New York: Macmillan-Atheneum, 1988.

Robinson, William H., ed. *Nommo: An Anthology of Modern Black African and Black American Literature.* New York: Macmillan, 1972.

Rosenberg, Jay F. *Beyond Formalism: Naming and Necessity for Human Beings.* Philadelphia: Temple Univ. Press, 1994.

Rosenburg, Ruth. " 'You Took a Name That Made You Amiable to the Music': Toni Cade Bambara's *The Salt Eaters.*" *Literary Onomastics Studies* 12 (1985): 165–94.

———. " 'And the Children May Know Their Names': Toni Morrison's *Song of Solomon.*" *Literary Onomastics Studies* 8 (1981): 195–219.

Russell, Bertrand. *Logic and Knowledge.* London: G. Allen & Unwin, 1956.

———. "On Denoting." In *Readings in Philosophical Analysis,* ed. Herbert Feigl and Wilfred Sellars, 103–15. New York: Appleton Century Crofts, 1949.

Saussure, Ferdinand de. *Course in General Linguistics.* Trans. Roy Harris. La Salle IL: Open Court, 1986.

Schwartz, Stephen P. *Naming, Necessity, and Natural Kinds.* Ithaca: Cornell Univ. Press, 1977.

Schwarz, David S. *Naming and Referring: The Semantics and Pragmatics of Singular Terms.* New York: de Gruyter, 1979.

Searle, John R. *Expression and Meaning: Studies in the Theory of Speech Acts.* Cambridge: Cambridge Univ. Press, 1979.

———. "The Logical Status of Fictional Discourse." In *Contemporary Perceptions in Philosophy of Language,* ed. Peter A. French, Theodore E. Uehling Jr., and Howard K. Wetstein, 240–68. Minneapolis: Univ. of Minnesota Press, 1979.

———. "Problems of Reference." In *Speech Acts: An Essay in the Philosophy of Language*, 157–74. Cambridge: Cambridge Univ. Press, 1969.

———. "Proper Names." *Mind: A Quarterly Review of Psychology and Philosophy* 67 (1958): 166–73.

Seed, David. "Naming and Identity in Modern American Fiction." *Dutch Quarterly Review of Anglo-American Letters* 20, no. 2 (1990): 120–37.

Seeman, M. V. "Name and Identity." *Canadian Journal of Psychiatry* 25 (1980): 129–37.

Seyffert, Oscar, Henry Nettleship, and J. E. Sandys. *Dictionary of Classical Antiquities*. New York: Meridian, 1956.

Shakespeare, William. *Romeo and Juliet*. In *The Complete Works of Shakespeare*, 3d ed., ed. David Bevington, 994–1031. Chicago: Univ. of Chicago Press, 1980.

Shanley, Kathryn. Conversation with author, Ford Fellows Conference, Washington DC, 14 Oct. 1995.

———. Letter to author, 13 Jan. 1997.

Simpson, Anne K. *A Gathering of Gaines: The Man and the Writer*. Lafayette LA: Center for Louisiana Studies, 1991.

Smith, Valerie. "Gender and Afro-Americanist Literary Theory and Criticism." In *Speaking of Gender*, ed. Elaine Showalter. Boston: Routledge, Chapman & Hall, 1988.

Smitherman, Geneva. *Talkin' and Testifyin': The Language of Black America*. Boston: Houghton Mifflin, 1977.

Solomon, J. Fisher. "Speaking of No One: The Logical Status of Fictional Proper Names." *Names* 33, no. 3 (1985): 145–57.

Spear, Chloe. *Memoir of Mrs. Chloe Spear, a Native African, Died in 1815 Aged 65, by a Lady of Boston*. Boston, 1815.

Spillers, Hortense. "Mama's Baby, Papa's Maybe: An American Grammar Book." *Diacritics* (summer 1987): 65–81.

———. " 'The Permanent Obliquity of the In(pha)llibly Straight': In the Time of the Daughters and the Fathers." In *Changing Our Own Words*, ed. Cheryl A. Wall, 234–35. New Brunswick: Rutgers Univ. Press, 1989.

Spillers, Hortense, and Marjorie Pryse, eds. *Conjuring: Black Women, Fiction, and Literary Tradition*. Bloomington: Indiana Univ. Press, 1985.

Spivak, Gayatri Chakravorty, trans. Intro. to *Of Grammatology*, by Jacques Derrida, ix–xc. Baltimore: Johns Hopkins Univ. Press, 1976.

———. *In Other Worlds: Essays in Cultural Politics*. New York: Routledge, 1988.

Stryz, Jan. "Inscribing an Origin in *Song of Solomon*." *Studies in American Fiction* 19 (spring 1991): 31–40.

Sundquist, Eric J. *Cultural Contexts for Ralph Ellison's* Invisible Man. Boston: St. Martin's Press, 1995.

Tate, Claudia. *Black Women Writers at Work*. New York: Continuum, 1990.

———. "Reshuffling the Deck: Or, (Re)Reading Race and Gender in Black Women's Writing." *Tulsa Studies in Women's Literature* 7, no. 1 (1988): 119–32.

Turner, Victor. *The Ritual Process: Structure and Anti-Structure*. 1969. Rpt., New York: Cornell Univ. Press, 1977.

Van Beek, Walter E. A. "Dogon Restudied: A Field Evaluation of the Work of Marcel Griaule." *Current Anthropology* 32, no. 2 (April 1991): 139–67.

Van Langendonck, Willy. "Pragmatics and Iconicity as Factors Explaining the Paradox of Quantified Proper Names." *Names* 33, no. 3 (1985): 119–26.

Voloshinov, V. N. *Marxism and the Philosophy of Language*. Trans. Ladislav Matejka and I. R. Tutunik. New York: Seminar Press, 1973.

Walker, Alice. *The Color Purple*. New York: Harcourt Brace Jovanovich, 1982.

———. "Everyday Use." In *In Love and Trouble*. New York: Harcourt Brace Jovanovich, 1967.

———. *In Search of Our Mother's Gardens*. New York: Harcourt Brace Jovanovich, 1984.

Walker, David. *David Walker's Appeal*. 1829. Rpt., with an introduction by Charles M. Witlse, New York: Hill and Wang, 1965.

Washington, Booker T. *Up from Slavery*, 1901. Rpt., in *Three Negro Classics*. New York: Hearst-Avon, 1965.

Washington, Mary Helen, ed. *Black-Eyed Susans/Midnight Birds: Stories by and about Black Women*. New York: Doubleday, 1990.

Weems, Renita J. *Just a Sister Away: A Womanist Vison of Women's Relationships in the Bible*. San Diego: LuraMedia, 1988.

Whiteside, Anna, and Michael Issacharoff, eds. *On Referring in Literature*. Bloomington: Indiana Univ. Press, 1987.

Wideman, John Edgar. *Brothers and Keepers*. New York: Viking Penguin, 1984.

Wilentz, Gay. *Binding Cultures: Black Women Writers in Africa and the Diaspora*. Bloomington: Indiana Univ. Press, 1992.

Williams, Bettye J. "Names and Naming." In *The Oxford Companion to African-American Literature*, ed. William Andrews et al., 523–26. New York: Oxford Univ. Press, 1997.

Williams, Sherley Anne. *Dessa Rose*. New York: William Morrow, 1986.

Wright, Richard. *Black Boy*. New York: Harper & Row, 1945.

Zabeeh, Farhang. *What Is in a Name? An Inquiry into the Semantics and Pragmatics of Proper Names*. The Hague: Martinus Nijhoff, 1968.

Index

absent presence, 18, 44, 58, 67, 90, 189

active reader, 13, 14, 29, 65, 66, 87, 104, 105, 123, 210

acts of resistance: absence of, 36; against white namers, 19, 44, 136, 174, 175, 188–91, 194, 202–4, 214; in alien spheres of influence, 18; biblical naming practices as, 55; cosmic forces and, 41; covert stories and, 7; created names as, 20; cultural imprints as, 31; in *Dessa Rose*, 131; "I am" as, 41–44; loud talking, 27, 139, 214; memory and, 141, 159; mnemonic phrase names as, 45; name-entities and, 141; namelessness and, 18; names and naming as, 5; name spelling or pronunciation as, 20; names that celebrate, 173; naming as, 41; nicknames as, 181, 185; nonviolent, 19, 181–85; Phillis Wheatley's, 51; secret name and, 19, 214; symbolic

gestures and, 48; the true-real and, 29, 114; within extended metatexts, 30

African Colonization Society, 47

African Dorcas Society, 47

African heritage, 1, 53, 118, 119, 120; Ibo, 55; naming practices and, 35–36, 54, 170, 199; nommo and, 28, 36–41, 44, 56; secret names and, 18, 44, 45, 51, 52, 184–85, 193; West Africa and, 35, 141, 214–15; Yoruba and, 54, 55

African names, 41, 54, 141, 185; Akan, 56; *Kiswana*, 54–55, 126–27, 198; Nigerian, 56; Tanzanian, 56

African philosophy, 28; *Beloved* and, 37–40; Dogon, 36; naming practices and, 44; nommo and, 28, 36–41, 56; Ogotemmêli, 28, 37–38

African tradition, 40, 54, 55; retention of, 55

allegory, 30, 80